eat *up* slim *down*™ Annual Recipes 2004

150 Simply Delicious Recipes for Permanent Weight Loss

Edited by KATHY EVERLETH

RODALE®

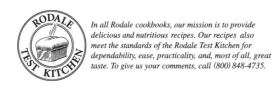

In all Rodale cookbooks, our mission is to provide delicious and nutritious recipes. Our recipes also meet the standards of the Rodale Test Kitchen for dependability, ease, practicality, and, most of all, great taste. To give us your comments, call (800) 848-4735.

Book design by Carol Angstadt and Faith Hague
Interior and cover photography credits for this book are on page 259.

Front cover recipes: No-Bake Cheese Pie (page 211), Greek Beef Stew (page 117), Chocolate-Walnut Cake (page 206), Ocean Garden Fettuccine (page 143), Toasted Vegetable Tacos (page 228)

ISBN 1–57954–758–3 hardcover

2 4 6 8 10 9 7 5 3 1 hardcover

WE **INSPIRE** AND **ENABLE** PEOPLE TO IMPROVE
THEIR LIVES AND THE WORLD AROUND THEM

FOR PRODUCTS & INFORMATION
WWW.RODALESTORE.COM
WWW.PREVENTION.COM
(800) 848-4735

Contents

Special Thanks

With grateful appreciation to all the supporters and sponsors of the Eat Up Slim Down Recipe Sweepstakes, we would like to thank . . .

The companies that so generously provided the terrific prizes for the sweepstakes:

Capresso, Chantal, EdgeCraft, Hamilton Beach, Kuhn Rikon, Meadowsweet Kitchens, Messermeister, Tilia, William Bounds, Wüsthof-Trident

The product representatives who were so generous with their time and talents:

Val Gleason from EdgeCraft, Loretta Towne from Field & Associates, Paul Ward-Willis from Wüsthof-Trident, Sue Haase from Hamilton Beach

And sincere, heartfelt thanks . . .

. . . to all of the readers of www.eatupslimdown.com and www.prevention.com, who were kind enough to share their delicious recipes, clever tips, and inspiring stories of weight-loss success for this book. We salute you and wish you continued success!

Acknowledgments

A very special thank you to everyone who had a hand in creating *Eat Up Slim Down Annual Recipes 2004*.

Carol Angstadt

JoAnn Brader

Leanne Coppola

Kathy Dvorsky

Tara Grill

Faith Hague

Kathleen Hanuschak, R.D.

Joely Johnson

Fran Kriebel

Miriam Rubin

Kimberly Tweed

Contributors

This book is a compilation of the delicious and creative recipes sent to us by weight-loss winners across the United States, and even beyond. The number of recipes we received was so great, it was a difficult task choosing 150. But after a careful selection process, we managed to whittle it down. Here are this year's recipe contributors. We salute their innovative efforts in the kitchen, and hope you'll enjoy eating up and slimming down with their recipes!

Name and Residence	Recipe	Page
Jean Adam, Orefield, Pennsylvania	Very Cherry Dessert	171
	Tasty Apple Dessert	173
Cynthia Adams, Greensboro, North Carolina	Berry Morning Mash	41
Marylinn Albert, Feura Bush, New York	Mexican Pie	122
Carolann Alexander, Houston, Texas	Chili Lime Snapper	138
Maryann Amburgey, Richardson, Texas	Spicy Black Bean and Artichoke Spaghetti	85
Suzanne Aycock, Annapolis, Maryland	Quick Spinach Sauté	156
Heather Balentine, Emory, Texas	Heather's First Cake	205
Nancy Ballard, Johnson City, Tennessee	Light Spinach Roll-Ups	233
Sarah Ballweg, Middleton, WI	Sautéed Bananas with Praline Sauce	175
Eileen Barringer, Leeds Point, New Jersey	Savory Grilled Tomatoes	243
Wanda Beeken, Goldsboro, North Carolina	Rice Pudding	192
Emily Bickell, Kitchener, Ontario, Canada	Meatless Tacos	230
Annette Boswell, Meadville, Pennsylvania	Piña Colada Cake	201
Lorelle Boxler, Salina, Kansas	Oatmeal-Raisin Cookies	166
Betty Brader, Allentown, Pennsylvania	Orange-Glazed Pork Tenderloin	128
Rick Brucker, Urbandale, Iowa	Light and Fluffy Pancakes	48
Joanne Burke, Panorama City, California	Island Rice with Turkey Kielbasa	133
Kathryn Burke, Portola Valley, California	Fulfilling Salad	64
MaryLou Burks, Minden, Nevada	Mary's Baked Italian Chicken	104
Kate Burrage, Exeter, New Hampshire	Guiltless Potato and Apple Salad	78
Jeanie Callaghan, Smyrna, Georgia	Meatless Mexican Lunch	89
Faye Canape, Englishtown, New Jersey	Apple Cake	194
Barbra Clark, River Falls, Wisconsin	Hot Roasted Vegetables	158

Name and Residence	Recipe	Page
Ellen Parodi, Philadelphia, Pennsylvania	Chicken-Pasta Salad	68
	Veggie Pizza	237
Amanda Parr, Mandeville, Louisiana	Ocean Garden Fettuccine	143
Judy Parsons, Surrey, British Columbia, Canada	Chocolate-Marshmallow Fudge	168
Misty Phillips, Port Gibson, Mississippi	Tex-Mex Chicken	102
Barbie Picciano, Wickliffe, Ohio	Roasted Red Pepper Chicken	98
Tracey Pintell, Valley Lee, Maryland	Pudding Cup with Bananas	191
Karen Preston, Stoney Creek, Ontario, Canada	Awesome French Toast	46
	Caesar Kebabs	247
Susie Raimi, San Diego, California	Apricot Chicken	101
Jenny Renedo, Columbia, South Carolina	Turkey Black Bean Soup	55
Monica Richards, Pearland, Texas	Tuna Patties	238
Stephanie Rothschild, New York City	Easy Baked Apples	172
	Heavenly Berries	178
Lisa Rothwell, Virginia Beach, Virginia	Fast Beef Stroganoff	120
Anne Roy, Ellicott City, Maryland	Greek Beef Stew	117
Patsy Roy-Turple, Belledune, New Brunswick, Canada	Chicken Parmesan Strips	106
Kim Russell, North Wales, Pennsylvania	Wild Rice Salad	76
Lesley Sawhook, Maineville, Ohio	Easy Tasty Cottage Fries	148
Jennifer Schuerer, Menasha, Wisconsin	Ground Turkey Lasagna	251
Rita Schwass, Kirkwood, Illinois	Reduced-Fat Chocolate Cake	204
Miran Sedlacek, Port Charlotte, Florida	Soy Bars	167
Roni Sharp, Thornhill, Ontario, Canada	Spaghetti Squash	151
Mycala Shaulis, Mechanicsburg, Pennsylvania	Couscous Salad	74
Shirley Slager, Edmonton, Alberta, Canada	Comfort Food Mashed Potatoes	149
Barbara Sloan, Wallingford, Connecticut	Spinach-Mushroom Lasagna	249
Gregory Smith, Washington, D.C.	Bacon Asparagus Wraps	227
Gudne Smyth, La Pine, Oregon	Holiday Pepper-Cheddar Muffins	52
Denise Sorino, Florence, South Carolina	Awesome Salad	75
Bonnie Steele, Grove Hill, New Brunswick, Canada	Beef and Vegetables	95
Linda Stretch, Pittsburgh, Pennsylvania	Spicy 'n' Light Shrimp Curry	145
Cary Sutherland, Christmas, Michigan	Healthy Brownie Cookies	165
Patti Tan, Richmond, British Columbia, Canada	Bean Dip	225
Paula Towery, Hopkinsville, Kentucky	Ice Cream Sandwich	188
JoAnn Tremel, Mint Spring, Virginia	Banana Cream "Pie"	185
Amy Tucker, Vancouver, British Columbia, Canada	Chinese Cabbage Salad	73

We were also gratified to encounter eight weight-loss winners who shared their stories of success with us in personal profiles. Look for their inspiring stories throughout the book.

Introduction

Here's your chance to break free! If you've ever felt tired of eating the same old foods every day, and if you're just not making the strides you'd like in your weight-loss efforts, take this opportunity to make a change for the better. Not only will you enjoy your meals more, but you'll also be shedding unwanted pounds and eating healthier.

This year's edition of *Eat Up Slim Down Annual Recipes* includes dozens of ideas to make cooking for weight loss easier and more enjoyable. We talked with food writer and cooking expert Miriam Rubin to find out virtually everything you need to know to make your time in the kitchen quicker, easier, and most of all, beneficial to your waistline. You'll find Miriam's advice invaluable as you wind your way through the supermarket aisles, and as you prepare new and exciting meals.

And if you're looking for innovative dishes to try out, feast your eyes on the 150 all-new recipes inside this book. Each recipe was submitted to us on our Web site, www.eatupslimdown.com, as part of the Eat Up Slim Down Recipe Sweepstakes. Visitors to the Web site shared their weight-loss recipes with us, and they could also enter our sweepstakes for a chance to win exciting prizes. As we tried out their dishes, we were overwhelmed by the creativity and the taste of these delicious weight-loss recipes. Please your family with satisfying dishes like Roasted Red Pepper Chicken and Stir-Fry Beef. Enjoy quick-fix dinners like Caesar Kebabs and Shrimp and Feta Spinach Fettuccine. And don't forget desserts like Chocolate-Marshmallow Fudge and Peanut Butter Pie.

We've also included stories of success from real-life weight-loss winners: a woman whose hospitalization for heart failure helped her revamp her cooking techniques; a mother of two who dropped 30 pounds and now trains for half-marathons; a confirmed "sweetaholic" who kicked her sugar habit, started a walking program, and watched the pounds fall away; and many others who will inspire you to succeed. In addition, dozens of weight-loss winners reveal clever tips you can use right now.

With each recipe, we've provided complete nutritional information, including both Diet Exchanges and Carb Choices for those who wish to track their intake of carbohydrates. Be sure to consult with your doctor about the amounts that are right for you.

So take a chance and break free from the everyday—you'll eat lots of wonderful food, you'll lose weight, and most of all, you'll enjoy every bite!

Wise Buys for Weight Loss

Your guide to hunting down the best low-calorie choices in the supermarket.

Before you can cook, you have to shop. To stay on track with your weight-loss goals and to avoid impulsive purchases at the super-market, you may want to try adopting these two mottos: Never go shopping when you're hungry, and never go without a list.

With so many choices available at super-markets, it's easy to get overwhelmed. So, to help you on your trip though the aisles, we've provided a selection of the best, the health-iest, and the most delicious foods to choose from to help you lose weight quickly and easily—and keep it off. Once you get a feel for the products you like the best, shopping will become a breeze. So grab your cart and let's get shopping.

Picking Produce

A leaner, healthier diet—which will lead to a leaner, healthier you!—needs to include plenty of vegetables and fruits. Not only do they taste great, but they're also chock full of nutrients your body needs. Best of all, they contain fiber that will help fill you up and keep you from overeating other, higher-calorie foods. Here are some tips for choosing the best produce.

Shop seasonally. Fruits and vegetables taste best and often are most nutritious when they're in season. They're very often less ex-pensive in season as well. So keep an eye out for what's really fresh, and, if possible, what's been grown locally. When food is bursting

1

FIBER-FULL FRUITS AND VEGGIES

Filling up on fiber is a great way to help you shed pounds, and eating more fruits and vegetables is a tasty—and nutritious—way to do it. Here are some commonly used fruits and veggies, along with their fiber content.

FRUITS			VEGETABLES		
Food	Portion	Fiber (g)	Food	Portion	Fiber (g)
Figs, dried	2	4.6	Peas, fresh, cooked	½ cup	4.4
Raspberries, red	½ cup	4.1	Sweet potato, with skin, baked	1 medium	3.4
Blackberries	½ cup	3.8	Potato, with skin, baked	1 medium	2.3
Apple, unpeeled	1	3.7			
Avocado, sliced	½ cup	3.6	Broccoli, cooked	½ cup	2.2
Dates	5 medium	3.1	Corn, cooked	1 ear	2.1
Orange	1	3.1	Brussels sprouts, cooked	½ cup	2.0
Banana	1	2.8			
Kiwifruit	1 medium	2.5	Green beans	½ cup	2.0
Nectarine	1 medium	2.1	Onion, sliced	½ cup	2.0
Blueberries	½ cup	1.9	Carrot, raw	1 medium	1.8
Peach	1 medium	1.9	Cabbage, shredded, cooked	½ cup	1.7
Strawberries	½ cup sliced	1.9			
Dried plums (prunes)	3 medium	1.7	Cauliflower, cooked	½ cup	1.6
Pineapple, cubed	½ cup	1.0	Asparagus, cooked	½ cup	1.4
Grapes, seedless	½ cup	0.8	Tomato	1 medium	1.3
Cantaloupe, cubed	½ cup	0.6	Celery, strips	½ cup	1.0
			Red bell pepper, raw, sliced	½ cup	0.9
			Green bell pepper, raw, sliced	½ cup	0.8
			Mushrooms, raw	½ cup	0.4

with flavor, such as a juicy ripe strawberry (instead of an out-of-season tasteless one), you won't need to slather on the hi-cal toppings just to make it palatable.

Look for fiber. Fiber-packed vegetables and fruits take longer to chew, fill you up more, and keep you feeling fuller longer. They are one of the best weight-loss tools. (See "Fiber-Full Fruits and Veggies" for suggestions.)

Shop by color. Sounds a little too easy, but for the best health and nutrition, aim to eat an array of different colors of fruits and vegetables every day. It's like a gorgeous fresh multivitamin. A quick rule of thumb: The most intensely colored fruits and vegetables are often the most healthful as well.

Buy by the bag. Bagged vegetables and especially bagged salads save you loads of time, and they're great for when you're in a hurry. The only drawback is that cut salads may turn brown more quickly than whole bunches. If you don't have the time to wash and cut your own greens, choose bagged whole intact leaves such as baby spinach, mâche, arugula, and baby lettuce mixes (mesclun), which remain fresher longer.

Organic baby lettuce mixes with herbs;

EATING BY COLOR: THE BEST CHOICES FOR NUTRITION

Here's a quick color guide to the wide variety of fruits and vegetables you'll find in the supermarket. Remember: The most vibrantly colored ones are often the most healthful.

Blue and purple: Blackberries, blueberries, dried plums (prunes), fresh plums, purple potatoes, raisins.

Green: Asparagus, avocado, broccoli, celery, green apples, green beans, green grapes, kiwifruit, leafy greens, peas, spinach, zucchini.

White: Bananas, cauliflower, jicama, mushrooms, onions, parsnips, white potatoes.

Yellow and orange: Apricots, butternut squash, cantaloupe, carrots, corn, mangoes, nectarines, oranges, papaya, peaches, pineapple, pumpkin, tangerines, yellow apples, yellow summer squash, yellow winter squash.

Red: Beets, cherries, cranberries, pink or red grapefruit, red apples, red cabbage, red grapes, red bell peppers, red raspberries, rhubarb, strawberries, tomatoes, watermelon.

Source: The Produce for Better Health Foundation

baby carrots (for snacking and cooking); fiber-packed broccoli slaw; and microwaveable-pack greens, such as kale, are also good choices.

Best Bets in the Bakery

The bakery department is the source of good-for-you whole-grain breads and rolls, along with much temptation and bad-for-you partially hydrogenated fat—think frostings, fillings, cookies, pastries, and pie crust. There are healthy choices to be had, however. Here are a couple of suggestions.

Go for the grain. When buying breads in the bakery department, for fiber's sake, look for those made primarily with whole grain flours. These will usually be darker, heavier loaves, often with a firmer crust. Labels should first list whole wheat flour or other whole grains instead of just wheat flour, which means plain old white flour. Note that pumpernickel bread is dark in color due mainly to added coloring (often cocoa), although it may contain some whole grain flour. Other good choices are fat-free, whole wheat, and regular flour tortillas and whole wheat pita pockets.

Got a sweet tooth? Choose an angel food cake from the bakery for dessert and the family will cheer. It's light because it's made with all egg whites, and it's fat-free! Cut a thin slice for each diner and freeze the rest. (It's easy to slice when frozen.) Serve with sliced fresh fruit, juice-packed canned fruit, or melted no-sugar fruit spread for a fantastic treat.

Deli Delights

There's a wonderful assortment of great choices in the deli department; you just need to know where to look for them. Here's a quick guide to picking the best.

Look for lean meats. Deli meats with the least processing will generally be lower in both fat and sodium. Avoid luncheon meats and fatty products such as salami and bologna. Instead, opt for fresh-roast turkey breast (remove the skin); smoked turkey breast (choose pepper- or herb-coated smoked turkey for even more flavor); turkey pastrami (high in sodium but lower in fat); lean roast beef; and reduced-fat, lower-sodium ham.

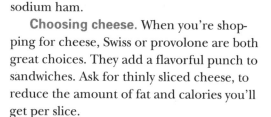

Choosing cheese. When you're shopping for cheese, Swiss or provolone are both great choices. They add a flavorful punch to sandwiches. Ask for thinly sliced cheese, to reduce the amount of fat and calories you'll get per slice.

Selecting salads. Look for vegetable, mixed bean, or bean-and-grain salads that are prepared with vinaigrette dressings, and drain off any excess dressing at home. Select vinaigrette-dressed pasta salads and add more veggies at home. Pick up small amounts of flavorful items such as olives and pickled vegetables or roasted peppers packed in water or vinegar, not in oil. They'll add zip to all your salads and sandwiches.

Avoid mayonnaise-dressed salads and pasta salads heavy with meat and cheese, as they contain loads of added fat and calories that will sabotage your weight-loss efforts.

Pick up a rotisserie chicken. Avoid breaded and fried fast-food chicken and pick up a rotisserie chicken for an easy dinner. One will feed a family of four. Before the chicken hits the platter, remove the skin and fat and tear it into portions, or cut it up with kitchen shears. But if you want to reheat the chicken, do so with the skin on or it will become dry. Set the oven to 350°F, wrap the chicken loosely in foil, place on a baking sheet, and bake for 20 minutes, or until warmed through. If you like, serve the chicken with salsa, barbecue sauce, or cranberry sauce.

The Fish Counter

Good for you and naturally low in fat and calories, fish is quick to prepare.

The fish department is a place you'll want to linger, but not if there's a fishy odor. Fish requires special handling, and you may prefer to buy it from a local fish market with a swifter turnover if you're not satisfied with the selection at your supermarket. Try these tips for making the best catch.

Be flexible. When purchasing fish, go to the store with an open mind: If you insist on a particular type of fish, you may end up with a less-than-fresh choice. A better way is to choose what is sparkling fresh—most fish can be mixed or matched in many recipes. The type of fish you choose is really a matter of personal preference, which is why recipes often call for something vague like "any mild white fish such as flounder or sole." Trying different varieties of fish will not only give you more choices at the supermarket, but it will also add more variety to your menu at home.

Use it quickly. Buy only the amount of fish you'll use in a day or so, unless it's

frozen. Insist on freshness and ask for a sniff—fish should smell like the ocean or a clean pond. If it smells overly fishy, it isn't fresh. Purchase fish with your eyes, too; if it looks dull, flabby, mushy, or dry, or if it isn't properly chilled, don't buy it.

Some fish may be labeled "previously frozen." If it's the type of fish you want, ask if there is some still frozen. Then you can thaw it yourself, often under better conditions.

Opt for oily over lean. Oily fish contain substances that are thought to benefit your health even more than leaner, white-fleshed fish, such as cod, halibut, bass, and flounder. Good oily fish choices include mackerel, bluefish, salmon, lake trout, tuna, and swordfish. But remember: All fish is still healthy and low in calories.

Choose steaks or fillets. Most fish on the market are boneless, skinless fillets that are easy for baking and broiling. Less often, you'll see fish steaks—thick slices cut across the width of the fish, generally a large fish such as salmon. Fish steaks are great for grilling. Check with your supermarket or fish

market when you want steaks; you may need to order them in advance.

Steer clear of breading. Avoid the added calories in breaded frozen fish and breaded formed fish or shellfish sticks and patties. If you prefer to buy frozen fish over fresh, opt for healthier varieties that won't pack on the pounds, such as haddock or orange roughy fillets without breading. They're just as tasty, and they cook just as quickly.

Pick up some shrimp. Shrimp are easy to cook, and they're naturally low in calories, so they fit perfectly into any weight-loss plan. You can steam, boil, broil, or grill them with terrific—and fast!—results. They're available in a wide range of sizes and are sold frozen in the shell, frozen shelled, defrosted from frozen, or cooked and peeled.

Shrimp freezes beautifully, so frozen uncooked, unpeeled shrimp is generally the best buy, quality-wise. When buying frozen shrimp, press on the bag or box. If you hear a crunchy covering of ice crystals, the shrimp have been partially thawed and refrozen. Look for a box or bag without a crunchy sound. If you can't find one, you may want to pass on it and stop at a local fish market on your way home.

Thawed uncooked shrimp should smell sweetly of the ocean. Avoid shrimp that have black spots or a pinkish cast. This means they've been sprayed with hot water so that they turn pink and are more "attractive" to the consumer. Go for gray shrimp instead, as they will turn pink when cooked anyway. When buying cooked shrimp, make sure that they look moist and plump.

Go for scallops. Scallops are delicious and a snap to prepare. They're best when cooked quickly, and work well with broiling,

grilling, steaming, baking, and sautéing. Watch them carefully, as they cook through in only a few minutes. (Overcooking can make them rubbery.) Cook them until they're just opaque. The larger sea scallops are those most often available. Scallops should be creamy white to pale pink. Avoid those that are bright white; this means that they have been soaked in a preservative solution, which causes them to them swell up. It also dilutes the flavor.

Other shellfish are great, too. The sea also holds other tasty, low-calorie shellfish, such as clams, mussels, and oysters. Keep in mind that shellfish doesn't travel well, so shop with your eyes and nose. Shellfish should be sweet-smelling and tightly closed. If slightly open, tap the shell; it should quickly close, indicating still-alive shellfish. Land-locked communities or rural areas may lack the high turnover necessary for stocking and selling good-quality shellfish, so be vigilant about freshness.

Pack shellfish on ice for the ride home,

and cook and enjoy it as soon as possible. If a clam or mussel remains closed after cooking, discard it.

Poultry and Meat Department

Meat and poultry are definitely on the menu, and there's an enormous variety to choose from. Just think lean, be sure to buy before the sell-by date, and make sure they're tightly wrapped. Here's a quick rundown of the best choices. (And remember, poultry is very perishable. If you've got a long trip home from the grocery store or if it's a warm day, plan on packing it on ice in a cooler.)

Chicken and Turkey

Skinless bone-in or boneless chicken and turkey breasts are the best choices calorie-wise. The breast contains less fat, and removing the skin further reduces calories by up to one-half. Whole roast chicken and turkey should be cooked with the skin on to retain moisture in the meat. Remove the skin just before eating. For quickest cooking and minimal preparation, select boneless breast halves, thin breast slices, cutlets, or tenders. Here are some other options:

Turkey breast roast is often overlooked, but it's delicious and lean—and it makes great leftovers. Sold bone-in, you can purchase the whole breast or just a half. The whole breast is generally a good buy; it's often sold frozen on sale, but it does provide quite a bit of meat, so for a small household, plan on delicious leftovers! As always, remove the skin before eating.

Ground chicken and turkey are tasty alternatives to higher-fat beef, but read the label to be sure they are made only from breast meat, with no added skin or fat, which are often ground in to provide moisture. Like all ground meats, they are quite perishable, so use or freeze within 2 days.

You can cut calories by making your next meatloaf with half ground turkey or chicken and half ground beef.

Poultry sausage is a wonderful alternative to higher-fat pork sausage. Some varieties are precooked, needing just a quick turn in a grill pan or skillet or over hot coals. Link turkey sausage is a raw product and must be thoroughly cooked. Broil it and add to pasta sauce, rice and beans, or soup. Or serve alongside waffles or French toast for a Sunday morning treat.

Lean turkey bacon, a delicious and lighter alternative to fatty pork bacon, means you can *really* enjoy your next BLT (the L stands for light!).

Beef

Look for beef with a bright red color. If it's beginning to darken and turn gray or brown, it has been sitting in the butcher case too long. Beef should be firm to the touch, neither soft nor mushy.

Look for "loin." The leanest cuts of beef have "loin" in their name. Sirloin and tenderloin as well as round are some of the low-fat cuts that'll help you cook up delicious dinners.

Choose "select." Also, reach for meat labeled "select." It is leaner than meat graded

COOKING LEAN CUTS OF BEEF

These beef cuts have the least fat. Check the list to see which cooking methods work best for each cut. In many cases, moist-heat methods, such as stewing or braising, are best for tenderizing them.

Cut of Beef	Best Cooking Method
Bottom round roast	Roast or braise large pieces
	Broil or grill steaks
Brisket	Braise
Chuck roast	Braise or stew
Eye of round	Roast large pieces
	Braise chunks
	Broil or grill steaks
Flank steak	Broil or grill
Round tip	Roast or braise large pieces
	Broil or grill steaks
	Sauté thin strips
Shank (cross cuts)	Braise
Sirloin steak	Broil or grill
Top round	Roast large pieces
	Broil or grill marinated steaks

"choice" and much leaner than "prime." Avoid heavily marbled cuts or those that are surrounded by a thick layer of fat. (See "Cooking Lean Cuts of Beef" for more information.)

For ground beef, choose extra-lean, round, or sirloin, and use or freeze it within 2 days.

Pork

When you're shopping for pork, look for moist meat that is firm to the touch. Cuts from the loin should be pale with a light tinge of pink, and the fat should be pure white, not yellow. Avoid any pork that is dry, gray, red, or discolored; it's been in the store too long.

Loin is leanest. As with beef, the leanest pork cuts generally have "loin" in their names. Whole pork tenderloin is a terrific cut to grill, roast, or broil, and it cooks quickly. Pork tenderloins often come in packages of two. One is the perfect size for a family of four; trim and freeze the other for another meal. Sometimes tenderloins come premarinated—convenient in a pinch, but for freshest flavor, marinate them yourself. (For more on marinating, see page 19.)

Pork loin roast, with or without the bones, is a fine choice for roasting. Center-cut pork loin chops are excellent sautéed, grilled, or broiled, and they're done in less than 10 minutes. Boneless pork cutlets or chops may also be cut into strips for stir-fries or skillet dinners.

Canadian bacon is best. When it comes to pork sausage, bacon, and ribs waltz right on by. They're way too fatty and loaded with calories. The poultry sausage and bacon mentioned earlier are fabulous alternatives guaranteed to please. One exception is Canadian bacon, a smoked cured pork loin that is naturally low in fat. Canadian bacon has a subtle smoky flavor, and it comes in slices or in cylindrical pieces that can be sliced or cut up at home. It is fully cooked, so all you need to do is heat it up. Try it sautéed, stir-fried, barbecued, baked, mixed into sauces, or added to sandwiches.

Lamb

Lamb is best when it's bright and moist. The fat on the surface should be white and waxy-looking. The color of the meat should range from pink to pale red. For the freshest flavor, cook lamb on the same day that you buy it. Whole cuts keep best—refrigerate them for up to 4 days. Ground lamb should be used or frozen within 2 days.

Again, look for "loin." As with beef and pork, the leanest lamb cuts also contain "loin" in their names. This includes loin chops and lamb loin, both tender cuts with hefty price tags, so you may want to reserve them for a special occasion.

Consider other cuts, too. A well-trimmed leg of lamb, cut from the sirloin end, is lean and delicious to roast or grill. If it's been butterflied (boned and opened up like a book), it grills more quickly and evenly, and it's easier to slice. It's also a great cut to marinate. But for daily cooking, check out lamb steaks or lamb sirloin chops; both are cut from the sirloin end of the leg and are very nice grilled or broiled.

Canned and Jarred Foods

This is a section of the supermarket where you'll find many excellent—and convenient—choices. Here's how to locate the slimmest, most healthful foods.

All Kinds of Oil

Vegetable oil is the most common oil used, but there may be a better choice for the dish you're preparing. Experiment with different types to see what flavorings you enjoy the most. One terrific pick is extra-virgin olive oil, a good-for-you fat that lends richness and depth to food, allowing you to use less oil and enjoy it more. Here are some other varieties to try:

Canola oil. This type is flavorless and has a light yellow color. It's often used to make salad dressings, as well as for sautéing and baking.

Corn oil. This mild-flavored oil has a yellow color and is great for dressings as well as for sautéing.

Olive oil. One of the most popular and widely used oils, olive oil has a mild to rich olive flavor, depending on what kind you buy. Its color can be pale yellow to deep green. Use it for anything from salad dressings and sautéing to drizzling over pasta or fresh tomato slices.

Peanut oil. Neutral-flavored peanut oil has a lovely golden color. It's often used for sautéing and stir-frying Asian-style dishes.

Safflower oil. Almost flavorless, safflower oil has a light texture and is great when used for sautéing.

Sesame oil (toasted). This type has a

strong, nutty flavor that dissipates with heat. It's great used in dressings and sauces.

Soybean oil. This oil has a very neutral flavor and is light in color. It's often used for sautéing. Incidentally, many "vegetable" oils on supermarket shelves are actually soybean oil or a combination of soybean oil and canola oil.

Sunflower oil. Light in flavor and color, the flavor of sunflower oil dissipates with heat. Use it for sautéing and for dressings.

Vinegar Varieties

There's more to vinegar than the ordinary white kind. When you sample all that's out there, you'll find that vinegars can add a great deal of zip and character to your cooking, without any added fat. When choosing a vinegar for a dish, remember that red wine vinegar and other intensely flavored varieties pair well with hearty, rich-flavored foods and dark leafy greens. White wine vinegar and other lighter-flavored types go well with more delicate foods such as chicken salads and mild salad greens. Here's a quick primer on some you may want to try.

Balsamic vinegar. This very distinctive Italian vinegar is aged for at least 10 years—some much longer. Commercial balsamic vinegar is made from red wine vinegar fortified with concentrated grape juice. It has a sweet, pungent quality that's good in a sauce or a salad dressing. The milder flavor of white balsamic vinegar is perfect with spring salads or on roasted asparagus.

Cider vinegar. Use in a deglazing sauce for a pork roast or in a vinaigrette. A mild vinegar, this is also good to use for homemade pickles.

Distilled vinegar. Made from commer-cially processed grain alcohol, distilled vinegar has a harsh, pungent flavor. Widely used in processed foods, at home, it's best reserved for washing down counters and cutting boards.

Flavored vinegars. These are made from wine vinegars (usually white wine) infused with fruits and/or fresh herbs. They add a subtle herbal or fruit flavor to salads, chicken, or fish. Raspberry vinegar has a particular affinity for beets. Tarragon vinegar lends fabulous flavor to salad greens, potato salad, and fish.

Malt vinegar. A classic condiment for fish and chips, malt vinegar is traditionally made from beer. Its mild flavor makes it a good choice for pickles and assertive salad dressings.

Sherry vinegar. Sweeter and more complex than red wine vinegar, sherry vinegar is aged for a minimum of 6 years. It's wonderful in a dressing for an avocado and grapefruit salad.

Red wine vinegar. A bold vinegar, this variety takes flavor nuances from the wine from which it was made. Combine red wine vinegar with fruity olive oil, mustard, and shallots for a lively vinaigrette.

Rice vinegar. Plain rice vinegar has a delicate flavor. It's so mild that it can be used with little to no oil for Asian-inspired salad dressings and dipping sauces. Rice vinegar is also sold flavored.

White wine and champagne vinegars. Use these subtle-flavored vinegars with delicate foods, such as seafood salads, or in a sauce for chicken or fish.

Salad Dressings

Prepared salad dressings, great for salads and for quick and easy marinades, can be a godsend on busy weeknights. There are plenty to choose from, but be mindful that dressings can be loaded with fat and calories. So select lighter versions that have less of both. Here are just a few of the standards—Italian and ranch—that you may want to try:

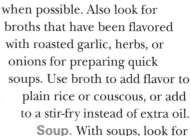

- Seven Seas Viva Italian Reduced-Fat Dressing (45 calories and 4 grams fat per serving)

- Kraft Light Done Right! Italian Reduced-Fat Dressing (40 calories and 3 grams fat per serving)

- Litehouse Lite Salsa Ranch Dressing and Dip (50 calories and 4.5 grams fat per serving)

- Kraft Light Done Right! Ranch Reduced-Fat Dressing (70 calories and 4.5 grams fat per serving)

And for something different, try the following fat-free dressing; it's great on greens and on fruit salads. Look for it refrigerated in the produce aisles.

- Litehouse Naturals Cranberry Vinaigrette, 25 calories and no fat per serving

Broths and Soups

Many people just don't have the time anymore to make their own broths and soups from scratch, so keeping a few cans in the cupboard can help streamline your efforts on those busy weeknights. Soups can be fat and calorie traps, though, so here's what to look for:

Broth. Choose fat-free, low-sodium broth when possible. Also look for broths that have been flavored with roasted garlic, herbs, or onions for preparing quick soups. Use broth to add flavor to plain rice or couscous, or add to a stir-fry instead of extra oil.

Soup. With soups, look for broth-based soups, bean or lentil soups, or reduced-fat or fat-free creamy soups, instead of the higher-fat versions. Be mindful of the sodium. Soups can add flavor to poultry, meat, and fish, and can make a quick and easy sauce for pasta.

Condiments, Spreads, and Sauces

Use these high-flavor items to perk things up. Check out mustards, with or without added herbs or onion; salsa; low-fat plain and flavored mayonnaise; soy sauce; plain and flavored teriyaki sauces; hot sauces of all types, from mild to super-spicy; roasted peppers; sweet and dill pickle relish; ketchup; and Asian chili and garlic sauce. Avoid anything that is very caloric or sugar-laden so the calories don't pile up.

For a treat. You can also choose pickles and pickled vegetables, olives, and olive spreads. These will be higher in calories, but since the flavors are so pronounced, just a touch will give you all the added zip you need without sabotaging your weight-loss efforts.

On the sweet side. Choose fruity no-sugar-added jams, syrups, and spreads to top anything from toast, muffins, and waffles to pancakes, angel food cake, and fat-free frozen yogurt.

Canned Fish

For a sandwich or salad, canned tuna, salmon, and sardines can't be beat. And they're good for you, but only if they're not weighed down with great spoonfuls of full-fat mayo.

Look for water-packed. For best nutrition, choose water-packed products and be sure to consume the calcium-rich bones found in canned salmon and sardines—they make you strong!

Pick up a pouch. The new flavored tuna in pouches is a tasty timesaver. Tuck some inside a whole wheat pita and top with plenty of fresh spinach, tomato, and sweet-onion slices.

Fruits

Juice-packed canned fruit is a terrific thing to have on the shelf. You can chill it and top with fat-free vanilla yogurt for dessert, enjoy it on cereal in the morning, or have some for a snack. Just avoid the calorie- and sugar-laden syrup-packed fruit.

A quick frozen treat. For a really quick sorbet, place the contents of one drained can and one undrained can of fruit in a metal pan in the freezer. When nearly frozen, puree in a food processor. Return to the pan and freeze until ready to serve. Voilà—instant sorbet!

A saucy snack. Natural applesauce has no added sugar, and it's very tasty. Keep a jar or two on the shelf for a quick snack or tasty dessert; a half-cup equals one fruit serving.

Tomatoes and Canned Vegetables

Probably one of the most frequently used canned products is canned tomatoes. They come in many varieties and are terrific to have on hand, especially when supermarket tomatoes aren't at their best or when you're just plain in a hurry. Canned vegetables are also a time-saver, providing quick and easy side dishes at a moment's notice.

Stock up on tomato products. Tomatoes are good for you and an essential ingredient in so many dishes. The very best tasting canned tomatoes are imported from Italy—see if your store carries them. Useful tomato products include whole tomatoes, crushed tomatoes, diced plain tomatoes, seasoned diced and stewed tomatoes (avoid those with added oil), and tomato paste.

Stock up on marinara or plain tomato-based pasta sauce, and check out the fat-free variety. Steer clear of pasta sauces with added cheese or meats, as they contain added calories and fat.

Keep canned veggies. If you can't seem to use up fresh vegetables fast enough before they spoil, canned vegetables are a convenient option. From corn to green beans to asparagus, the choices are many. Keep in mind that canned produce often contains excess sodium, so check labels, or rinse the produce before cooking.

Canned Beans

These are a wonderful convenience item. Keep a variety on hand for soups, salads, and dips. They're a great way to get your fiber! Look for beans without added pork products or fat. Rinse and drain them before using, and you'll reduce the amount of sodium. Stock up also on fat-free refried pinto and black beans for fast dinners and snacks.

Packaged Foods

There's no doubt about it: Packaged foods are quick and convenient, and they can make

LABEL LINGO

Don't worry—there's no need to go through a litany of confusing numbers and terminology to interpret food labels. This is the short version so you'll be able to quickly spot trouble areas. Reading a label is especially important when choosing packaged and canned foods. When you look at a label, first check out the serving size. Compare the food manufacturer's serving size to the size that you'll actually eat. For instance, if you usually eat 1 cup of ice cream, that's twice the usual serving size on a container, so you'll need to double all the figures or decide to reduce your serving size. Here's what else to look for as you continue reading the label:

Calories. Are they reasonable for the item and the serving size? And remember that many boxed mixes require added fats or eggs in the preparation, so check the "as prepared" column to find the calories for the finished product.

Total fat. If you're looking at a bottle of oil, this number will be high. Look for very low numbers for other foods, however, such vegetables, soups, crackers, or cereal. As with calories, double-check the "as prepared column" to be certain you're aware of the final fat count.

Saturated fat. This follows the figure given for fat on the label. Saturated fats, or "sat fats," are bad fats and can raise cholesterol levels, so keep this number as low as possible. And again, follow the "as prepared" rule.

Sodium. Your daily intake of sodium should not exceed 2,400 milligrams, so take that into consideration when looking at a label. Many packaged and prepared foods contain large amounts of sodium, so your daily total can add up quickly before you realize it.

Ingredients. Take a quick glance: What comes first? Ingredients are listed in order of use from greatest to smallest. If sugar is first or prominent, make another choice.

For breads, cereals, and crackers, the first ingredients should be whole grain flour or a whole grain. "Wheat" flour translates to white flour. Do your best to avoid products, especially breads and cereals, that contain partially hydrogenated oils.

Dietary Fiber. Fiber is an important weight-loss tool, and you'll want to try and get at least 25 grams per day. Cereal is an excellent way to start.

cooking infinitely easier. They can also harbor plenty of added fat and calories that can pack on the pounds. There's no need to avoid them completely; it's just a matter of steering clear of the fat traps. Here's a run-down of the best choices:

Rice, Grains, and Pasta

Carbohydrates, especially those from whole grains, are important components of low-calorie eating. They're a great base for many a delicious stir-fry, sauté, or stew, to name just a few serving options. Portion control is the key, along with low-fat preparation. Here are some good choices:

- Brown rice (look for the type that cooks in 30 minutes)

- Rice and bean mixes (read the labels for excess calories, fat, and sodium from added sauces and flavorings)
  - Barley, bulgur, and quinoa
    - Polenta, sold dry or prepared in the refrigerated section
    - Whole wheat and regular pasta
    - Whole wheat and regular couscous (watch for extra calories, fat, and sodium from seasoning packets)

Crackers

The buzzwords here are *whole grain* and *fiber*. Here's a list of good cracker picks,

GREAT CRACKER CHOICES

Cracker	Serving size	Fiber (g)	Calories
Ry Krisp Cracker	2	4	60
Kavli Whole Grain Crispbread, Hearty Thick	2	3	70
Ryvita Dark Rye Whole Grain Crispbread	2	3	70
Triscuit Reduced-Fat Baked Whole Wheat Crackers*	7	3	120
Wasa Original Crispbread Fiber Rye	1	2	30
Health Valley Low-Fat Whole Wheat Crackers	6	2	60
Nabisco Reduced-Fat Wheat Thins*	16	1	130

*Contains partially hydrogenated oil

SUPER CEREALS

Cereal	Serving size	Fiber (g)	Calories
Kellogg's All-Bran Original	½ cup	10	80
Kashi Good Friends	¾ cup	8	90
Barbara's Bakery Grain Shop	⅔ cup	8	90
Post Shredded Wheat 'N Bran, Original Spoon Size	1¼ cups	8	200
Kellogg's Two Scoops! Raisin Bran	1 cup	7	190
Post Shredded Wheat, Original	2 biscuits	6	160
Kellogg's Complete Wheat Bran Flakes	¾ cup	5	90
Post Grape Nuts	½ cup	5	210

starting from the most fiber to the least. Check labels for serving sizes.

Cereal

Many of us begin our mornings over a bowl of cereal. Instead of spooning up artificially flavored, oversweetened flakes, dig in to a satisfying, fiber-rich, nutritious whole grain bowlful. Your body will thank you!

Avoid prepared cereals with high amounts of sugar and those containing partially hydrogenated oils. Cereal should have least 3 grams of fiber per serving. And don't forget hot oatmeal and oat bran, with fat-free milk, a touch of brown sugar, and a sliced banana.

Frozen Foods

This section of the supermarket stocks some good staple items along with things you just don't need, such as frozen french fries, pizza, macaroni and cheese, lasagna, and fat-laden frozen dinners. Pass them by. Here are the smartest choices:

Find fruits and vegetables. Choose frozen vegetables and vegetable mixtures without added fat or sauces, fruits packed without sugar, and juice concentrates.

Pull breakfast from the freezer. Frozen whole grain toaster waffles are terrific for on-the-go breakfasts.

Hankering for dessert? Check out the ever-growing sorbet selection or take a peek at the frozen yogurt display. Read the labels to get the lowest fat and calories. Fruit pops or frozen low-fat fudge pops can be an occasional, welcome treat.

In the Dairy Case

The best way for men and women to get enough calcium in their diets is by consuming low-fat dairy products. Supermarkets are brimming with appealing choices in this area. Here's how to sift through the array to find the slimmest selection.

Drink your milk. Fat-free milk is best, but 1% looks and tastes better in coffee, especially if you're used to cream. You may want to give fat-free half-and-half a try, but nix the nondairy creamers. Avoid 2% milk; it's not low-fat because it has more than 3 grams of fat per serving.

Get some culture. Choose fat-free plain yogurt with active cultures for toppings and dressings. Stock up on small containers of fat-free flavored yogurt for effortless breakfasts and snacks. Avoid the sugary high-fat dessert-like yogurt products. They may look healthy, but they're really just extra calories in disguise.

Sour cream selections. Reach for low-fat sour cream instead of the high-fat version. The low-fat version is tasty and creamy—and much slimmer. Fat-free sour cream can taste disappointing, however.

Cottage cheese choices. When choosing cottage cheese, look for 1% instead of the high-fat version. A nice treat for breakfast: a bowl of 1% cottage cheese mixed with fresh or juice-packed canned fruit, such as pineapple chunks, and a light dusting of ground cinnamon.

Better ways with butter. A little butter on your whole wheat toast can't hurt. But re-member to use just a little. If you heat a stick of butter for a few seconds in the microwave, it'll soften up so you can easily slice off a very thin sliver. Keep in mind that unsalted butter has a fresher flavor than salted, so you may want to give it a try.

Eggs are *really* okay. It's official: Eggs are back. Enjoy one for your next breakfast. If you like, make a veggie-filled frittata for dinner. Serve with salsa, boiled potatoes, and a crisp salad—delicious!

Cheese it. Fresh whole blocks of full-fat cheese are often a better choice than low-fat cheeses, which can be rubbery, or pre-shredded cheeses, which tend to lack flavor. Cheese shreds are also expensive, you are tempted to use more, and they can go moldy quickly. A smaller amount of the real thing is more flavorful and much more satisfying.

Looking for a schmeer? Spread your whole wheat bagel half with whipped low-fat plain or flavored cream cheese instead of the high-fat variety. Add a slice of tomato or a little fruit spread, and you'll never miss the fat.

Grab a carton of juice. Choose chilled fresh-squeezed juices that have been fortified with calcium. Avoid juice drinks.

Note: Grapefruit juice reacts with certain medications, so ask your doctor if anything you take might pose a problem.

Storing and Freezing Food

Keeping your purchases fresher, longer.

Once you've unloaded the groceries from the car, take a moment to stretch before you begin the next step: putting them away.

We all know that milk goes in the fridge, sorbet and frozen peas in the freezer, cereal on the shelf. But there are a few things you'll need to store more carefully so they stay fresh and are easy to cook.

Meat and Poultry

These items are all highly perishable and need to be properly stored as soon as you get home. Here are tips for keeping them at their freshest.

Refrigerating. Store meat and chicken in their original packaging in the coldest part of the fridge (usually the bottom, toward the back), placing a plate or tray underneath in case of leakage. Cook or freeze chicken within 2 days, cuts of meat within 4 days, and ground meat or poultry within 2 days.

Freezing. Meat or poultry that you don't plan to cook within the above time frame should be frozen. But don't simply toss it in the freezer in the store wrapping; take the time to trim and portion it so that it's ready to cook when thawed. Wrap it properly in a zip-top freezer bag. Clearly label and date the item, even if you're sure you'll remember later. Freeze it in the coldest part of the freezer, at 0°F or colder.

For whole chicken or turkey, remove the giblet bag and interior fat around the cavity

17

HOW LONG CAN I KEEP IT?

Here's how long you can expect meat, poultry, and fish to last in the freezer. The shelf lives given here assume that the food has been properly wrapped and tightly sealed. If you haven't written a date on a frozen item, keep in mind the cardinal rule of food safety: When in doubt, throw it out.

Food	Average Freezer Shelf Life
Beef and lamb (steaks, roasts)	1 year
Chicken and turkey (whole)	1 year
Chicken and turkey (parts)	6 months
Ground meat	3 months
Pork (chops, roasts)	4–8 months
Fish, lean white	6 months
Fish, oily	2 months

and neck. For poultry parts, grasp the skin (if any) with a paper towel and pull it off. Also trim off the fat. If removing bones, freeze them separately for stock. For meats, trim off any fat, gristle, or silver skin.

Divide the meat or poultry into recipe- or meal-size portions. Place in zip-top freezer bags, press to squeeze out the air, and seal the bags completely.

Ground beef or other ground meats or poultry should be pressed out flat in a freezer bag so that they store flat and thaw rapidly. If you like, form ground beef or turkey into patties. Or mix up a favorite meatball recipe, shape the meatballs, and freeze them, uncooked, in single layers in zip-top freezer bags, or freeze first on a baking sheet, then transfer to bags.

Chops, cutlets, and small pieces or cubes should be spread out in a zip-top freezer bag in a single layer. They'll thaw much more quickly if they're not on top of each other, and you won't be hacking at frozen chunks, trying to separate the pieces. Freeze them flat; once frozen, the bags can be stacked, saving valuable space.

Thawing. It is safest to thaw meat and poultry in the refrigerator to reduce any chance of contamination. Plus, the ice crystals will melt slowly, allowing the food to re-absorb the liquid, so it is less likely to be dry. Place on a tray to catch any seepage. It is not safe to thaw at room temperature or to re-freeze thawed meat or poultry.

Thin steaks, cutlets, chops, cubes, parts, and ground meats and poultry can be thawed in a container of cold water if sealed *completely* in a zip-top bag, changing the water if it gets lukewarm. Or, thaw them in the microwave according to the manufacturer's directions.

Fish and Shellfish

Fish and shellfish are also highly perishable, but the steps for storing them differ a bit from that of meat and poultry. Here's how to maintain optimum freshness.

Refrigerating. If the fish is sparkling fresh, it's generally safe to keep it for 2 days; however, it's best to cook it the day it was purchased. To store fish, fill a colander with ice and set over a large bowl. Seal the fish securely in a zip-top bag. Put the fish on top of the ice, cover with more ice, and refrigerate until ready to cook. Avoid storing fish directly in a bowl of ice; the fish will end up sitting in a puddle of water, which can harm both its texture and flavor. Replenish the ice and drain the water if storing fish for an extra day.

Alternately, you can place the wrapped fish between two ice packs in a baking dish and put the whole thing in the fridge. In other words, keep fish cold, cold, cold.

Place mussels, clams, and oysters in a single layer on a tray covered with a damp towel. Refrigerate for up to 2 days. If they are packed in perforated plastic or net bags, place the bags on a tray in the refrigerator. Scallops should be refrigerated in the container in which they were purchased.

Freezing. Trim the fish, if necessary. Remove any bones that run partway down the center of fillets by pulling them out with clean needlenose pliers or tweezers. Cut the fish into portions. Pack in single layers, divided in meal-size batches in zip-top freezer bags. Don't stack thin fillets on top of each other; you'll never get them separated intact. Freeze the fish flat; then stack the bags for easy storage.

ADDING EXTRA FLAVOR

Here's a neat trick: Add an oil-based marinade to a bag of meat or poultry before freezing. Once it's thawed, the marinade will have penetrated with a deep, rich flavor, and the item is ready to hit the grill or broiler.

Bone-in chicken pieces and large cuts of meat, such as butterflied leg of lamb or London broil, are good choices for freezer marinating. They'll keep for up to a month without detriment to the texture. Freezer-marinate thinner cuts and chops for only a week; otherwise, the meat may become mushy.

Thaw the item in the refrigerator in its marinade, placing the unopened bag in a dish to catch any drips. Thicker pieces of meat may take at least a day to thaw in the refrigerator.

Keep frozen shrimp well-wrapped in the freezer, defrosting just what you need for a meal. For scallops, clean as you would before cooking: Remove the little tendon along the side; swish the scallops in a bowl of cold water, and lift them out, leaving any grit behind. Pat dry on paper towels and pack in meal-size batches in single layers in freezer bags.

Thawing. Most fish should be thawed before cooking, as should shrimp and scallops. Thin fish fillets or cubes of fish that are to be simmered in liquid, say for a chowder, need not be thawed. Commercially frozen fish fillets (often sold in boxes) should be cooked while still partially frozen to avoid overcooking; follow package directions.

Thaw fish or shellfish overnight in the refrigerator, placed in a colander over a bowl to catch drips. Fish and scallops may be thawed in the microwave according to manufacturer's instructions. Or, if completely sealed in zip-top bags, they can be thawed in a container of cold water. To quickly thaw shrimp, unwrap them and let stand in a bowl of cold water for about 30 minutes. Never leave fish or shellfish to thaw on the counter at room temperature; it's not safe.

Vegetables

When vegetables are picked, they are at their peak of ripeness. To prevent decay, they should be refrigerated as soon as possible, loosely packed in plastic bags or store wrappings. Of course, there are a few exceptions to this rule.

Winter squash, potatoes, onions, garlic, and shallots should be stored at a cool room temperature, as refrigeration causes them to deteriorate. Choose a wicker basket that allows some air exchange or store in paper bags. Wire baskets that hang in tiers from the ceiling are perfect.

If you like having frozen vegetables on hand, it's convenient to stock bags and boxes of commercially frozen vegetables. They're frozen almost immediately after harvest, so they're at their peak of freshness. Most often, you can simply toss them as they are into a dish you're cooking—no thawing required. In addition to packages of individual vegetables, such as broccoli and spinach, try

stocking up on frozen veggie mixes as well (the ones without the added sauces). They come in very handy for quick stir-fries.

Fruit

Most fruit, with notable exceptions, is picked unripe and should be left to ripen at room temperature.

Refrigerating. Once ripe, fruit should be refrigerated loosely packed in plastic bags to preserve flavor and texture.

Citrus fruits do not ripen once they have been picked. They will keep for a few days in a basket at a cool room temperature, but they will last longer if refrigerated.

Grapes, cherries, and berries will not ripen once picked and are extremely perishable. Refrigerate berries in the baskets in which they were sold, covered with the store cellophane, or sort them and transfer to covered plastic containers—this works especially well for large quantities. Store cherries and grapes loosely covered in plastic bags.

Apples are picked when they are ripe,

and they'll stay crisp if stored in the refrigerator. However, pears and other tree fruits, such as peaches, apricots, plums, and nectarines, often need to ripen at room temperature before they are ready to eat. Once ripe, store these fragile fruits in the refrigerator to eat soon.

Melons need to sit at room temperature until fragrant and ripe, but should then be kept chilled. Cut melons should always be refrigerated. Watermelon needs no refrigeration until it has been cut. Always wash a melon prior to cutting it to avoid transferring any bacteria from the rind to the fruit.

Tropical fruits, such as pineapple, persimmons, papaya, and mangoes, should not be chilled for more than a day or so. Bananas will blacken in the refrigerator. If very ripe, freeze them to use in banana bread. When thawed, they will turn to puree and be ready to add to the batter.

Large tomatoes should never be refrigerated; that blunts their flavor. Very ripe cherry tomatoes will spoil quickly and need to be refrigerated and eaten soon, especially in 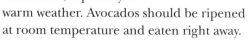 warm weather. Avocados should be ripened at room temperature and eaten right away.

Freezing. Berries are the easiest fruits to freeze because they require the least amount of processing, so they fit right in to your busy lifestyle. Berries have a short season, so buy during their peak. Perhaps you're planning a trip to a pick-your-own farm, dreaming of baskets filled with ripe berries? Here is how to preserve those treasures.

Except for strawberries, berries shouldn't be washed before they are frozen. Freeze blueberries in a zip-top bag, and pop cranberries into the freezer in their bags, or transfer to freezer bags in measured amounts.

Sort raspberries, huckleberries, and blackberries, discarding any that are not sound. Place measured amounts in freezer bags, or freeze them flat on jelly-roll pans and then transfer to bags. For strawberries, rinse first and pat dry. Hull and pack in freezer bags. Be sure to label bags with the date and amount.

Add frozen berries, except large whole strawberries, as they are to baked goods, smoothies, or yogurt. Whole strawberries should be partially thawed before adding to a smoothie. If you're cooking with them, it's best to leave them frozen. You may want to slice any large strawberries into smaller pieces before freezing.

Using Your Frozen Assets

Your freezer can go a long way toward helping you make nutritious meals quickly. Here's how to use those frozen assets to your best advantage:

Freeze some grains. Cook a double or triple amount of brown rice, barley, or quinoa and freeze in measured amounts (1 cup is handy) in zip-top freezer bags. There is no need to thaw before adding to soups or stews. If you're serving them as a side dish, just warm up in the microwave according to manufacturer's directions.

Save leftover canned goods. Freeze what's left in a can of beans, broth, corn, tomatoes—or whatever. Measure the food

and label the bag with content, amount, and date. In most cases, there will be no need to thaw the item before adding to a recipe in which it will be cooked or heated.

Make some planned-overs. Make a large batch of a favorite stew, chili, casserole, or soup. Freeze in meal-size or single-serving portions for easy dinners or lunches.

Solve the paste quandary. What to do with the rest of a can of tomato paste? Before you toss it, try this: Spoon it into a zip-top freezer bag and press the outside of the bag to spread it flat. When you need some, rap the bag on the counter to break off a chunk. If you prefer measured amounts, drop the tomato paste in tablespoons onto a baking sheet. Freeze the drops, then transfer to a freezer bag. No need to thaw before using.

Do some pre-prep. If you are chopping an onion, why not chop two and freeze the extra? The next time you need chopped onion, you won't shed any tears. No need to thaw first.

Save some money. Red bell peppers are delicious—but often they're pricey. When they're on sale or locally grown at the farmers' market, stock up. Rinse, cut into halves or wide strips, seed, and freeze. Don't thaw before adding to stir-fries. They're also delicious roasted until tender with olive oil and a sprinkle of thyme.

Get ready for breakfast. Make big batches of your own healthy waffles or pancakes. Freeze flat on trays, then stack in freezer bags with waxed paper in between. For a quick breakfast, pop a waffle into the toaster or toaster oven or heat a pancake in the microwave.

Crafting Your Kitchen Space

Putting the keys to low-cal cooking at your fingertips.

The more pleasant your kitchen is to work in and the more organized it is, the more you will enjoy preparing meals. To start cooking low-calorie meals, you won't need to renovate your kitchen or restock every cupboard. In fact, you probably already own most of the really useful fat-fighting and timesaving equipment you'll need. All it takes is a little bit of planning.

Get Organized

Deciding how to organize your kitchen is a personal decision, and it's largely dictated by the space you have to work with. Regardless of your kitchen's size, there are ways to make it work to your advantage. Here are a few things you can do right now:

Claim some space. Remove nonessential items from countertops that can go elsewhere. Shelving and cabinets can help clear countertops for much-needed work space. If you don't have shelving in your kitchen, inexpensive units are widely available and easy to install. Can you fit a butcher-block cart with underneath shelves in your kitchen? It can become a movable (or stationary) working island with the bonus of extra storage.

Slim down your drawers and cupboards. Get rid of things that you never use, that are broken, or that never worked in the first place. Stow rarely used items that you just can't part with—be they pasta makers or ice crushers—in another room or an out-of-the-way place, so they don't take up valuable cupboard space needed for the items you use more frequently.

Add some compartments. Instead of tossing all manner of cooking utensils in a random drawer, decide which drawers will hold which tools, and then add compartments to help organize everything. Plastic utensil trays are available in many department stores and cooking supply stores. Or, you may want to look for pretty baskets to line the drawers. Both choices are easily removable, so you can always change your mind as to how things are organized.

Make it logical. Hang pots on racks or hooks near the stove, or keep them in heavy-duty drawers beneath or next to the stove. Keep knives near cutting surfaces. Store them in a knife block or sheathed and stowed in nearby drawers. Store often-used utensils, including measuring cups and spoons, next to your work area.

Place metal spatulas, tongs, slotted spoons, and stirring spoons upright in a pretty crock, jar, or earthenware flowerpot near the stove. Whisks, rubber scrapers, and mixing spoons can go in another crock near the prep area, to keep them from getting coated with grease.

Shelve it. Store cookbooks in bookcases, not on the counter. No need to worry then about spills, plus your counter won't be so cluttered. Also, make photocopies of your favorite recipes. When cooking, tape the recipe on the wall in front of your work space; if the refrigerator is close to that space, anchor the copy at eye level with a magnet. If you like working directly from cookbooks, consider buying a cookbook stand, which will prop the book up, keep it clean, and hold open the page, taking up less counter space.

Work Smart

Once you have your general work space set up, it's time to think about making your actual cooking efforts easier. Here are some tips to get you started:

Keep your feet on the ground. Place some nonslip, washable rugs in front of the stove and sink to keep your feet cushioned and in place while you prepare your meals.

Cover up. Most of us drip and splatter a bit while we cook, so invest in a few large bib aprons to keep your clothes looking nice.

Cover counters, too. The counter next to the stove or the space in the center of the stove often becomes a resting spot for cooking implements, such as greasy spoons. Spoon rests are handy, but they never seem large enough. Try this if you have a counter adjoining your stove: Cover it with a sheet of aluminum foil. Spoons, spatulas, measuring cups, and tongs that you are using can rest there, instead of balanced in a small dish. As an added bonus, the counter will stay grease-free. When you are done, drop the utensils in the sink and toss the foil. Clean counter, cleaner stove. Less clean-up later!

Streamline prep time. Nothing slows you down more than slicing or dicing at awkward angles to avoid piles of food on your cutting board. Instead, keep small bowls or a few paper plates near the cutting area to transfer prepped food. Also, have a scrap bowl or a bucket lined with a plastic bag on hand to readily dispose of or to compost waste such as vegetable trimmings.

Keep it clean. This is a cardinal rule of cooking, even if space is abundant. Keep a large bowl of sudsy water in your sink (or fill the whole sink) and place dirty utensils, bowls, and dishes—but **never** knives—in it as soon as you're done with them. Keep a trash receptacle nearby. Load the dishwasher as you go. Cooking will be so much easier when piles of dirty dishes and waste aren't edging into your space.

Get the Right Tools

Good-quality pots and pans, well-crafted sharp knives, and a cutting board or two are a great investment in your cooking future. You may even want to ask for cookware for birthdays, or for an anniversary or other special occasion. Again, you probably already have a lot of these items, but if you'd like to add to your collection, here are some ideas:

Saucepans, Dutch Ovens, and Stockpots

The type and quality of pots and pans you use have a dramatic effect on the quality of your cooking. It's not necessary to invest a lot of money in an expensive matched set. A few well-chosen pieces are all that's needed. Buy the heaviest-gauge cookware you can afford. Heavy-gauge pots and pans deliver heat more evenly and will last longer. Often, the best all-purpose cooking choice is stainless steel with a copper or aluminum core. Look for sales or special offers, or scour catalogs for special deals.

Heavy-gauge pans, as described above, are the best choices for saucepans and Dutch ovens. Avoid pure aluminum pans, as the interior can pit. It may also react with acidic foods, such as tomatoes, and impart a tinny taste. Instead, select pans made of or lined with stainless steel. Some saucepans and Dutch ovens have a nonstick coating, which is nice, but not necessary. Do make sure all parts of a Dutch oven are ovenproof. (Many are made with plastic handles or lids, which cannot withstand the heat of an oven, so they're only useful on the stove top.)

For a stockpot, used mainly for boiling large amounts of water or simmering stock, a thinner gauge pot is acceptable and much easier to hoist.

Here are some items that get lots of use in the kitchen. Start small, with only a few items that you know you'll use frequently, then add to your kitchen collection when you feel the need to expand.

• 2-quart saucepan with lid

• 3½- to 4-quart saucepan with lid

- 6- to 8-quart ovenproof Dutch oven with lid
- 8-quart or larger stockpot

Skillets

A large skillet is the workhorse of the kitchen. In this simple piece of cookware, you can prepare an entire meal. For excellent performance and even heat distribution, choose a heavy-gauge skillet with a stainless steel or brushed or anodized aluminum exterior and an aluminum inner core or heavy aluminum disk on the bottom. Thinner-gauge pans hold heat unevenly and may scorch the food.

Choose skillets with nonstick coatings—they allow you to cook with much less fat. A good nonstick pan has a coating that's been applied several times, so it will hold up to longer use.

Never heat a nonstick-coated pan dry, without even a light coat of oil, and don't exceed medium-high temperature. If you like to cook at a high sear, do so in an uncoated pan. Always use nylon or wooden utensils, and don't put the pan in the dishwasher, no matter what the manufacturer claims.

If you're in the market for one or more skillets, here are a few to consider:

- 12" nonstick skillet with lid
- 12" anodized steel or aluminum or nonstick grill pan
- 10" nonstick skillet
- 6" to 8" nonstick skillet

Ovenware

Good-quality ovenware helps foods cook evenly, and with the myriad nonstick products available, it can also speed cleanup time—always a plus! Here are a few items you may want to consider:

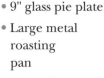

- 13" × 9" metal baking pan
- 8" or 9" square metal baking pan
- 9" round metal cake pan
- 9" × 5" and/or 8½" × 4½" metal loaf pan
- 13" × 9" glass baking dish
- 8" or 9" square glass baking dish
- 9" glass pie plate
- Large metal roasting pan

- Jelly-roll pan or other baking pan with shallow sides
- Baking (cookie) sheet

Also Nice to Have

These items will have endless use in your kitchen and will pay for themselves.

- Selection of nested stainless steel bowls
- Colanders, sieves, and strainers
- Food processor/ blender/ electric mixer

Knives

Almost any good cook will tell you that a good-quality knife is the single most important tool in the kitchen. There's no reason to buy a lot of knives. Just be sure to stock three top-quality ones: a paring knife; a chef's knife for chopping, slicing, and dicing; and a serrated knife for bread and tomatoes. The chef's knife is most important. Men are usually comfortable with an 8" or 10" chef's knife; many women prefer a 6" knife for its lighter weight. Hold the knife in your hand. It should feel comfortable and be easy to grip. The knife that feels good in your hand is the right knife for you. Purchase knives made of high-carbon stainless steel, which keeps its edge longer and won't stain or discolor food.

To properly care for your knives, never use them for any other purpose (opening jars, tightening screws, etc.), don't throw them carelessly into a drawer or toss them into a sink of sudsy water, and never put them in the dishwasher. Always cut on a wooden or plastic cutting board; never cut directly on a marble or a metal surface, which could damage the knife blade. If you take good care of your knives and use them properly, they can last for years.

Cutting Boards

When it comes to cutting boards, what's better, wooden or plastic? The truth is, it doesn't much matter as long as the board is properly cleaned after each use. For food safety reasons, especially after cutting raw meat, fish, or poultry, all cutting boards must be thoroughly cleaned before they are used again.

Wooden boards can be more aesthetically pleasing, and they are nicer to cut upon, but they must be scrubbed and sanitized by hand after each use, and they can absorb the odors of onion and garlic. Most plastic boards, on the other hand, can go into the dishwasher for thorough cleaning and deodorizing.

Wooden boards are often used for slicing breads, rolling out pie doughs, and stamping out biscuits. They also can do double-duty as platters at large parties—they look good, and they are functional.

Plastic boards are often used for most everything else. And afterward, there's usually no elbow grease required; just pop them into the dishwasher for cleaning.

When choosing and buying your own cutting boards, keep the size of your countertop in mind. You want the most cutting surface possible, but remember that the board has to fit on your countertop—and in the dishwasher, if you're choosing plastic. Thicker is better in both plastic and wood, so that the board won't warp, but it should not be too heavy to move easily. A good, sturdy plastic board is about ½" thick. To keep your board from slipping while you work, or to steady a warped board, place a damp sheet or two of paper towel underneath.

Quick and Easy Meal Planning

Simple suggestions for eating your fill while still slimming down.

You've purchased the food, the kitchen is stocked, and you're psyched to get started. A newer, thinner, healthier, and more energetic you (and family) is within your grasp. But how do keep your resolve to eat better?

To borrow a phrase, you do it one meal at a time. One snack at a time. One victory and one pound at a time. And pretty soon, making better and slimmer food choices will become second nature.

The key to a healthy eating plan is to eat plenty of fruits and vegetables, enjoy modest amounts of whole grains, include fish and seafood, and opt for low-fat dairy products and lean meats. And by using herbs, spices, and healthful condiments, you can pack your food with flavor, while watching your waistline shrink.

To shift the focus of your diet around, make an effort to get one or two servings of fruits and vegetables at each meal or snack. By making this simple change, one meal at a time, it will soon be easy to reach a goal of at least eight vegetable and fruit servings per day.

Why load up on fruits and vegetables? As good sources of fiber, they'll fill you up and keep you feeling fuller longer, with fewer calories. Rich in vitamins and nutrients, fruits and veggies can also aid in maintaining good health.

To help you start a day of meal planning, let's start at the beginning and continue

29

through the day. These simple tips and tricks will easily fit into your daily routine.

Breakfast: Ideas for A.M. Eating

Mom was right: Never skip breakfast. It really is the most important meal of the day. If you miss it, chances are you'll get extremely hungry later on and give in to a fattening craving. Think of breakfast as fuel for your body: Like a car with an empty tank, without breakfast, you'll simply come to a halt. Here are some ideas to try.

Fiber up. Breakfast is a great time for fiber. Have a serving of high-fiber cereal (see page 15 for some terrific selections), add

fruit, fat-free or 1% milk, and a slice of whole grain toast, and you're well on your way to a daily goal of at least 25 grams of fiber. And remember, it takes a little while for your body to adjust to getting more fiber, so be sure to add it to your diet gradually.

Have some juice. Drink a glass of juice at breakfast, but avoid juice the rest of the day, opting instead for the whole fruit (more fiber!). If you prefer, divide your juice into two portions, saving some to drink later over ice, perhaps mixed with sparkling water.

Spread it thinner. If the butter you spread on your toast is rock-hard, you might use too much. Microwave it for 5 to 10 seconds, until slightly soft, and less butter will spread much further.

Whip up a smoothie. Hate to eat in the morning? Drink your breakfast instead. Make a smoothie with fruit, yogurt, and frozen juice concentrate (see smoothie recipes beginning on page 218). Too much work? Put the fixings in the blender container the night before, chill it, and whirl it up for breakfast. Pour into a tall glass and sip through a straw. Or, pour into a travel cup with a lid and straw for a quick breakfast on the go.

Craving a bagel? Today's bagels are actually twice their former size. Instead of eating the whole thing, enjoy half a whole wheat bagel and share or freeze the rest. Top with light whipped cream cheese and sliced strawberries or peaches, a favorite fruit spread, or a schmeer of light chive cream cheese and sliced tomatoes. Munch with fruit or juice and a cup of coffee.

More fruit! In summer, top mixed fresh fruit with fat-free plain or lemon yogurt and a handful of slivered almonds or low-fat granola. In winter, simmer mixed dried fruit in

WHAT'S IN A SERVING?

It's amazing how easy it is to rack up servings of fruits and vegetables in a day. Serving sizes are relatively small, so before you know it, you'll reach a goal of at least 8 servings per day. The examples below show just how easy it is to get a serving:

• One serving of cooked or uncooked vegetables or fruit is ½ cup (chopped or sliced, if applicable) or 1 medium piece

• One serving of raw leafy greens or salad is 1 cup

• One serving of dried fruit is ¾ ounce

• One serving of fruit or vegetable juice is ¾ cup

orange juice and water until soft. Sweeten lightly with honey or brown sugar and chill. Serve with fat-free vanilla yogurt and a slice of toast or over a bowl of oatmeal.

Crack an egg. Eggs are a wonderful source of nutrients. Fry or scramble one per person in cooking spray in a nonstick skillet. If you like, sprinkle a little shredded cheese on top. Serve on a slice of whole grain toast with salsa or ketchup for a better breakfast sandwich.

Be selective with sides. Sausage or bacon can be an occasional treat, but make it turkey sausage and turkey or lean Canadian bacon. (For more breakfast ideas, see the recipes beginning on page 41.)

Lunch: Tips for Midday Dining

Lunch can be a minefield—fat traps at every turn. Even if you lunch at home because you work in a home office or are retired or a stay-at-home parent, you probably don't want to spend a lot of time making lunch. But wherever you're lunching, make sure you have a serving of veggies—it could be a side salad with low-fat dressing, a microwaved vegetable, or raw veggie sticks. Finish lunch with a piece of fruit for a little something sweet.

Since lunch is often something served between bread, let's begin there.

Build a better sandwich. For fiber's sake, have your sandwich with whole wheat bread, pita pockets, or tortillas. Choosing a smart spread will add flavor instead of just fat. Have less meat and cheese—about 2 ounces of meat and ½ ounce of cheese per sandwich. Meat options could include roasted or smoked turkey, turkey pastrami, lean roast beef, or lean, lower-sodium ham.

SMART SPREADS

If you're used to full-fat mayo, make a switch to fat-free mustard. The gain? Full-bodied flavor. The loss? Per tablespoon, a whopping 110 calories and 11 grams of fat! Ketchup and salsa are also terrific as spreads and won't cost you in calories or fat. Here are some other spread choices:

- Regular or flavored reduced-fat mayonnaise
- Olive spread
- Hummus (great for salad-based pita sandwiches)
- Thousand Island or salsa-ranch reduced-fat dressing
- Olive oil and vinegar

Avoid fatty meats, salami, and luncheon loaves. Since you're adding less cheese, make it a tasty one—try Cheddar, Pepper Jack, Jarlsberg, Swiss, or provolone.

For crunch and zip, pile on the healthful additions. Try roasted red or yellow bell peppers, pickled banana peppers, sliced tomato, crunchy cucumber, pickles, and sweet onion slices—and go green with spinach leaves, shredded romaine, or red-leaf lettuce. And if your veggie add-ons equal ½ cup, that's a serving of veggies!

Share it or save it. Most deli sandwiches could easily serve two, so find a lunch buddy to share your sandwich, or save half for tomorrow's lunch. Some delis sell half sand-

QUICK AND LEAN SANDWICH IDEAS

Tired of the same old sandwich every day? Here are three unique ideas that will add some zip to your lunch.

- Spread a whole wheat, fat-free tortilla with fat-free refried beans. Sprinkle with a little shredded cheese and heat in the microwave. Top with chopped romaine or baby spinach leaves, chopped or sliced tomato, and salsa. Eat with a knife and fork, or roll it up and eat out-of-hand.

- Spread a halved whole wheat pita pocket with hummus and add a little crumbled feta cheese, mixed greens, sliced cucumber, and sliced red bell pepper. Spritz with lemon.

- Spread one slice of whole wheat toast with mustard, and one slice with low-fat mayo. Add ripe tomato slices and torn fresh basil. For protein, add a sliced hard-cooked egg or ½ ounce sliced fresh mozzarella cheese.

wiches served with soup or salad, which is a great idea. Avoid the chips offered with a sandwich; crunch on an apple instead. If you can't resist, give in to a few chips and share the rest.

Have some soup. Begin your meal with a cup of lentil or bean soup, or broth-based veggie soup (another vegetable serving!). Or have a heartier serving of soup with a side salad and a whole grain roll or crackers.

Enjoy a slice. Pizza can also be part of a healthy lunch. Order a single plain or veggie slice but nix the extra cheese and fat-laden meats. Round out the meal with a nice side salad.

Go green. Fast-food restaurants are making an effort to attract health- and weight-conscious consumers by offering meal-size salads, which can be good low-cal choices. Be wary of the bacon bits, fried chicken toppings, croutons, shredded cheese, and large servings of full-fat dressings. Request lower-fat alternatives, such as grilled chicken, and have them make the salad with half the cheese, bacon, and no croutons. Ask for the nut toppings on the side. And inquire about low-cal dressings, or bring your own. Or simply dress your salad with half the amount of dressing you've been given and skip the remaining dressing. Out goes temptation.

Bar none. Salad bars are good lunch spots, if you pick carefully. Load up first on dark-colored greens, such as romaine, spinach, and watercress. Add fiber with beans. Be generous with the fresh steamed veggies, such as broccoli, green beans, and carrots. Build in color and vitamins with beets, tomatoes, red cabbage, melon, berries, and red bell peppers. Add cucumbers, celery, and sweet onions for crunch.

Avoid the fat traps like bacon bits and predressed salads and prepared foods, unless they are low-cal choices, such as vegetable or crab rolls—without mayo. Sprinkle on a little bit of cheese, if you please, especially feta, which adds loads of flavor. Get some protein with tofu, a hard-cooked egg, or lean, skinless chicken.

Dress your salad with vinegar (try rice vinegar) and a touch of oil, a low-fat dressing, or a small amount of regular dressing, remembering that it's the dressing that packs the most fat. That innocent-looking ladle may hold 2 ounces, which is ¼ cup dressing, about 3 tablespoons more than necessary.

Snacks: Playing It Smart

Healthful snacks can and should be part of your weight-loss plan. They give you that boost of energy you need at times of the day when you feel your stamina waning. They also can prevent you from getting too hungry for main meals, eliminating the possibility of overeating at those meals. Plan snack breaks into your day so you're not mindlessly munching on a bag of something salty, sweet, greasy, and fattening. To avoid this trap, eat without engaging in any other simultaneous activity, such as reading, watching TV, or sitting at the computer.

Banish foods that you know you can't control from the house or desk drawer; otherwise, they may beckon you. If you get a craving you just have to feed, buy a tiny package of whatever it is and eat it all. Craving over. Here are some tips for handling snack time wisely:

Do a soda switch. Cut back on or cut out soda, sweetened iced tea, and lemonade for snacks. They're all loaded with calories. If you have a 20-ounce bottle of cola every day, switch to the diet variety. You could lose 25 pounds in a year.

Snack on protein. In a study, high-carbohydrate snackers got hungry as quickly as subjects who had no snack at all. Those who ate lean protein, such as chicken, stayed full nearly 40 minutes longer. Here are some ideas for protein-packed snacks:

- 1 cup prebaked chicken strips, such as Perdue
- 1 cup low-fat cottage cheese
- 2 string cheese sticks
- 1 hard-cooked egg topped with salsa
- 1-ounce wedge of cheese
- 2 tablespoons peanut butter spread on 1 medium apple

Stock up. Keep healthful shelf-stable or refrigerated foods—such as fat-free yogurt, ready-cut vegetables, fresh or dried fruits, and whole grain cereal—that are ready to grab and eat on busy days. Try to include foods that provide a variety of textures, including chewy, crunchy, and smooth.

Avoid the chip trap. If you often crave salty (and fatty!) snacks like potato chips or corn chips, try alternatives like pretzels or air-popped popcorn. Dress up your popcorn by spritzing it with low-fat butter spray and then sprinkling with your favorite seasoning mix.

Feed a sweet tooth. Almost all candy is empty sugar calories, but when only something sweet will do, choose licorice, gumdrops, or jelly beans, which all have a negligible amount of fat. Small, individually wrapped candies offer built-in portion control.

Have a cup of tea. How about adding a tea to your list of snacks? Traditionally served in Chinese restaurants but also sold in super-markets, oolong tea may be a great fat fighter. In a small study, men who drank 5 cups of oolong tea a day burned 80 more calories over 24 hours. That's enough to lose 8 pounds in a year! Researchers believe that compounds in the tea work to promote weight loss by speeding up metabolism and turning on your body's fat burners.

Eat only when empty. Don't force a snack; wait until you want it. Your body is least likely to store food as fat if you eat only when you are physically hungry.

Dinner: Taking Control

Let's face it, dinner is the meal that often presents the biggest challenges. Perhaps you are pressed for time and cooking feels like a burden. It may seem easier to order in or go out. Maybe you've been cooking dinner for years and your repertoire feels stale—the same old dishes, many of them too high in fat and calories. But if you're trying to lose weight, keep it off, or just stay healthy, you know that what you eat matters, so what you make for dinner is extremely important.

It really is possible to take control over dinner—to ease the preparation along and make it go more smoothly. Here you'll find a few tricks and shortcuts so that you can have a good time while you cook. So browse through the tips and leaf through the deli-cious recipes in this book. You'll see that

meal-making time can be your own stress-free, special time of the day.

Create a mood. Put on a favorite CD—soothing mellow music or some upbeat tunes. Fill an attractive glass with ice; add herbal tea, sparkling water with a twist, or a spoonful of frozen cranberry juice concen-trate, spring water, and a lime wedge. Sip your drink as you cook so you don't nibble. Or have a healthful snack first (see snack sug-gestions on page 33), and then get started.

Spice it up. Getting more flavor into your food will help you cook with less fat. If your dishes seem bland and dull, spice them up. When food is more delicious, you'll savor every bite, and you'll have more control over your cravings. Here are some easy ideas:

- Investigate hot sauces (many are actually quite mild).

- Buy a pepper mill to add fresh-ground flavor at the table.

- Experiment with different vinegars (see page 10 for suggestions).

- Serve food garnished with pretty wedges of lemon, lime, or orange to squeeze over servings.

- Invest in a garlic press; fresh garlic has more punch than the powdered or pre-chopped versions.

- Grow some fresh herbs on your windowsill and snip a few leaves into dishes. Throw out any dried herbs and spices that are over a year old; they've long since lost their inten-sity. Buy a new fresh batch, and don't keep them over the stove, as heat withers their flavor. Check out intriguing spice blends at the supermarket.

EYES ON THE SIZE

You may know that you want to eat ½ cup of pasta with your pork dinner, but dishing out ½ cup is another matter entirely. That doesn't mean you have to pull out the measuring cups. Use a few visual cues instead. Picture the following objects when serving up your favorite foods:

- Lightbulb = 1 cup
- Closed fist = 1 cup
- Tennis ball = ½ cup
- Ping-Pong ball = 2 tablespoons
- Deck of cards = 3 ounces (of cooked meat, fish, or chicken, for instance)

- Woman's palm = 3 ounces
- Top of thumb (from tip to 2nd joint) = 1 teaspoon
- Top of thumb (from tip to 2nd joint) = 1 ounce (of cheese, for instance)

Timing is everything. Cooking will be more fun if you combine tasks to work efficiently. For instance, many recipes use the term *meanwhile*. What this means is that while the pasta water is coming to a boil, you should be sautéing the mushrooms for the sauce, or while the rice is simmering, you should be toasting and chopping the cashew garnish.

A recipe is a game plan, an outline of what you need to do to complete a dish. The key to making dinner preparation easier is to think of the whole process as a recipe, or a game plan. Soon, you'll understand what to do when, and what to do "meanwhile," and preparations will speed right along. Here are some more tricks:

- Cook grains first. Once done, keep them off the heat, covered. Rice, barley, and couscous will remain warm for a long time. Fluff with a fork before serving.

- Roasting a chicken for dinner? Baking a casserole or a meatloaf? The oven is already on, so use it to prepare the sides: Try roasted carrots or mixed roasted veggies, baked white or sweet potatoes or winter squash, or a mushroom-barley or rice pilaf.

- Baked fish has a shorter cooking time, but since the oven will be on anyway, start the oven-baked sides first. When they're about done, it's time to put in the fish. They'll stay warm while the fish finishes cooking.

- Roasted meat and poultry need 10 to 15 minutes resting time after cooking. This redistributes the juices and makes them more tender and easier to slice. Even if you're not planning on slicing them, allow them to rest anyway. If the room is cold, cover loosely with foil. Meanwhile, do the final meal prep.

Streamline pasta dishes. Hard to believe, but making pasta can be even easier than it already is! Try these streamlining tips:

- Soon as you're in the kitchen, put on the pasta water. If it comes to a boil before you're ready to add the pasta, simply turn the water to low.

- If vegetables are part of your pasta recipe, it's efficient to cook them with the pasta. Stir them into the pasta water during the last few minutes of cooking. Timing depends on the vegetable. Frozen peas can be added when you're about to drain the pasta. Broccoli florets will need about 5 minutes. Drain the vegetable and pasta together.

- If you're adding tender greens to a pasta dish, such as arugula or spinach, arrange the greens in a large colander in the sink. Drain the pasta over the greens, and the heat of the water will wilt them beautifully.

- Just before draining the pasta, scoop out ½ cup of the cooking water. If the pasta is dry or a bit sticky, mix some cooking water with

the drained noodles instead of adding extra oil or butter.

- If you're not using the pasta pot to warm the sauce, return the drained pasta to the pot. Covered, the pasta will keep warm for at least 10 minutes. And don't worry; slightly tepid pasta will warm up quickly if the sauce is piping hot.

- If you're using a jarred pasta sauce or making a quick pasta sauce, heat or make it in the pasta-cooking pot to save cleanup. Add the drained pasta to the sauce, toss, and serve it from the pot.

Get out the fat. Most recipes can easily be slimmed down. Here are some quick switches and fast tricks for trimming:

- If a recipe calls for sautéing in 2 tablespoons oil, knock that down to 1 tablespoon.

- For dishes spread with sour cream, halve the amount, and use the reduced-fat version.

- In casseroles spiked with cheese, cut back by a half, and be sure to use a really flavorful cheese. Or, sprinkle the cheese only on the top, and add a tablespoon of Parmesan into the mix for lots more taste.

- For dishes calling for a can of "cream of" soup, use the fat-free version. Do you stir in whole milk? Try fat-free or 1% instead.

- Instead of adding evaporated milk to a sauce, try fat-free evaporated milk.

- In meatloaf recipes, cut the fat by using half beef and half ground turkey breast.

- For stir-fries, use a little less meat than the recipe calls for and increase the vegetables instead, or toss in some tofu.

- Make a 4-serving omelet using 3 eggs and 1 egg white, and fill it with sautéed vegetables instead of loads of cheese.
- Stretch out pasta portions by pumping up the veggies or adding some drained canned beans.

Start with soup. It can't be said enough: Soup can be a waist-watcher's best friend. Hearty soups, rich with beans, meat, and/or grains, can be the main dish. (Just avoid the creamy, fat-laden kinds.) Round out the meal with a green salad and whole grain bread or rolls.

Begin with fruit. Fruit is a healthful, refreshing start to dinner. And it'll help fill you up so you won't overdo on the main course or side dishes. Try grapefruit, papaya, fruit salad, chilled juice-packed canned fruit, or melon. It's yet another way to get in a fruit serving, along with essential vitamins and fiber. Add elegance with a lime or lemon wedge, a mint sprig, a dusting of ground cinnamon or ginger, a little black pepper, or a dollop of vanilla yogurt.

Try fish. Enjoy fish on your road to weight loss. It's delicious, easy to cook, and it packs healthy "good" fats that your body needs. (For more on fish, see page 5.)

Eat less meat. Go meatless one or two nights a week, and you'll be eating less saturated fat. Make the main event a baked squash or sweet potato, rice and beans, polenta or whole wheat pasta with chunky tomato sauce and a little cheese, or quinoa with a vegetable stir-fry. (For more filling meatless ideas, see the recipes beginning on page 80.)

Pass the veggies. When it comes to second helpings, provide ample servings of vegetables. Add interest to vegetables with a sprinkle of fresh Parmesan, a light drizzle of fruity olive oil, a shower of sliced scallions or chopped parsley, or a squeeze of fresh lemon or orange juice.

Wrap it up. Instead of placing a whole roast or meatloaf on the table, prepare individual portions in the kitchen andserve everyone at the table. Wrap up and refrigerate the rest so that you don't even think about second helpings. It's easy to eat too much when it's in front of you. The bonus: You'll have plenty left over for a quick and easy lunch or dinner the next day.

Focus on your food. Eat dinner sitting down at the table, not leaning up against the counter. Engage all of the senses in the pleasure of nourishing your body. It'll also help you gain more awareness of what you're eating and how much.

Set a nice table. Pretty china, cloth napkins, cut fresh flowers—it can't hurt to make dinnertime something special. And turn off the television. Play music instead, or review the day. Add some atmosphere to your meal and take the time to really enjoy yourself.

Don't forget dessert. Dessert definitely has a place in your weight-loss plan. Fresh fruit and fruit packed in water or juice (not syrup) are always good choices, but you can also try the many varieties of fat-free frozen yogurt. Top the yogurt with some fruit to get another fruit serving into your day. Also check out the easy dessert recipes beginning on page 161.

Lighter Fare

Berry Morning Mash

—Cynthia Adams, Greensboro, North Carolina

"This is something I can create quickly and easily and dash out. I dislike eggs, and I find it difficult to get enough protein into my morning meals. This has been a real boon to staying healthier and getting in more protein, plus I don't get hungry for carbs in the late morning when I have this dish."

Prep time: 7 minutes

- 1 **cup fat-free blueberry yogurt**
- ½ **cup reduced-fat cottage cheese**
- ½ **cup blueberries and/or sliced strawberries**
- 1–2 **tablespoons fat-free granola**
- 1 **teaspoon crushed walnuts or almonds**
- 2 **teaspoons grated dark chocolate**

In individual cups or a large bowl, combine the yogurt, cottage cheese, berries, granola, and nuts. Grate the chocolate over the top.

Makes 2 servings

Per serving: *159 calories, 11 g protein, 22 g carbohydrate, 3 g fat, 11 mg cholesterol, 258 mg sodium, 1 g dietary fiber*

Diet Exchanges: *1 milk, 0 vegetable, ½ fruit, 0 carbohydrate, 1 meat, ½ fat*

1½ Carb Choices

Kitchen Tip

Cynthia likes to use a Dove Promise dark chocolate bar for this recipe.

Microwave Oatmeal

—Rena Zayit, Toronto, Ontario, Canada

"This is a fast and very filling morning meal."

Prep time: 4 minutes; Cook time: 3 minutes

1 cup fat-free milk

¼ cup + 2 tablespoons old-fashioned rolled oats

6 dried apricots, chopped

1 teaspoon vanilla extract

1 teaspoon chopped walnuts

Pinch of ground cinnamon

In a microwaveable bowl, combine the milk, oats, apricots, and vanilla extract. Cover with plastic wrap and microwave for 3 minutes. Sprinkle with the walnuts and cinnamon.

Makes 1 serving

Per serving: *383 calories, 15 g protein, 65 g carbohydrate, 6 g fat, 10 mg cholesterol, 126 mg sodium, 6 g dietary fiber*

Diet Exchanges: *1 milk, 0 vegetable, 2 fruit, 1 carbohydrate, 0 meat, ½ fat*

4 Carb Choices

300-CALORIE BREAKFASTS

It's easy to overeat at breakfast, when you're probably in a hurry to get out the door and don't have a whole lot of time to put a healthy meal together. Here are five easy 300-calorie breakfasts to add to your repertoire—no counting required!

- 1 cup Cheerios with 1 small sliced banana, 1 tablespoon chopped walnuts, and ½ cup fat-free milk
- Quaker Oat Bran hot cereal with 1 cup fat-free milk and ½ cup orange juice
- 1 low-fat apple bran muffin from McDonald's and hot tea
- 1 egg, 2 slices whole wheat toast, and ½ cup orange juice
- 8 ounces fat-free French vanilla yogurt with 1 tablespoon slivered almonds, ½ medium apple, sliced, 1 tablespoon raisins, and 1 tablespoon ground flaxseed

Shirley's Omelet

—Shirley Hill, Chatham, Ontario, Canada

"This omelet gives me a good start to my day. It carries me through until lunch and satisfies my tastebuds. I just love the combinations!"

Prep time: 3 minutes; Cook time: 4 minutes

2 **large eggs, well beaten**
  Salt, to taste
  Ground black pepper, to taste
1 **slice reduced-fat Cheddar or mozzarella cheese**
1 **teaspoon salsa**

Heat a medium skillet coated with cooking spray over medium heat. Add the eggs, allowing them to cover the bottom of the pan. Cook for 1½ minutes, or until the bottom begins to set. Using a spatula, lift the edges to allow the uncooked egg to flow to the bottom of the pan. Cook for 1 minute longer, or until set. Sprinkle with salt and pepper and top with the cheese. Cover and cook for 1 minute, or until the cheese is melted and the eggs are cooked through. Fold the egg mixture in half and invert onto a serving plate. Top with the salsa.

Makes 1 serving

Per serving: *200 calories, 19 g protein, 2 g carbohydrate, 12 g fat, 431 mg cholesterol, 333 mg sodium, 0 g dietary fiber*

Diet Exchanges: *0 milk, 0 vegetable, 0 fruit, 0 carbohydrate, 3 meat, 1½ fat*

0 Carb Choices

Vegetable Omelet

—Roanne Latner, Toronto, Ontario, Canada

*" I use this as a quick and easy dinner. Serve with
a mixed green salad and a light dressing. "*

Prep time: 10 minutes; Cook time: 5 minutes

3 **eggs, well-beaten**
3 **tablespoons chopped red bell pepper**
2 **tablespoons chopped green bell pepper**
2 **tablespoons chopped tomato, seeded**
2 **tablespoons chopped mushrooms**
2 **tablespoons chopped zucchini**
   Salt, to taste
   Ground black pepper, to taste

Heat a large skillet coated with olive oil
cooking spray over medium heat. Add the
eggs, allowing them to cover the bottom of
the pan. Cook for 3 minutes, or until the
bottom begins to set. When nearly cooked,
top one half of the omelet with the bell peppers, tomato, mushrooms, zucchini, salt, and
black pepper. Carefully fold the
remaining half over the filling and cook for
2 minutes, or until cooked through.

Makes 1 serving

Per serving: *257 calories, 21 g protein, 9 g carbohydrate, 15 g fat, 637 mg cholesterol, 194 mg
sodium, 2 g dietary fiber*

Diet Exchanges: *0 milk, 1½ vegetable, 0 fruit,
0 carbohydrate, 3 meat, 2 fat*

1 Carb Choice

Awesome French Toast

—Karen Preston, Stoney Creek, Ontario, Canada

Prep time: 4 minutes; Cook time: 6 minutes

2 egg whites, beaten
½ cup 1% milk
¼ teaspoon vanilla extract
⅛ teaspoon ground cinnamon
4 slices bread

In a shallow bowl, combine the egg whites, milk, vanilla extract, and cinnamon. Beat until frothy. Dip the bread into the egg-white mixture, turning to coat both sides.

Heat a large skillet coated with cooking spray over medium heat. Working in batches if necessary, place the bread in the pan and cook for 3 minutes. Turn the bread. Cook for 3 minutes longer, or until golden brown on both sides.

Makes 2 servings

Per serving: *174 calories, 11 g protein, 28 g carbohydrate, 3 g fat, 2 mg cholesterol, 339 mg sodium, 3 g dietary fiber*

Diet Exchanges: *½ milk, 0 vegetable, 0 fruit, 1½ carbohydrate, ½ meat, 0 fat*

2 Carb Choices

Kitchen Tip

Try serving this French toast with a drizzle of low-calorie maple syrup and some fresh fruit.

Light and Fluffy Pancakes

61 Calories

—Rick Brucker, Urbandale, Iowa

"My wife loves having pancakes on the weekends, but I didn't like the ingredients in the prepackaged mixes. This recipe uses more baking powder and soda than usual to make them fluffy without buttermilk."

Prep time: 12 minutes; Cook time: 8 minutes

¾ **cup bread flour**

¼ **cup ground rolled oats**

4 **teaspoons sugar or 4 packets sugar substitute**

2 **teaspoons baking powder**

1 **teaspoon baking soda**

¼ **teaspoon salt**

1 **cup fat-free milk**

2 **egg whites**

1 **tablespoon vegetable oil**

In a large bowl, combine the flour, oats, sugar, baking powder, baking soda, and salt. Add the milk, egg whites, and oil and mix well.

Coat a griddle or nonstick skillet with cooking spray. Preheat the griddle according to the manufacturer's directions, or place the skillet over medium heat.

Using a ¼-cup measure, pour the batter onto the griddle to make 3" to 4" pancakes. Cook for 2 minutes, or until tiny bubbles appear on the surface and the edges begin to look dry. Flip the pancakes. Cook for 2 minutes longer, or until golden on the bottom. Remove to a plate, cover, and keep warm. Repeat with the remaining batter.

Makes 12 pancakes

Per pancake: *61 calories, 3 g protein, 10 g carbohydrate, 2 g fat, 0 mg cholesterol, 254 mg sodium, 0 g dietary fiber*

Diet Exchanges: *0 milk, 0 vegetable, 0 fruit, ½ carbohydrate, 0 meat, ½ fat*

½ Carb Choice

Kitchen Tip

Rick serves these fluffy pancakes with fat-free butter spray and low-calorie Vermont maple syrup.

Apple Matzoh

—Marilyn Goran, Poughkeepsie, New York

" This is a very satisfying and tasty breakfast. It is low-fat and has the protein and fiber to keep me going all morning. "

Prep time: 3 minutes; Cook time: 4 minutes

½ **cup fat-free or reduced-fat cottage cheese**
1 **packet sugar substitute**
⅛ **teaspoon ground cinnamon**
1 **matzoh (whole wheat preferred)**
1 **apple, thinly sliced**

In a small bowl, combine the cottage cheese, sugar substitute, and cinnamon. Evenly spread over the matzoh to the edges. Top with the apple slices in slightly overlapping rows. Toast in the toaster oven for 4 minutes, or until the cottage cheese is warm and the apple is soft.

Makes 1 serving

Per serving: *276 calories, 16 g protein, 53 g carbohydrate, 0 g fat, 5 mg cholesterol, 441 mg sodium, 6 g dietary fiber*

Diet Exchanges: *0 milk, 0 vegetable, 1½ fruit, 2 carbohydrate, 2 meat, 0 fat*

3½ Carb Choices

SECRETS OF WEIGHT-LOSS WINNERS

• I keep changing my routine, and it helps me stay motivated and fight boredom. I walk, dance, and do videos, which I borrow free from the library. I am learning new things and also doing the old reliable long walk for those days when I just feel like doing the familiar.

—Marie Haley, Berne, New York

• Consider taking up activities you haven't tried for a while. I have started ice-skating again, and it makes me feel so young and fit.

—Liz Ritchie, Brampton, Ontario, Canada

• One thing I am doing is swimming for 30 to 45 minutes, 3 to 5 times a week (or more). Swimming helps me to feel more alert, it boosts my metabolism, it gives me more endurance throughout the day, and it makes me a happier person.

—Suzanne Long, Eureka, California

Blueberry Tea Scones

—Julia Zinzow, Waukesha, Wisconsin

"These scones are great to have as a snack between meals rather than a junk-food item. With a nice snack to look forward to, it is easier to keep smaller portions at regular meals."

Prep time: 20 minutes; Cook time: 12 minutes

- ½ **cup dried blueberries**
- 1 **cup boiling water**
- 1 **egg**
- ½ **cup soy milk**
- ¼ **cup fat-free milk**
- 2 **cups unbleached or all-purpose flour**
- ¼ **cup sugar**
- 1½ **teaspoons baking powder**
- 6 **tablespoons margarine, such as Smart Balance**
- ¼ **cup English toffee chips**
- 2 **tablespoons ground flaxseed**
- 1 **tablespoon wheat germ**

Preheat the oven to 400°F. Coat 2 large baking sheets with cooking spray.

Place the blueberries in a bowl and cover with the boiling water. Set aside.

Beat the egg in an 8-ounce measuring cup and add the soy milk to the ¾ cup line. Fill to the 1-cup line with fat-free milk. Set aside.

In a large bowl, sift together the flour, sugar, and baking powder. Add the margarine using a pastry blender or fork until the mixture resembles coarse meal.

Drain the blueberries. Add the blueberries to the flour mixture along with the toffee chips, flaxseed, and wheat germ. Stir to distribute evenly. Stir the egg and milk mixture and add to the dough. Stir until the dough just clings together; do not overmix. Drop by ¼ cupfuls onto the prepared baking sheets.

Bake for 12 minutes, or until golden brown. Serve warm.

Makes 12 scones

Per scone: *200 calories, 4 g protein, 28 g carbohydrate, 8 g fat, 19 mg cholesterol, 127 mg sodium, 2 g dietary fiber*

Diet Exchanges: *0 milk, 0 vegetable, ½ fruit, 1½ carbohydrate, 0 meat, 1½ fat*

2 Carb Choices

Kitchen Tip

Julia notes that these scones can be reheated and enjoyed the next day as well.

Holiday Pepper-Cheddar Muffins

—Gudne Smyth, La Pine, Oregon

" My weakness is bread, and these muffins help satisfy that hunger. These are so good, I never feel that I am eating a reduced-fat product. "

Prep time: 20 minutes; Cook time: 15 minutes

1 cup unbleached or all-purpose flour

1 cup yellow cornmeal

2 teaspoons sugar

2 teaspoons baking powder

½ teaspoon salt

1 cup (4 ounces) shredded fat-free Cheddar cheese

⅓ cup grated reduced-fat Parmesan cheese

1 cup fat-free milk

½ cup liquid egg substitute

¼ cup canola oil

⅛ teaspoon hot-pepper sauce

½ green bell pepper, finely chopped

½ red bell pepper, finely chopped

½ small onion, finely chopped

Preheat the oven to 400°F. Coat a 12-cup muffin pan with cooking spray.

In a large bowl, combine the flour, cornmeal, sugar, baking powder, salt, Cheddar, and Parmesan.

In a small bowl, combine the milk, egg substitute, oil, and hot-pepper sauce. Add to the flour mixture and stir just until blended. Stir in the bell peppers and onion. Evenly divide the batter among the prepared muffin cups.

Bake for 15 minutes, or until a wooden pick inserted in the center of a muffin comes out clean. Cool slightly on a rack. Serve warm.

Makes 12 muffins

Per muffin: *161 calories, 8 g protein, 18 g carbohydrate, 6 g fat, 4 mg cholesterol, 348 mg sodium, 1 g dietary fiber*

Diet Exchanges: *0 milk, 0 vegetable, 0 fruit, 1 carbohydrate, 1 meat, 1 fat*

1 Carb Choice

Kitchen Tip

Gudne suggests serving these delicious muffins warm with soup, chili, stew, or salad. They're also wonderful cold.

Oatmeal and Wheat Maple Muffins

—Jennifer Lamontagne, Stratford, Connecticut

" Adding yogurt and applesauce instead of all that fattening oil allows one to indulge in a tasty treat and not feel deprived. The yogurt gives it a nice texture and moistness that would be lost normally if all of the oil was eliminated. "

Prep time: 18 minutes; Cook time: 20 minutes

1 cup white flour
¾ cup whole wheat flour
¾ cup rolled oats
2 teaspoons baking powder
2 teaspoons ground cinnamon
1 teaspoon ground nutmeg
½ teaspoon baking soda
½ teaspoon salt
½ teaspoon cloves
1 cup unsweetened applesauce
1 cup fat-free plain yogurt
½ cup maple syrup
½ cup packed dark brown sugar
¼ cup reduced-fat sour cream
1 egg or ¼ cup liquid egg substitute
2 teaspoons vanilla extract

Preheat the oven to 375°F. Coat two 12-cup muffin pans with cooking spray.

In a large bowl, combine the white flour, whole wheat flour, oats, baking powder, cinnamon, nutmeg, baking soda, salt, and cloves.

In a medium bowl, combine the applesauce, yogurt, syrup, brown sugar, sour cream, egg or egg substitute, and vanilla extract. Add to the flour mixture and stir just until blended. Evenly divide the batter among the prepared muffin cups.

Bake for 20 minutes, or until a wooden pick inserted in the center of a muffin comes out clean. Cool on a rack.

Makes 24 muffins

Per muffin: *94 calories, 2 g protein, 20 g carbohydrate, 1 g fat, 10 mg cholesterol, 128 mg sodium, 1 g dietary fiber*

Diet Exchanges: *0 milk, 0 vegetable, 0 fruit, 1 carbohydrate, 0 meat, 0 fat*

1 Carb Choice

Kitchen Tip

To make ladling the batter into the muffin cups easier, Jennifer suggests coating the ladle with cooking spray.

Turkey Black Bean Soup

—Jenny Renedo, Columbia, South Carolina

"This soup is tasty, filling, and liked by the whole family."

Prep time: 12 minutes; Cook time: 1 hour 5 minutes

1 tablespoon olive oil

4 cloves garlic, minced

1 onion, chopped

3 cans (10¾ ounces each) fat-free chicken broth

2 cans (14–19 ounces each) black beans, rinsed and drained

1 can (10 ounces) niblet corn, rinsed and drained

2 tomatoes, chopped, or 1 can (14½ ounces) diced tomatoes

½ pound smoked turkey breast

¼ teaspoon ground cumin

Reduced-fat sour cream, for garnish

Heat the oil in a large skillet over medium heat. Add the garlic and onion and cook, stirring occasionally, for 4 minutes, or until the onion is soft. Add the broth, beans, and corn and cook, stirring occasionally, for 45 minutes. Remove 1 cup of the soup to a blender and puree. Return to the pot. Add the tomatoes, turkey, and cumin and simmer for 15 minutes, or until heated through. Serve with the sour cream.

Makes 8 servings

Per serving: *180 calories, 14 g protein, 24 g carbohydrate, 3 g fat, 8 mg cholesterol, 785 mg sodium, 7 g dietary fiber*

Diet Exchanges: *0 milk, 1 vegetable, 0 fruit, 1½ carbohydrate, 1½ meat, ½ fat*

2 Carb Choices

Erin's Minestrone

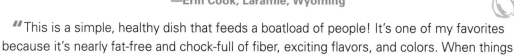

—Erin Cook, Laramie, Wyoming

"This is a simple, healthy dish that feeds a boatload of people! It's one of my favorites because it's nearly fat-free and chock-full of fiber, exciting flavors, and colors. When things are tantalizing, it helps me enjoy eating healthy and consequently lose weight."

Prep time: 15 minutes; Cook time: 6–8 hours

- 2 cans (10¾ ounces each) low-sodium chicken or vegetable broth
- 1 can (14–19 ounces) red kidney beans, rinsed and drained
- 1 can (14–19 ounces) white kidney beans, rinsed and drained
- 2 cans (14½ ounces each) diced tomatoes
- 6 carrots, peeled and sliced
- 1 bunch scallions, sliced
- ¾ teaspoon dried Italian seasoning
- ¼ teaspoon salt
- ¼ teaspoon ground black pepper
- 12 ounces rotini pasta
- 1 package (10 ounces) frozen spinach, thawed and squeezed dry
- Fat-free Parmesan cheese, for garnish (optional)

In a large pot, combine the broth, beans, tomatoes (with juice), carrots, scallions, Italian seasoning, salt, and pepper. Cover and cook on the low heat setting for 6 to 8 hours.

Prepare the pasta according to package directions. Drain and stir into the soup along with the spinach until heated through. Serve sprinkled with the cheese, if using.

Makes 10 servings

Per serving: *117 calories, 7 g protein, 22 g carbohydrate, 1 g fat, 1 mg cholesterol, 394 mg sodium, 8 g dietary fiber*

Diet Exchanges: *0 milk, 2 vegetable, 0 fruit, 1 carbohydrate, ½ meat, 0 fat*

1½ Carb Choices

Kitchen Tip

Erin says that after the flavors have a chance to mingle in the fridge, this minestrone gets even better! To round out this classic Italian meal, Erin suggests serving it with some warm French wheat bread to sop up every drop.

Vegetable Soup

—Jo Mathews, Chandler, Arizona

"I refuse to eat canned soup because of all the sodium in it. We eat only homemade soup. This has been the only way that we consistently get vegetables in our diet. My daughter and I love the stuff. My parents, aunts, and coworkers are also making it. It is very filling because of all the liquid and fiber, yet low in calories."

Prep time: 30 minutes; Cook time: 1 hour

7 cups water

2 cans low-sodium chicken broth

1 pound carrots, chopped

2 large sweet potatoes, peeled and cubed

2 large ribs celery, chopped

1 red, green, or yellow bell pepper, chopped

1 can (14½ ounces) diced tomatoes

1 box (10 ounces) frozen chopped spinach, thawed and squeezed dry

8 ounces frozen peas

1 can (14–19 ounces) great Northern beans, rinsed and drained

¼ cup chopped fresh cilantro leaves

1 pound cooked boneless, skinless chicken breast, cut into bite-size pieces

Bring the water and broth to a boil in a large pot over medium-high heat. Add the carrots, sweet potatoes, celery, pepper, tomatoes (with juice), spinach, peas, beans, cilantro, and chicken and bring to a boil. Reduce the heat to low and simmer for 45 minutes, or until the vegetables are tender.

Makes 10 servings

Per serving: *255 calories, 27 g protein, 28 g carbohydrate, 4 g fat, 59 mg cholesterol, 240 mg sodium, 7 g dietary fiber*

Diet Exchanges: *0 milk, 2 vegetable, 0 fruit, 1 carbohydrate, 3 meat, ½ fat*

2 Carb Choices

Kitchen Tip

Jo makes this soup about once a month and freezes it in serving-size portions so it's always handy. She also notes that you can add whatever vegetables you like in this soup for variety. She likes to include broccoli florets and cut-up asparagus.

Taco Soup

—Joni Goeders, Fort Worth, Texas

*"*This is a very limited calorie food. It keeps me from snacking between meals.*"*

Prep time: 12 minutes; Cook time: 20 minutes

- **2 cans (10¾ ounces each) reduced-sodium chicken broth**
- **2 cans (14½ ounces each) tomatoes with chile peppers**
- **1 can (14–19 ounces) pinto or black beans, rinsed and drained**
- **1 can (8 ounces) sliced mushrooms**
- **1 can (8 ounces) French-style green beans, drained**
- **1 large onion, finely chopped**
- **1 tablespoon taco seasoning**
- **1 tablespoon ranch salad dressing mix**

In a large pot over medium-high heat, combine the broth, tomatoes (with juice), pinto or black beans, mushrooms, green beans, onion, taco seasoning, and salad dressing mix. Bring to a boil. Reduce the heat to low and simmer for 15 minutes, or until heated through.

Makes 6 servings

Per serving: *119 calories, 6 g protein, 22 g carbohydrate, 1 g fat, 0 mg cholesterol, 890 mg sodium, 6 g dietary fiber*

Diet Exchanges: *0 milk, 2 vegetable, 0 fruit, 1 carbohydrate, 0 meat, 0 fat*

1½ Carb Choices

Barley-Lentil Soup

—Tara Forster, London, Ontario, Canada

"This soup is full of fiber and protein, and it's really filling."

Prep time: 15 minutes; Cook time: 1 hour

> 2 **quarts beef broth**
> 1 **can (28 ounces) crushed tomatoes**
> ¾ **cup red lentils, sorted and rinsed**
> ¾ **cup hulled or pearl barley**
> 10–15 **ready-to-eat baby carrots**
> 3 **ribs celery, finely chopped**
> 1 **onion, finely chopped**
> 1 **teaspoon ground black pepper**
> 1 **teaspoon dried rosemary**
> 1 **teaspoon dried oregano**

In a large pot over medium-high heat, bring the broth, tomatoes, lentils, barley, carrots, celery, onion, pepper, rosemary, and oregano to a boil. Reduce the heat to low and simmer for 50 minutes, or until the vegetables, beans, and barley are tender. The soup will thicken on standing.

Makes 8 servings

Per serving: *189 calories, 13 g protein, 35 g carbohydrate, 1 g fat, 0 mg cholesterol, 1,163 mg sodium, 9 g dietary fiber*

Diet Exchanges: *0 milk, 2 vegetable, 0 fruit, 1½ carbohydrate, 1 meat, 0 fat*

2½ Carb Choices

300-CALORIE LUNCHES

Lunchtime is filled with fat traps, especially if you dine out frequently. Here are some quick 300-calorie meals for midday dining:

- 1 cup Nile Spice Sweet Corn Chowder, 1 cup skim milk, and 1 large apple
- 1 tablespoon peanut butter and 1 tablespoon grape jelly on 2 slices whole wheat bread, and 1½ celery stalks
- 1 cup Boston Market chicken chili, and 1 cup Boston Market broccoli with red peppers
- Subway Veggie Delight 6" sub, and 1 cup diet soda

Bachelor Noodle Soup

—Paul Grooms, Philadelphia, Pennsylvania

"This fills me up and requires less than 10 minutes to prepare. It's very cheap and uses staples that are always on hand with lots of variety."

Prep time: 10 minutes; Cook time: 12 minutes

4–5 **cups water**
  8 **ounces frozen mixed vegetables**
  1 **teaspoon dried oregano**
  ½ **teaspoon chopped fresh thyme**
  1 **package (3½ ounces) ramen noodles**
  1 **small onion, chopped**
2–3 **low-sodium bouillon cubes**
  1 **teaspoon grated fresh ginger**
  2 **cloves garlic, minced**
    Dash of lemon juice

Bring the water to a boil in a large saucepan over high heat. Add the mixed vegetables, oregano, and thyme and return to a boil. Add the noodles (discard the seasoning packet) and cook for 4 minutes. Add the onion, bouillon cubes, ginger, garlic, and lemon juice and cook for 4 minutes, or until cooked through. Remove from the heat.

Makes 4 servings

Per serving: *89 calories, 3 g protein, 16 g carbohydrate, 2 g fat, 1 mg cholesterol, 842 mg sodium, 3 g dietary fiber*

Diet Exchanges: *0 milk, 0 vegetable, 0 fruit, 1 carbohydrate, 0 meat, ½ fat*

1 Carb Choice

Kitchen Tip

Paul notes that if you allow the soup to steep for 15 minutes before serving, the results will be similar to a casserole. He sometimes stirs in chopped cooked chicken or beef—a hearty addition!

Creamy Potato-Cheddar Soup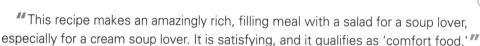

—Tara Leo, Misissauga, Ontario, Canada

"This recipe makes an amazingly rich, filling meal with a salad for a soup lover, especially for a cream soup lover. It is satisfying, and it qualifies as 'comfort food.'"

Prep time: 8 minutes; Cook time: 30 minutes

  1 **large onion, chopped**
  2 **cloves garlic, minced**
3–4 **small potatoes, chopped**
 1½ **cups fat-free chicken broth**
 2½ **cups fat-free milk**
  ¾ **cup shredded reduced-fat Cheddar cheese**
  ¼ **teaspoon salt**
  ¼ **teaspoon ground black pepper**

Heat a large saucepan coated with cooking spray over medium heat. Add the onion and garlic and cook, stirring occasionally, for 3 minutes, or until the onion is soft. Add the potatoes and mix thoroughly. Add the broth, reduce the heat to low, and simmer for 20 minutes, or until the potatoes are tender. Remove from the heat.

Working in batches, puree the soup in a blender and return to the pot over low heat. Slowly add the milk and cook, stirring occasionally, for 5 minutes, or until heated through. Add the cheese, salt, and pepper and heat through.

Makes 6 servings

Per serving: *97 calories, 9 g protein, 10 g carbohydrate, 2 g fat, 7 mg cholesterol, 280 mg sodium, 2 g dietary fiber*

Diet Exchanges: *½ milk, ½ vegetable, 0 fruit, 0 carbohydrate, 1 meat, 0 fat*

1 Carb Choice

Kitchen Tip

If you're reheating the soup, Tara suggests stirring in a little water, broth, or milk.

Totally Tomato Soup

—Gail Hayes, Breckenridge, Minnesota

"Soup is such a great addition to my meals. It's so satisfying and helps to fill me up so I don't overeat. It also makes a great snack."

Prep time: 10 minutes; Cook time: 12 minutes

3–4 **cloves garlic, finely chopped**
2 **tablespoons water**
1 **tablespoon dehydrated onion**
2 **teaspoons dried Italian seasoning**
1 **teaspoon olive oil**
2 **cans (15 ounces each) diced tomatoes**
1 **cup fat-free chicken broth**
1 **tablespoon sugar**
½ **cup 2% milk**

In a medium saucepan, combine the garlic, water, onion, Italian seasoning, and oil. Let stand off the heat for 5 minutes. Place over medium-high heat and cook for 1 minute, or until fragrant (be careful not to let it burn). Add the tomatoes (with juice), broth, and sugar and simmer for 10 minutes. Working in batches if necessary, puree the soup in a blender or food processor. Return to the pot and stir in the milk.

Makes 4 servings

Per serving: *94 calories, 4 g protein, 16 g carbohydrate, 2 g fat, 2 mg cholesterol, 329 mg sodium, 4 g dietary fiber*

Diet Exchanges: *0 milk, 2 vegetable, 0 fruit, ½ carbohydrate, 0 meat, ½ fat*

1 Carb Choice

Kitchen Tip

For a special presentation, Gail suggests serving this soup with a few croutons and a sprinkling of freshly grated Parmesan cheese.

Fulfilling Salad

—Kathryn Burke, Portola Valley, California

92 Calories

"I eat this salad every day for lunch, and it has helped me lose excess weight from my stomach and thighs, as well as enabling me to maintain my figure."

Prep time: 4 minutes; Cook time: 5 minutes

2　slices turkey bacon
3　large leaves green leaf lettuce
1　tomato, chopped
3–4　slices avocado, halved
½　cup sliced strawberries
1　tablespoon balsamic vinegar
　　or rice vinegar

Prepare the turkey bacon according to package directions. Slice into bite-size pieces.

Line 2 plates with the lettuce leaves. Top with the tomato, avocado, bacon, and strawberries. Drizzle with the vinegar.

Makes 2 servings

Per serving: *92 calories, 3 g protein, 9 g carbohydrate, 6 g fat, 12 mg cholesterol, 195 mg sodium, 3 g dietary fiber*

Diet Exchanges: *0 milk, ½ vegetable, ½ fruit, 0 carbohydrate, ½ meat, 1 fat*

1 Carb Choice

SHOPPING SAVVY

Great Greens

Expand your salad repertoire with mâche. This gorgeous green, formerly available only at top produce stores, is now sold prewashed and ready to go in 4-ounce plastic bags. Mâche has a nutty flavor and a velvety, yet sturdy texture. Sauté it like spinach or sprinkle with a fruity olive oil vinaigrette and toasted walnuts to make a lovely salad. Look for Epic

Roots Mâche at Whole Foods, Trader Joe's, and other stores nationwide. To locate a store near you, go to www.epicroots.com.

Photo courtesy of Epic Roots

Orange Balsamic Chicken Salad

181 Calories

—Jacquelynn Novak, Loveland, Ohio

"Decadent taste and texture! Except for assembly, everything can be made in advance, and can await you at the end of a long day."

Prep time: 15 minutes; Cook time: 9 minutes

¼ **cup balsamic vinegar**

¼ **cup orange juice**

5–6 **spears asparagus**

¼ **teaspoon salt**

¼ **teaspoon ground black pepper**

1 **bag (8 ounces) mixed baby greens**

1 **cooked boneless, skinless chicken breast**

1 **can (11 ounces) mandarin orange sections, rinsed and drained**

2 **tablespoons olive oil**

Chopped scallions and/or chopped water chestnuts, for garnish (optional)

In a small saucepan over medium heat, combine the vinegar and orange juice. Cook for 2 minutes, or until it just begins to bubble. Continue cooking until reduced by half and the glaze coats a spoon.

Preheat the oven to 500°F.

Place the asparagus on a baking sheet and coat with cooking spray. Season lightly with the salt and pepper. Roast for 5 minutes, or until tips are crispy and stalks are roasted.

Evenly divide the greens among 4 salad plates. Top with the asparagus. Brush some of the vinegar glaze over the chicken. Shred the chicken and divide the pieces among the plates. Top with the oranges. Whisk the oil into any remaining glaze and season with salt and pepper, if desired. Pour over the salads. Serve sprinkled with the scallions and/or water chestnuts, if using.

Makes 4 servings

Per serving: *181 calories, 10 g protein, 15 g carbohydrate, 9 g fat, 24 mg cholesterol, 244 mg sodium, 3 g dietary fiber*

Diet Exchanges: *0 milk, ½ vegetable, 1 fruit, 0 carbohydrate, 1½ meat, 1½ fat*

1 Carb Choice

Chicken-Pasta Salad

—Ellen Parodi, Philadelphia, Pennsylvania

203 Calories

"This can be lunch or dinner, and the entire taste changes according to the dressing you use. You don't need much dressing on this to enjoy it. It is filling, so you don't feel you have to eat a lot to be satisfied."

Prep time: 15 minutes; Cook time: 13 minutes; Chill time: 30 minutes

1½ **cups rotini pasta**
1 **package (6 ounces) cooked chicken breast, cut into bite-size pieces**
2 **cups broccoli florets**
½ **green bell pepper, chopped**
½ **red bell pepper, chopped**
½ **red onion, finely chopped**
¾ **cup light salad dressing, such as Italian or ranch**

Prepare the pasta according to package directions. Drain and place in a serving bowl. Add the chicken, broccoli, bell peppers, onion, and salad dressing. Toss to combine. Refrigerate for 30 minutes, or until chilled.

Makes 6 servings

Per serving: *203 calories, 13 g protein, 25 g carbohydrate, 6 g fat, 26 mg cholesterol, 264 mg sodium, 2 g dietary fiber*

Diet Exchanges: *0 milk, ½ vegetable, 0 fruit, 1½ carbohydrate, 1½ meat, 1 fat*

2 Carb Choices

Kitchen Tip

Ellen says this salad is just as tasty the next day, so you could easily make it ahead. She also notes that you can substitute elbow macaroni for the rotini pasta.

Noodle-Crab Salad

—Teresa Wargo, Pulaski, Wisconsin

"This recipe uses all low-fat ingredients."

Prep time: 8 minutes; Cook time: 13 minutes; Chill time: 2 hours

1 pound tricolor rotini pasta
1 package (16 ounces) imitation crabmeat, flaked
1 rib celery, chopped
1 green bell pepper, chopped
½ small onion, chopped
½ cup reduced-fat mayonnaise
½ cup reduced-fat ranch salad dressing
1 teaspoon dried dillweed

Prepare the pasta according to package directions. Drain, rinse with cold water, and place in a serving bowl. Add the crabmeat, celery, pepper, and onion.

In a small bowl, combine the mayonnaise, salad dressing, and dill. Pour over the pasta mixture and toss to coat. Cover and refrigerate for at least 2 hours before serving.

Makes 8 servings

Per serving: *338 calories, 16 g protein, 58 g carbohydrate, 5 g fat, 31 mg cholesterol, 287 mg sodium, 2 g dietary fiber*

Diet Exchanges: *0 milk, ½ vegetable, 0 fruit, 3½ carbohydrate, 1 meat, ½ fat*

4 Carb Choices

SLIM DOWN WITH ROASTED VEGETABLES

Most vegetables can be oven-roasted, a technique that uses very little fat. Roasting intensifies the flavor of the vegetables, bringing out their natural sweetness. Mix the following combos in a baking pan with a little olive oil plus seasoning. Bake at 425°F until tender and lightly browned. Timing depends on vegetables; stir them occasionally to prevent burning.

• Broccoli florets, sliced red bell peppers, and onion wedges; season with oregano and red-pepper flakes.

• Cauliflower florets, plum tomato halves, and sliced yellow bell peppers; season with minced garlic and marjoram.
• Sliced zucchini, coarsely chopped yellow summer squash, halved cherry tomatoes, asparagus cut into 2" pieces, and halved scallions; season with fresh thyme sprigs.
• Halved baby carrots, new potato wedges, and onion wedges; season with rosemary sprigs and smashed garlic cloves (add broth, if necessary).

pinach Salad

254 Calories

...net, Massachusetts

"...ar by modifying my diet to include a salad at lunch ...erg lettuce (necessity being the mother of invention), , interesting combinations, this recipe being one of them."

...n
...ced
..., sliced
s **grilled or broiled salmon fillet**
..spoon **crumbled feta cheese**
..lespoons **fat-free red wine vinaigrette**

Place the spinach on a plate. Arrange the mushroom and onion slices on top. Top with the salmon and cheese and drizzle with the vinaigrette.

Makes 1 serving

Per serving: *254 calories, 24 g protein, 11 g carbohydrate, 12 g fat, 62 mg cholesterol, 786 mg sodium, 4 g dietary fiber*

Diet Exchanges: *0 milk, 2 vegetable, 0 fruit, 0 carbohydrate, 3 meat, 1 fat*

1 Carb Choice

— SHOPPING SAVVY —

Polenta!

Dinner just got much easier, thanks to Frieda's Organic Parmesan Polenta. Here's how: Slice the log of premade polenta, arrange in a lightly oiled baking dish, top with your favorite tomato sauce, and bake. Sprinkle with grated Parmesan and chopped fresh basil or parsley. One serving of polenta, without the sauce, cheese, or herb, is a modest, very delicious 90 calories. Frieda's Organic Polenta comes in other flavors, including Mushroom and Onion, Sun Dried Tomato and Garlic, and Green Chili and Cilantro. It's found in the produce aisles of most supermarkets, or go to www.friedas.com.

Photo courtesy of Frieda's®

It Worked for Me!

Jeanie Callaghan

VITAL STATS

Weight lost: 40 pounds

Time to goal: 8 months

Unique secret to success: Never going hungry; eating more frequently means eating less at each sitting.

Affirmation: *"Weighing daily encourages me and keeps me on track."*

Following her marriage in 1998, Jeanie's weight ballooned from an optimal 130 to over 180 pounds. The weight gain made a chronic back injury worse and contributed to a painful foot condition. She needed to reverse the trend, and fast.

"I'm only 5 feet 3 inches tall, so many people automatically think of me as petite. In fact, I spent most of my life being skinny and never had to worry about what I ate. At 55, I find my metabolism has slowed considerably. Combine this with my love of baking cookies, cakes, and pies, and suddenly I found myself facing a weight problem.

"I had no idea how to lose weight and doubted that I even had the self-discipline necessary to succeed. My oldest daughter had lost a lot of weight through a popular program. I never actually joined the group but I did do my best to follow the tips my daughter shared with me. In particular, confronting the actual number of calories, fat, and (lack of) fiber in my regular diet made it clear to me just why my weight had gotten so out of control.

"For the first few months, I was often hungry between meals—something I didn't really enjoy. But you can't imagine my elation the first time I stepped on the scale to discover I was actually losing weight! I realized then that I really could do it. I was in no rush, however. I didn't want to starve myself; I wanted to find a lifestyle I could live with permanently.

"Because of my lower back problems, my doctor recommended swimming as a safe exercise. I found a pool near my house and began to attend classes whenever I could.

"The big breakthrough for me was discovering that I didn't have to completely give up the foods I enjoyed to lose weight. I still have a steak now and then, but grilled chicken is now my favorite dish. I adapted my baking recipes to fit my new lower-calorie, lower-fat approach. And since I am allergic to artificial sweeteners, I rely on recipes that are sweetened with fruit or contain real sugar, but in lesser amounts.

"I eat my meals at regular times and never allow myself to get hungry. I still have 10 pounds to go, and as I approach my fifth wedding anniversary, I am thrilled to find that I can fit into my wedding dress again.

Chinese Cabbage Salad

—Amy Tucker, Vancouver, British Columbia, Canada

"This meal is very satisfying and keeps the cravings at bay."

Prep time: 15 minutes; Cook time: 4 minutes

¼ **cup slivered almonds**

¼ **cup sesame seeds**

1 **package (13 ounces) Chinese noodles, broken**

1 **large head Chinese cabbage, chopped**

2 **large bunches scallions, chopped**

⅓ **cup canola oil**

¼ **cup vinegar**

2 **tablespoons sugar**

1 **tablespoon soy sauce**

Preheat the oven to 350°F.

Place the almonds, sesame seeds, and noodles on a baking sheet. Bake for 4 minutes, or until just beginning to brown.

Combine the cabbage and scallions in a large serving bowl. In a small bowl, combine the oil, vinegar, sugar, and soy sauce. Pour over the lettuce mixture and toss to combine. Add the nut mixture and toss to combine.

Makes 10 servings

Per serving: *267 calories, 7 g protein, 37 g carbohydrate, 12 g fat, 0 mg cholesterol, 202 mg sodium, 8 g dietary fiber*

Diet Exchanges: *0 milk, 1 vegetable, 0 fruit, 2 carbohydrate, ½ meat, 2 fat*

2½ Carb Choices

Kitchen Tip

If you're making this ahead to serve the next day, Amy recommends keeping the cabbage, dressing, and nut mixture separate until just before serving.

Couscous Salad

—Mycala Shaulis, Mechanicsburg, Pennsylvania

"I came up with this recipe when I had an overabundance of tomatoes in the garden. While this does have some fat in it, it's the heart-healthy kind. When regular salads get boring, this is one of my favorite recipes to turn to."

Prep time: 10 minutes; Cook time: 7 minutes

- **2 cups hot cooked couscous**
- **2 roma tomatoes, cored, seeded, and chopped**
- **¼ cup fresh basil leaves, snipped**
- **1 clove garlic, minced**
- **3 tablespoons balsamic vinegar**
- **2 tablespoons olive oil**

In a large serving bowl, combine the couscous, tomatoes, basil, garlic, vinegar, and oil. Toss to coat.

Makes 4 servings

Per serving: *163 calories, 3 g protein, 22 g carbohydrate, 7 g fat, 0 mg cholesterol, 10 mg sodium, 2 g dietary fiber*

Diet Exchanges: *0 milk, ½ vegetable, 0 fruit, 1½ carbohydrate, 0 meat, 1½ fat*

1½ Carb Choices

SECRETS OF WEIGHT-LOSS WINNERS

• I eat desserts only on the weekends, Friday at 5:00 P.M. to Sunday at midnight. This rule in my head helps me deflect offers of dessert during the week, control my sugar cravings, and enjoy dessert guilt-free.

—**Jane Meier, Silver Spring, Maryland**

• Buy only foods that are on the perimeter of the grocery store. No canned goods, only fresh foods.

—**Maria Rudnick, Oshawa, Ontario, Canada**

Awesome Salad

—Denise Sorino, Florence, South Carolina

"This is refreshingly slim eating!"

Prep time: 10 minutes; Chill time: 4 hours

- **3 small zucchini, sliced**
- **1 small green bell pepper, chopped**
- **½ small onion, chopped**
- **1 can (14–19 ounces) red kidney beans; rinsed and drained**
- **2 tablespoons olive oil**
- **1 tablespoon vinegar**
- **1 teaspoon garlic salt**
- **¼ teaspoon ground black pepper**

In a large serving bowl, combine the zucchini, bell pepper, onion, beans, oil, vinegar, garlic salt, and black pepper. Cover and refrigerate for at least 4 hours, stirring occasionally, to blend the flavors.

Makes 8 servings

Per serving: *87 calories, 4 g protein, 11 g carbohydrate, 3 g fat, 0 mg cholesterol, 361 mg sodium, 3 g dietary fiber*

Diet Exchanges: *0 milk, ½ vegetable, 0 fruit, ½ carbohydrate, 0 meat, ½ fat*

1 Carb Choice

Kitchen Tip

If you like, you can sprinkle this delightful salad with chopped fresh cilantro and parsley, or a teaspoon each of dried oregano and cumin.

Wild Rice Salad

—Kim Russell, North Wales, Pennsylvania

222 Calories

"This recipe has multiple tastes and textures that satisfy hunger for variety. It's also a good party dish."

Prep time: 20 minutes; Cook time: 1 hour; Chill time: 2 hours

¼ cup almonds, pecans, walnuts, and/or cashews
1 box (4 ounces) wild rice
3 ribs celery, chopped
1 red bell pepper, finely chopped
1 yellow bell pepper, finely chopped
1 bunch scallions, chopped
1 small red onion, chopped
¼ cup balsamic vinegar
2 tablespoons finely chopped fresh basil
2 tablespoons finely chopped parsley
1 tablespoon Dijon mustard
1 clove garlic, minced
½ teaspoon kosher salt
⅛ teaspoon freshly ground black pepper
⅛ teaspoon dried oregano
1 teaspoon sugar
¼ cup extra virgin olive oil
3 cups assorted salad greens

Preheat the oven to 425°F.

Spread the nuts in a single layer on a baking sheet. Bake for 3 minutes, or until they begin to brown. Remove and set aside.

Prepare the wild rice according to package directions.

In a large serving bowl, combine the rice, celery, bell peppers, scallions, onion, and nuts.

In a measuring cup, combine the vinegar, basil, parsley, mustard, garlic, salt, black pepper, oregano, and sugar. Gradually add the oil. Stir to combine. Pour all but 2 table-spoons of the dressing over the rice mixture. Cover and refrigerate for at least 2 hours or overnight.

Serve the rice salad over the greens. Drizzle with the reserved dressing.

Makes 6 servings

Per serving: *222 calories, 5 g protein, 25 g carbohydrate, 12 g fat, 0 mg cholesterol, 264 mg sodium, 4 g dietary fiber*

Diet Exchanges: *0 milk, 1 vegetable, 0 fruit, 1½ carbohydrate, 0 meat, 2½ fat*

2 Carb Choices

Guiltless Potato and Apple Salad

—Kate Burrage, Exeter, New Hampshire

"Whenever my family craves a potato salad or we are invited to a barbecue, I whip up this high-flavor treat. It cannot be beat!"

Prep time: 20 minutes; Cook time: 18 minutes; Chill time: 2 hours

1½ **pounds red potatoes, scrubbed and halved**

3 **carrots, scrubbed and thinly sliced**

2 **ribs celery, finely chopped**

2 **Granny Smith apples with skin, cored and finely chopped**

½ **small onion, sliced**

½ **cup light mayonnaise**

½ **cup fat-free plain yogurt**

¼ **cup fat-free lemon yogurt**

1 **tablespoon chopped fresh dill**

1 **tablespoon finely chopped parsley**

1 **tablespoon Dijon mustard**

¼ **teaspoon salt**

Place the potatoes in a large saucepan with enough water to cover. Cook over medium heat for 10 minutes. Add the carrots and cook for 8 minutes. Drain and rinse with cold water. Allow to cool.

In a large serving bowl, combine the celery, apples, onion, mayonnaise, plain yogurt, lemon yogurt, dill, parsley, mustard, and salt. Add the potato mixture and stir to combine. Cover and refrigerate for 2 hours before serving.

Makes 8 servings

Per serving: *121 calories, 3 g protein, 18 g carbohydrate, 5 g fat, 5 mg cholesterol, 270 mg sodium, 5 g dietary fiber*

Diet Exchanges: *0 milk, 1 vegetable, ½ fruit, ½ carbohydrate, 0 meat, 1 fat*

1 Carb Choice

Citrus Salad

—Wanda Cribb, Rome, Georgia

"This is a very nice light meal to have on a hot summer day. It's nice served with wheat crackers. It has helped me cut calories and shed those extra pounds that were put on during the winter."

Prep time: 10 minutes; Chill time: 1 hour

3 cups cubed fresh pineapple

3 cups grapefruit sections

8 ounces vanilla or lemon yogurt

Lettuce leaves

Combine the pineapple and grapefruit in a large bowl. Cover and refrigerate for 1 hour, or until chilled.

Line 6 plates with lettuce leaves. Evenly divide the fruit and yogurt among the plates.

Makes 6 servings

Per serving: *111 calories, 3 g protein, 24 g carbohydrate, 2 g fat, 4 mg cholesterol, 25 mg sodium, 3 g dietary fiber*

Diet Exchanges: *0 milk, 0 vegetable, 1½ fruit, ½ carbohydrate, 0 meat, ½ fat*

2 Carb Choices

SECRETS OF WEIGHT-LOSS WINNERS

• You have to start thinking that losing weight and getting into better, heart-healthy shape is not done by dieting. It starts with taking control of your life, your own thinking, and your own emotions. It is a complete lifestyle change that can start with just one or two little steps. You have to do it for yourself. You have to want to!

—Darla Stanton, Coldwater, Michigan

• I am convinced that keeping a daily food journal is the number 1 way to keep yourself on track and deter you from eating "just one more snack." I keep a small weekly diary in my purse and jot down every meal and snack consumed throughout each day.

—Donna Marrin, Markham, Ontario, Canada

Italian Medley

—Kay Franz, Richmond, Virginia

345 Calories

"This is a quick dish I can make in 45 minutes or less. It solves the after-work time crunch and avoids the temptation of fattening takeout foods. For myself, I often eliminate the pasta, but it's a mandate for my 9-year-old son, who often won't consider eating a meal that doesn't include pasta."

Prep time: 15 minutes; Cook time: 25 minutes

- **12 ounces elbow macaroni or other shape pasta (optional)**
- **1 tablespoon olive oil**
- **2 medium zucchini, sliced**
- **2 small or 1 medium eggplant, cubed**
- **2–3 cloves garlic, minced**
- **1 can (28 ounces) diced tomatoes**
- **1 teaspoon dried oregano**
- **1 teaspoon dried basil**
- **¼ teaspoon salt**
- **¼ teaspoon ground black pepper**
- **1 can (14–19 ounces) white or navy beans, rinsed and drained**

Prepare the macaroni according to package directions, if using.

Meanwhile, heat the oil in a large skillet over medium-high heat. Add the zucchini, eggplant, and garlic and cook, stirring frequently, for 5 minutes, or until tender-crisp. Add the tomatoes, oregano, basil, salt, and pepper and bring to a boil. Reduce the heat to low and simmer for 10 minutes. Add the beans and cook for 3 minutes, or until heated through. Serve over the macaroni, if using.

Makes 6 servings

Per serving: *345 calories, 14 g protein, 67 g carbohydrate, 4 g fat, 0 mg cholesterol, 280 mg sodium, 11 g dietary fiber*

Diet Exchanges: *0 milk, 2 vegetable, 0 fruit, 4 carbohydrate, 0 meat, ½ fat*

4½ Carb Choices

Pasta Ceci

—Bonni Ernst, Charlotte, North Carolina

"This recipe is easy to prepare, nutritious, and awfully good!"

Prep time: 15 minutes; Cook time: 13 minutes

- 12 ounces shell or bow-tie pasta
- 2 tablespoons olive oil
- 5 cloves garlic, minced
- 1 small onion, chopped
- 1 can (14–19 ounces) chickpeas (ceci beans), rinsed and drained
- 1 tomato, chopped
- 1 cup water
- 1 chicken bouillon cube
- ¼ teaspoon salt
- ¼ teaspoon ground black pepper
- 1 tablespoon chopped fresh parsley
- ¼ cup freshly grated Parmesan or Romano cheese

Prepare the pasta according to package directions. Drain and place in a serving bowl.

Meanwhile, heat the oil in a large skillet over medium-high heat. Add the garlic and onion and cook, stirring frequently, for 5 minutes, or until the onion is translucent. Add the chickpeas and tomato and cook for 3 minutes. Add the water and bouillon cube and bring to a boil. Reduce the heat to low and simmer for 5 minutes. Add to the bowl with the pasta and toss to combine. Season with the salt, pepper, and parsley. Sprinkle with the cheese.

Makes 4 servings

Per serving: *525 calories, 19 g protein, 89 g carbohydrate, 12 g fat, 4 mg cholesterol, 800 mg sodium, 8 g dietary fiber*

Diet Exchanges: *0 milk, ½ vegetable, 0 fruit, 5½ carbohydrate, ½ meat, 1½ fat*

6 Carb Choices

Black Beans and Bow Ties

—Amy Miller, Madison Heights, Michigan

"This takes so little time and effort to prepare, I can never say I don't want to cook. It's low-fat and packed with flavor."

Prep time: 5 minutes; Cook time: 15 minutes

- 1 **can (14–19 ounces) black beans, rinsed and drained**
- 1 **can (14½ ounces) diced tomatoes with Italian herbs**
- 1 **can (14½ ounces) fat-free reduced-sodium chicken broth**
- 1 **cup bow-tie pasta**
- 1 **clove garlic, minced**
- ¼ **cup chopped fresh basil leaves**
  Ground black pepper, to taste
  Shredded mozzarella cheese

In a 3-quart saucepan over medium-high heat, combine the beans, tomatoes (with juice), and broth. Add the pasta and bring to a boil. Reduce the heat to low and add the garlic, basil, and pepper. Cover and cook, stirring occasionally, for 10 minutes, or until the pasta is al dente. Sprinkle with the cheese.

Makes 2 servings

Per serving: *322 calories, 19 g protein, 54 g carbohydrate, 2 g fat, 0 mg cholesterol, 1,030 mg sodium, 12 g dietary fiber*

Diet Exchanges: *0 milk, 3 vegetable, 0 fruit, 2½ carbohydrate, 1½ meat, 0 fat*

4 Carb Choices

Kitchen Tip

Amy suggests serving this dish with a fresh green salad for a well-balanced, healthy meal.

Chinese Peanut Butter Noodles

329 Calories

—Caroline Wang, San Jose, California

"I usually mix 1 cup of noodles and 1 cup of shredded veggies with just a little peanut sauce, and it tastes great. I even use the sauce for dipping with raw or cooked veggies. I always make a whole lot to last 2 or 3 days. This way, I always have something quick and yummy to eat for lunch or a snack."

Prep time: 20 minutes; Cook time: 10 minutes

8 ounces thin spaghetti

¼ cup reduced-fat peanut butter

2 tablespoons warm water

1 scallion, finely chopped

2 tablespoons soy sauce

1 teaspoon brown sugar

1 teaspoon vinegar

1 teaspoon minced garlic

1 teaspoon sesame seeds (optional)

4 teaspoons ground flaxseed (optional)

½ cup shredded carrot

1 English cucumber, shredded

1 cup bean sprouts

Prepare the spaghetti according to package directions. Drain, rinse with cold water, and drain again. Place in a large serving bowl.

Meanwhile, in a small bowl, combine the peanut butter and water and stir until smooth. Add the scallion, soy sauce, brown sugar, vinegar, garlic, sesame seeds (if using), and flaxseeds (if using) and stir to combine.

To the bowl with the pasta, add the carrot, cucumber, and bean sprouts. Top with the sauce and toss to combine.

Makes 4 servings

Per serving: *329 calories, 13 g protein, 55 g carbohydrate, 7 g fat, 0 mg cholesterol, 795 mg sodium, 4 g dietary fiber*

Diet Exchanges: *0 milk, 1½ vegetable, 0 fruit, 3 carbohydrate, ½ meat, 1 fat*

3½ Carb Choices

Kitchen Tip

Make all the ingredients ahead, as Caroline does, and you'll have a meal at the ready on a busy day. Toss everything together just before serving. The ingredients will keep in the refrigerator for about 2 days. For a different twist, Caroline also enjoys tossing in some shredded cooked chicken breast or ham or sliced hard-boiled eggs.

Spicy Black Bean and Artichoke Spaghetti

—Maryann Amburgey, Richardson, Texas

"Since this doesn't take long to make, I can get home from work and have dinner ready in half an hour. That cuts down on my snacking before dinner. I usually have leftovers that I can reheat easily in the microwave at work for lunch the next day."

Prep time: 5 minutes; Cook time: 20 minutes

12 ounces thin spaghetti or angel hair pasta

1 can (14 ounces) artichoke hearts packed in water, drained and quartered

1 can (14–19 ounces) black beans with jalapeño chile pepper, rinsed and drained

2 cans (14½ ounces each) Mexican-style stewed tomatoes

1 small onion, chopped

1 small clove garlic, minced (optional)

¼ teaspoon salt

¼ teaspoon ground black pepper

¼ cup low-fat Parmesan or Asiago cheese

Prepare the pasta according to package directions.

Meanwhile, heat a large saucepan over medium-high heat. Add the artichokes, beans, tomatoes (with juice), onion, garlic (if using), salt, and pepper and bring to a boil. Reduce the heat to low and simmer for 15 minutes.

Serve over the pasta. Sprinkle with the cheese.

Makes 8 servings

Per serving: *255 calories, 12 g protein, 49 g carbohydrate, 2 g fat, 2 mg cholesterol, 610 mg sodium, 8 g dietary fiber*

Diet Exchanges: *0 milk, 2 vegetable, 0 fruit, 2½ carbohydrate, ½ meat, 0 fat*

3 Carb Choices

┌─ *Kitchen Tip* ─────────────────┐

Maryann notes that if you don't care for jalapeño chiles, you can substitute a can of plain black beans.

└──────────────────────────────────┘

Fettuccine Alfredo Light

421 Calories

—Julie McKenzie, Aliquippa, Pennsylvania

" I love rich, creamy foods and sauces, so this recipe allows me to have them without all of the fat and calories! "

Prep time: 8 minutes; Cook time: 14 minutes

12 ounces fettuccine

1 cup fat-free ricotta cheese

¾ cup fat-free milk

1 tablespoon butter-flavored sprinkles

⅛ teaspoon ground white pepper

¾ cup (3 ounces) grated reduced-fat Parmesan cheese

Prepare the pasta according to package directions. Drain, return to the pot, and cover to keep warm.

Meanwhile, in a blender or food processor, combine the ricotta, milk, butter-flavored sprinkles, and pepper. Process until smooth. Place in a saucepan over low heat and cook, stirring constantly, for 5 minutes, or until heated through (do not boil). Pour over the pasta and toss to coat. Sprinkle with the Parmesan.

Makes 4 servings

Per serving: *421 calories, 26 g protein, 67 g carbohydrate, 4 g fat, 21 mg cholesterol, 499 mg sodium, 3 g dietary fiber*

Diet Exchanges: *½ milk, 0 vegetable, 0 fruit, 4 carbohydrate, 1½ meat, 1 fat*

4½ Carb Choices

FOUR QUICK WAYS WITH RICE

Add one of these to 3 cups cooked, fluffed brown rice. Each mini recipe serves 6.

Curried Coconut Rice. Toast 3 tablespoons shredded coconut in small skillet over medium heat. Stir in 1 teaspoon curry powder; remove from the heat. Add to rice with ⅓ cup slivered dried apricots or golden raisins.

Latin Rice and Black Beans. Heat 15 ounces rinsed and drained canned black beans, 14 ounces drained canned diced tomatoes, and ⅓ cup medium salsa. Stir into rice with ½ cup chopped fresh cilantro.

Pecan Rice. In a small skillet, toast 3 tablespoons chopped pecans. Stir into rice with 3 tablespoons chopped fresh parsley and 1 teaspoon grated orange zest.

Mushroom-Sesame Rice. Toast 2 tablespoons sesame seeds in a small skillet. Sauté 8 ounces sliced white or cremini mushrooms in 1 tablespoon olive oil in a medium skillet until tender. Stir mushrooms and seeds into rice.

Easy Stir-Fry with Rice

—Charlene Ihrig, Virginia Beach, Virginia

"This is very filling, while getting lots of vegetables, using little fats, and reducing sodium. It makes good use of leftover rice and veggies."

Prep time: 25 minutes; Cook time: 20 minutes

2 tablespoons canola oil

1 onion, sliced

4 stalks celery hearts, chopped

2 carrots, chopped

1 clove garlic, minced

2 cups chopped bok choy

2 cups chopped mustard greens

8 ounces chopped cabbage and broccoli mix

4 scallions, chopped

2–3 drops hot-pepper sauce

2 cups cooked brown rice

Low-sodium soy sauce, to taste

Heat the oil in a large skillet or wok over medium-high heat. Add the onion and cook, stirring constantly, for 2 minutes, or until browned. Add the celery, carrots, and garlic and cook, stirring constantly, for 4 minutes, or until tender-crisp. Reduce the heat to medium-low. Add the bok choy, mustard greens, cabbage and broccoli mix, and scallions. Drizzle with hot-pepper sauce. Cook, stirring, for 5 minutes, or until the greens are wilted.

Heat another large skillet coated with cooking spray over medium-high heat. Add the rice and cook, stirring occasionally, for 5 minutes, or until slightly browned. Drizzle with soy sauce. Add the rice to the skillet with the vegetables and stir to combine. Cook, stirring frequently, for 4 minutes.

Makes 4 servings

Per serving: *251 calories, 7 g protein, 40 g carbohydrate, 8 g fat, 0 mg cholesterol, 155 mg sodium, 8 g dietary fiber*

Diet Exchanges: *0 milk, 3 vegetable, 0 fruit, 1½ carbohydrate, 0 meat, 1½ fat*

2½ Carb Choices

Kitchen Tip

Charlene suggests cooking the rice the night before so it's on hand when you're ready to start cooking. She also notes that you can add sliced cooked chicken or fish to this recipe.

Fast Tempeh Stir-Fry

—Wendi Jones, Cottonwood Falls, Kansas

380 Calories

"This recipe fills me up and provides a combination of nutrients that makes me feel satisfied. My children enjoy eating this with chopsticks."

Prep time: 5 minutes; Cook time: 45 minutes

- **1 cup brown rice**
- **2 tablespoons olive oil**
- **8 ounces tempeh, cubed**
- **2 cloves garlic, minced**
- **8 ounces your favorite frozen Asian vegetable mix**
- **3 tablespoons low-sodium soy sauce or tamari**
- **3 tablespoons apple juice or orange juice**
- **1 tablespoon cornstarch**

Prepare the rice according to package directions.

Meanwhile, heat the oil in a large nonstick skillet over medium-high heat. Add the tempeh and cook, stirring occasionally, for 5 minutes, or until cooked through. Add the garlic and vegetables and cook, stirring frequently, for 5 minutes, or until the vegetables are tender-crisp. Add the soy sauce or tamari, apple juice or orange juice, and cornstarch. Cook until the sauce thickens. Serve over the rice.

Makes 4 servings

Per serving: *380 calories, 16 g protein, 49 g carbohydrate, 14 g fat, 0 mg cholesterol, 271 mg sodium, 6 g dietary fiber*

Diet Exchanges: *0 milk, ½ vegetable, 0 fruit, 3 carbohydrate, 1 meat, 1½ fat*

3 Carb Choices

Kitchen Tip

Wendi's favorite vegetable mix for this recipe includes broccoli, carrots, soy beans, bok choy, and snow peas.

Meatless Mexican Lunch

—Jeanie Callaghan, Smyrna, Georgia

"I developed this recipe in my search for a fast, inexpensive, and easy meatless protein dish to take to work for lunch. I credit this recipe with helping me lose 40 pounds. It's low in fat and high in fiber. I often add odds and ends of leftover veggies to this dish as well."

Prep time: 10 minutes; Cook time: 13 minutes; Stand time: 10 minutes

½ **small onion, chopped**

1 **can (15½ ounces) crushed tomatoes**

¾ **cup frozen corn kernels**

1 **can (3½ ounces) chopped green chile peppers**

1 **can (14–19 ounces) black beans, rinsed and drained**

½ **cup instant rice**

1 **teaspoon ground cumin**

¼ **cup + 2 tablespoons fat-free shredded Cheddar or Monterey Jack cheese**

Heat a 2-quart pot coated with cooking spray over medium-high heat. Add the onion and cook, stirring, for 1 minute. Stir in the tomatoes, corn, and chile peppers and bring to a boil. Add the beans, rice, and cumin. Remove from the heat, cover, and let stand for 10 minutes. Serve sprinkled with the cheese.

Makes 4 servings

Per serving: *216 calories, 13 g protein, 40 g carbohydrate, 1 g fat, 2 mg cholesterol, 543 mg sodium, 10 g dietary fiber*

Diet Exchanges: *0 milk, 2 vegetable, 0 fruit, 2 carbohydrate, 1 meat, 0 fat*

3 Carb Choices

Kitchen Tip

Jeanie suggests serving this dish with low-fat taco chips. She also uses it for a quick and easy burrito filling.

It Worked for Me!

Lori Lefort

VITAL STATS

Weight lost: 30 pounds

Time to goal: 2 years

Unique secret to success: Taking advantage of an unforeseen opportunity; if you find yourself down a few pounds, use that as your invitation to lose more.

Affirmation: *"Losing weight is life-affirming."*

A personal life crisis brought Lori to a turning point. She used this unexpected jump-start to make other changes that have led her to lasting weight loss and better health.

"My husband passed away unexpectedly 7 years ago. It was a very emotional and difficult time for me. I was at my heaviest then and had a 6-year-old daughter to focus on, but quickly lost 15 pounds due to my grief. I only noticed the weight loss when my size-16 clothes started feeling loose on me. This turned out to be the push I needed to eat better and think about exercising.

"I realize now that carbohydrates are not something that I can eat a lot of. I don't avoid them completely, the way some dieters do, but I do try to limit the amount of carbs I eat each day. For example, if I have a starch for lunch,

I won't eat any carbs for dinner. If I do eat something like bread, I opt for whole wheat instead of white. Luckily, I love salads and vegetables, so it's really not hard for me to eat carbohydrate-free meals a lot of the time.

"I also totally changed my breakfast habits. I used to be a classic breakfast-skipper. But by lunchtime, I would be starving and ready to eat whatever was available. Now I have a simple breakfast every day. I make my own granola and eat that with fat-free, sugar-free yogurt that I buy in small containers for easy portion control. And I make sure to drink water all day long.

"I used to overeat regularly. Now, if I eat too much at a meal, I feel uncomfortable. I have learned to be aware of how much I eat in addition to improving the quality of the foods I choose."

spaghetti Squash with Veggie Gratin

—Ronni Mayer, Baltimore, Maryland

"This dish is my favorite way of eating vegetables. It makes a great meal for dinner, and leftovers are great to take to work. I get all my servings of veggies in one sitting without consuming a lot of calories. And it tastes yummy!"

Prep time: 20 minutes; Cook time: 1 hour 15 minutes

- **1 spaghetti squash (about 3 pounds)**
- **1 teaspoon olive oil**
- **2 medium zucchini, finely chopped**
- **1 cup sliced mushrooms**
- **¼ cup chopped spring onion**
- **2 cloves garlic, minced**
- **1 can (14½ ounces) no-salt-added diced tomatoes with Italian seasonings**
- **¾ cup (3 ounces) shredded reduced-fat mozzarella cheese**
- **¼ cup chopped parsley**
- **½ teaspoon salt**
- **½ teaspoon ground black pepper**

Preheat the oven to 350°F.

Slice the squash in half lengthwise and scoop out the seeds. Place the squash, cut sides down, in a 13" × 9" baking dish. Add water to the dish to a depth of ½". Bake for 50 minutes, or until fork-tender. Increase the oven temperature to 450°F.

When the squash is cool enough to handle, scrape with a fork to remove the spaghetti-like strands. Coat the baking dish with cooking spray. Return the pulp to the baking dish.

Meanwhile, heat the oil in a large nonstick skillet over medium-high heat. Add the zucchini, mushrooms, onion, and garlic and cook, stirring frequently, for 10 minutes, or until the vegetables are tender. Remove from the heat. Stir in the tomatoes (with juice), cheese, parsley, salt, and pepper. Add to the baking dish with the squash and toss to combine. Spread evenly in the baking dish.

Bake for 15 minutes, or until hot and bubbly.

Makes 6 servings

Per serving: *145 calories, 7 g protein, 23 g carbohydrate, 5 g fat, 7 mg cholesterol, 361 mg sodium, 6 g dietary fiber*

Diet Exchanges: *0 milk, 4 vegetable, 0 fruit, 0 carbohydrate, 1 meat, ½ fat*

1½ Carb Choices

Hearty Meals

Beef and Vegetables

—Bonnie Steele, Grove Hill, New Brunswick, Canada

"This recipe is easy and very, very good!"

Prep time: 10 minutes; Cook time: 1 hour 30 minutes

1 tablespoon vegetable oil
1½ pounds eye of round roast, trimmed
2 onions, cut into wedges
3 carrots, coarsely chopped
1 green bell pepper, coarsely chopped
1 quart beef broth
2 heads broccoli, coarsely chopped

Preheat the oven to 350°F.

Heat the oil in an ovenproof Dutch oven over medium-high heat. Add the beef and onions and cook for 7 minutes, or until browned. Add the carrots, bell pepper, and broth and bring to a boil. Remove from the heat and place in the oven.

Bake for 1 hour. Stir in the broccoli and bake for 20 minutes longer, or until a thermometer inserted in the center of the beef registers 160°F for medium doneness. Let stand for 10 minutes before slicing.

Makes 6 servings

Per serving: *293 calories, 30 g protein, 19 g carbohydrate, 12 g fat, 55 mg cholesterol, 160 mg sodium, 8 g dietary fiber*

Diet Exchanges: *0 milk, 4 vegetable, 0 fruit, 0 carbohydrate, 5 meat, 1½ fat*

1 Carb Choice

Spaghetti Squash Chicken Parmesan

395 Calories

—Naomi Olson, Sumas, Washington

"I am always looking for gluten-free recipes. I also want meals that aren't so hard to digest. This is a great alternative to the usual heavy chicken Parmesan and pasta."

Prep time: 20 minutes; Marinate time: 1 hour; Cook time: 25 minutes

- 4 boneless, skinless chicken breast halves
- ½ cup buttermilk or ½ cup fat-free milk + 1 tablespoon lemon juice
- 1 large spaghetti squash, cut in half
- ½ cup rice flour or unbleached or all-purpose flour
- ⅓ cup grated Parmesan cheese
- 1 teaspoon garlic powder
- ½ teaspoon seasoning salt
- 1¾ cups spaghetti sauce

Place the chicken in a 13" × 9" baking dish and pierce in several places with a fork. Pour the buttermilk over the chicken and turn to coat both sides. Cover and refrigerate for 1 hour.

Place the squash, cut sides up, in a microwaveable dish. Cover with plastic wrap and microwave for 25 minutes, or until fork-tender. Using a fork, scrape the flesh from the squash. Keep warm.

Meanwhile, preheat the oven to 375°F.

In a shallow dish, combine the flour, ¼ cup of the cheese, the garlic powder, and seasoning salt. Dredge the chicken in the flour mixture, then return to the pan with the buttermilk, then coat again with flour. Place in another large baking dish coated with cooking spray. Spoon about 2 tablespoons spaghetti sauce onto each chicken breast and sprinkle with the remaining cheese.

Bake for 25 minutes, or until a thermometer inserted in the thickest portion registers 160°F and the juices run clear.

Meanwhile, heat the remaining sauce in a medium saucepan over medium heat. Serve with the chicken and spaghetti squash.

Makes 4 servings

Per serving: *395 calories, 35 g protein, 48 g carbohydrate, 7 g fat, 72 mg cholesterol, 742 mg sodium, 7 g dietary fiber*

Diet Exchanges: *0 milk, 4 vegetable, 0 fruit, 2 carbohydrate, 4 meat, ½ fat*

3 Carb Choices

Roasted Red Pepper Chicken

315 Calories

—Barbie Picciano, Wickliffe, Ohio

"This is a great way to enjoy low-fat chicken that is juicy and tasty. Grilled chicken was getting boring, and I incorporated my vegetable and a small portion of dairy into the meal. My husband loves it, too."

Prep time: 10 minutes; Marinate time: 1 hour; Cook time: 50 minutes

4 boneless, skinless chicken breast halves
1 bottle (8 ounces) fat-free Italian dressing
4 large red bell peppers
4 thin slices fresh mozzarella cheese
   Fresh basil leaves, for garnish

Place the chicken in a 13" × 9" baking dish and pierce in several places with a fork. Pour the dressing over the chicken and turn to coat both sides. Cover and refrigerate for 1 hour.

Preheat the broiler.

Cut the tops off the peppers and cut the peppers in half. Remove the cores and seeds. Place the peppers, cut sides down, on a baking sheet. Broil for 10 minutes, or until the skins are charred. Place in a paper bag and allow to cool. When cool enough to handle, remove and discard the skins. Cut the pepper halves into ½" strips.

Change the oven temperature to 350°F.

Cut a pocket into the thick end of each chicken breast half. Stuff each piece with some of the sliced peppers. Place a slice of cheese on top of each piece. Top with the remaining pepper strips, covering the cheese.

Place the chicken in a clean 13" × 9" baking dish and bake for 40 minutes, or until a thermometer inserted in the thickest portion registers 160°F and the juices run clear. Let stand for 5 minutes before serving.

Makes 4 servings

Per serving: *315 calories, 33 g protein, 27 g carbohydrate, 8 g fat, 88 mg cholesterol, 714 mg sodium, 4 g dietary fiber*

Diet Exchanges: *0 milk, 1½ vegetable, 0 fruit, 1 carbohydrate, 4½ meat, 1 fat*

2 Carb Choices

(shown with Dirty Rice, page 147)

Apricot Chicken

—Susie Raimi, San Diego, California

Prep time: 5 minutes; Cook time: 1 hour

- 1 **jar (12 ounces) apricot preserves**
- 1 **bottle (8 ounces) low-fat French salad dressing**
- 1 **package dry onion soup mix**
- 1 **small whole chicken, skinned, or 4 bone-in chicken breasts, skinned**

Preheat the oven to 350°F.

In a small bowl, combine the apricot preserves, dressing, and soup mix. Place the chicken in a large baking dish or roasting pan. Pour the sauce over the chicken.

Bake for 1 hour, basting every 15 minutes, or until a thermometer inserted in the thickest portion registers 180°F (for whole chicken) or 170°F (for bone-in breasts) and the juices run clear.

Makes 4 servings

Per serving: *411 calories, 27 g protein, 68 g carbohydrate, 5 g fat, 66 mg cholesterol, 706 mg sodium, 1 g dietary fiber*

Diet Exchanges: *0 milk, 0 vegetable, 0 fruit, 4½ carbohydrate, 4 meat, ½ fat*

4½ Carb Choices

Kitchen Tip

You can also make this recipe using boneless, skinless chicken breast halves. Just reduce the baking time to 30 minutes, or until a thermometer inserted in the thickest portion registers 160°F and the juices run clear.

Tex-Mex Chicken

—Misty Phillips, Port Gibson, Mississippi

"This summer, I discovered that hot peppers seem to diminish my cravings for sweets and high-fat foods. By incorporating zest and flair into my diet with peppers, I have had fewer cravings and have felt much more satisfied after a meal."

Prep time: 25 minutes; Cook time: 1 hour

- **4 boneless, skinless chicken breast halves**
- **½ cup fat-free Italian dressing**
- **1 can (16 ounces) Mexican-style stewed tomatoes**
- **2 cloves garlic, minced**
- **2 jalapeño chile peppers, minced (wear plastic gloves when handling)**
- **¼ teaspoon dried cilantro**
- **¼ cup (1 ounce) freshly grated Parmesan cheese or shredded reduced-fat Monterey Jack cheese**
- **1 cup brown rice**

Place the chicken in a 13" × 9" baking dish. Pierce in several places with a fork. Pour the dressing over the top, turning to coat both sides. Cover and refrigerate for at least 15 minutes.

Meanwhile, preheat the oven to 400°F. In a medium saucepan over medium heat, combine the tomatoes (with juice), garlic, peppers, and cilantro. Simmer for 20 minutes. Reserve ¼ cup of the tomato mixture. Pour the remaining tomato mixture over the chicken.

Bake the chicken for 40 minutes, or until a thermometer inserted in the thickest portion registers 160°F and the juices run clear. Sprinkle with the cheese.

Meanwhile, prepare the rice according to package directions. Stir in the reserved ¼ cup tomato mixture. Serve with the chicken.

Makes 4 servings

Per serving: *417 calories, 34 g protein, 57 g carbohydrate, 5 g fat, 71 mg cholesterol, 900 mg sodium, 4 g dietary fiber*

Diet Exchanges: *0 milk, 2 vegetable, 0 fruit, 3 carbohydrate, 4 meat, 0 fat*

4 Carb Choices

Kitchen Tip

Misty completes this meal by serving it with steamed fresh vegetables or a side salad.

Mary's Baked Italian Chicken

266 Calories

—MaryLou Burks, Minden, Nevada

"This recipe is so delicious and is a break from ordinary broiled chicken breast. It is so tasty, you'll forget that it is low-fat and also low-calorie. The mushrooms and onions add a lot of flavor."

Prep time: 15 minutes; Cook time: 45 minutes

1 tablespoon olive oil

1 onion, thinly sliced

2 cups mushrooms, sliced

1 egg, beaten

½ cup 1% milk

½ cup plain dried bread crumbs

4 boneless, skinless chicken breast halves or thighs

Preheat the oven to 350°F. Drizzle the oil into a 13" × 9" baking dish.

Place the onion and mushrooms in a medium nonstick skillet over medium heat. Cook, stirring frequently for 5 minutes, or until soft but not fully cooked.

In a shallow bowl, whisk together the egg and milk. Place the bread crumbs in another shallow bowl.

Rinse the chicken and pat dry with paper towels. Dredge the chicken first in the egg mixture, turning to coat both sides, then in the bread crumbs until coated. Place in the prepared baking dish. Top with the onion mixture.

Bake for 40 minutes, or until a thermometer inserted in the thickest portion registers 160°F and the juices run clear.

Makes 4 servings

Per serving: *266 calories, 32 g protein, 17 g carbohydrate, 7 g fat, 120 mg cholesterol, 220 mg sodium, 2 g dietary fiber*

Diet Exchanges: *0 milk, 1 vegetable, 0 fruit, 1 carbohydrate, 4 meat, 1 fat*

1 Carb Choice

Kitchen Tip

MaryLou notes that you can serve this dish with any green vegetable, such as fresh green beans and a green salad. Everyone will enjoy!

Chicken Vegetable Pot Pie

—Sheila Groskin, Tuxedo Park, New York

"I find this recipe to be 'comfort food!' My children have always loved it. I can substitute with other vegetables like broccoli, potatoes, or green beans for variety. It is filling and healthy, and using the low-fat and low-calorie gravy helps with weight control."

Prep time: 15 minutes; Cook time: 57 minutes

1 teaspoon olive oil

2 carrots, thinly sliced

2 ribs celery, thinly sliced

1 pound cooked chicken, chopped

½ cup peas

1 can (15 ounces) fat-free chicken gravy

¼ teaspoon salt

¼ teaspoon ground black pepper
   Parsley, to taste

1 deep-dish frozen double pie crust

Preheat the oven to 350°.

Heat the oil in a medium skillet over medium-high heat. Add the carrots and celery and cook, stirring frequently, for 7 minutes, or until tender. Place in a large bowl. Add the chicken, peas, gravy, salt, pepper, and parsley. Place in the bottom pie crust. Top with the second crust, trim the edges according to package directions, and crimp the edges. Place on a baking sheet.

Bake for 50 minutes, or until brown and bubbly.

Makes 8 servings

Per serving: *292 calories, 21 g protein, 22 g carbohydrate, 13 g fat, 53 mg cholesterol, 635 mg sodium, 2 g dietary fiber*

Diet Exchanges: *0 milk, ½ vegetable, 0 fruit, 1 carbohydrate, 2½ meat, 2 fat*

1½ Carb Choices

Chicken Parmesan Strips

—Patsy Roy-Turple, Belledune, New Brunswick, Canada

"I have maintained my weight loss with the help of recipes that I have made with skim milk and chicken, plus my daily walk and cross-country skiing in the winter."

Prep time: 12 minutes; Marinate time: 15 minutes; Cook time: 20 minutes

- 1 **pound boneless chicken strips**
- ½ **cup fat-free milk**
- ⅓ **cup seasoned dried bread crumbs or cereal crumbs**
- 3 **tablespoons grated Parmesan cheese**
- 2 **teaspoons parsley**
- ¼ **teaspoon ground black pepper**

Preheat the oven to 400°F. Coat a baking sheet with cooking spray.

Place the chicken in a shallow bowl. Pierce in several places with a fork. Pour the milk over the top. Cover and refrigerate for at least 15 minutes.

In another shallow bowl, combine the bread crumbs, cheese, parsley, and pepper. Remove the chicken from the milk mixture and dip into the bread crumb mixture, turning to coat well. Place on the prepared baking sheet.

Bake for 10 minutes. Turn the chicken pieces and bake for 10 minutes longer, or until the chicken is no longer is pink.

Makes 4 servings

Per serving: *191 calories, 30 g protein, 8 g carbohydrate, 3 g fat, 70 mg cholesterol, 240 mg sodium, 0 g dietary fiber*

Diet Exchanges: *0 milk, 0 vegetable, 0 fruit, ½ carbohydrate, 4 meat, 0 fat*

½ Carb Choice

Spicy Meatballs

—Roselyne Kirchoff, Vancouver, Washington

"By cutting down my red meat intake and on fat, I am slowly losing weight.
This recipe is good enough for me to forget about the fatty meatballs I used to love.
The potatoes work as a binder, and you can't tell they are in the recipe. My family
is eating healthy, and they don't miss all the fat and red meat."

Prep time: 35 minutes; Cook time: 45 minutes

- **2 pounds ground turkey breast**
- **2 small potatoes, boiled with skin, cooled, peeled, and grated**
- **1 large carrot, grated**
- **1 medium onion, finely chopped**
- **1 tablespoon minced garlic**
- **1 teaspoon dried marjoram**
- **½ teaspoon ground black pepper**
- **½ teaspoon salt**
- **1 teaspoon celery salt or powder**
- **1 can (15 ounces) cream soup, such as cream of celery, mushroom, or chicken**

Preheat the oven to 350°F.

In a large bowl, combine the turkey, potatoes, carrot, onion, garlic, marjoram, pepper, salt, and celery salt. Form the mixture into balls. Place in a 13" × 9" baking dish (use 2 dishes if necessary). Pour the soup over the meatballs. Fill the soup can with water and pour over the meatballs.

Bake for 45 minutes, turning once halfway through cooking, or until a thermometer inserted in a meatball registers 180°F, the meatballs are no longer pink, and the soup has reduced and thickened.

Makes about 55 meatballs

Per meatball: *35 calories, 3 g protein, 1 g carbohydrate, 2 g fat, 14 mg cholesterol, 99 mg sodium, 0 g dietary fiber*

Diet Exchanges: *0 milk, 0 vegetable, 0 fruit, 0 carbohydrate, ½ meat, 0 fat*

0 Carb Choices

Kitchen Tip

Roselyne notes that these meatballs freeze well, so she often freezes any extra to have on hand for another day. Sometimes she even uses them to make delicious meatball subs. (Freeze them before pouring the soup over them and cooking them.)

It Worked for Me!

Jean Zelios

VITAL STATS

Weight lost: **30 pounds**

Time to goal: **6 months**

Unique secret to success:
Having a weight-loss partner
made it possible to both give
and get support along the way.

Affirmation: *"The things I do today affect how I look and feel tomorrow."*

A common combination of factors—having children, getting older, exercising less—put Jean in a position where she felt the urge to lose weight. Partnering with her sister, who was in a similar situation, made the process easier for each of the women.

"My sister and I had been talking to each other about getting back into shape. We had each gained some weight after having kids, and we both knew about our dad's diabetes. Dropping some pounds would be good for our looks and our health. We decided to support each other and make it a joint effort.

"I started reading a lot about weight loss and about the glycemic index—a way of ranking the sugar content of foods. As I became more aware of the things I was eating, I realized that I always felt lousy after eating foods with a high glycemic index—high sugar content.

"I made major diet changes. I added more fruits and vegetables and whole grains, which seemed to stick with me longer and keep me from getting hungry too soon. Oatmeal or bran cereal became the perfect breakfast. I also drank a lot of water every day. My sister was doing similar things.

"I added exercise, too. I used to run years ago, and I thought it would be great to get back into doing that. I was afraid, though, that if I jumped in too fast, I might give up. So I started slowly, by walking on a treadmill and then adding short bursts of running. It was a while before I could just run, and now I am actually training for a half-marathon. I can't believe I am going to run 13.1 miles!

"My sister and I differed in one aspect of losing weight that was important to me: I wrote down everything that I ate, and my sister didn't. I found that keeping a food journal was very helpful to me and worth the time it took. My sister didn't feel the need for that kind of record-keeping. I guess everyone has his or her own personal formula for success."

Mexican Turkey Meatloaf

—Jennifer Lamontagne, Stratford, Connecticut

"I like this recipe because although ground turkey tends to be very dry and flavorless, the salsa keeps it moist and tasty. I don't miss the more fattening beef version."

Prep time: 15 minutes; Cook time: 1 hour

1½ **cups chunky medium salsa**
1 **egg white**
1 **pound ground turkey breast**
1–1½ **cups old-fashioned rolled oats**
¼ **teaspoon ground black pepper**
½ **cup (2 ounces) shredded reduced-fat Cheddar or soy cheese alternative**
5 **black olives, finely chopped**
2–3 **scallions, finely chopped**

Preheat the oven to 350°F. Coat a loaf pan with cooking spray.

In a large bowl, combine 1 cup of the salsa and the egg. Add the turkey and mix in by hand. Add 1 cup of the oats, mixing in by hand. Add up to ½ cup more oats if needed to reach desired consistency. Place in the prepared loaf pan (it will be a little messy), allowing ½" of space along the side of the pan. Sprinkle with the pepper. Top with the remaining ½ cup salsa.

Bake for 50 minutes. Top with the cheese, olives, and scallions. Bake for 10 minutes longer, or until a thermometer inserted in the center registers 165°F and the turkey is no longer pink.

Makes 8 servings

Per serving: *157 calories, 14 g protein, 10 g carbohydrate, 6 g fat, 46 mg cholesterol, 339 mg sodium, 2 g dietary fiber*

Diet Exchanges: *0 milk, ½ vegetable, 0 fruit, ½ carbohydrate, 2 meat, ½ fat*

1 Carb Choice

Stuffed Peppers

—Lynn McFedries, Maple Ridge, British Columbia, Canada

"This is very tasty and doesn't make you feel like you have to sacrifice taste for health."

Prep time: 25 minutes; Cook time: 57 minutes

½ cup brown rice

8 large bell peppers (any color)

1 pound ground turkey breast

1 onion, chopped

3 cloves garlic, chopped

½ teaspoon seasoning salt

½ teaspoon ground black pepper

½ teaspoon dried thyme

½ teaspoon dried basil

½ teaspoon dried oregano

⅛ teaspoon ground red pepper

1 teaspoon parsley

1 can (8 ounces) tomato sauce

1 cup salsa

2 tablespoons Worcestershire sauce

1 can (11 ounces) corn niblets, drained

1 cup (4 ounces) shredded low-fat or fat-free mozzarella cheese

Prepare the rice according to package directions.

Meanwhile, cut the tops from the peppers and remove and discard the stems and seeds. Chop the tops.

In a large nonstick skillet over medium heat, cook the turkey for 5 minutes, or until no longer pink. Add the pepper tops, onion, garlic, seasoning salt, black pepper, thyme, basil, oregano, ground red pepper, and parsley. Cook for 7 minutes, or until the vegetables are soft. Remove to a large bowl.

In a small bowl, combine the tomato sauce, salsa, and Worcestershire sauce. Reserve 1½ cups; set aside.

Preheat the oven to 400°F.

To the bowl with the turkey mixture, add the rice, corn, ½ cup of the cheese, and the 1½ cups reserved sauce mixture. Stir to combine. Spoon into the pepper shells. Top with the remaining ½ cup sauce mixture. Place in two 13" × 9" baking dishes.

Cover with foil and bake for 35 minutes. Sprinkle with the remaining ½ cup cheese and bake for 10 minutes longer, or until the cheese is melted.

Makes 8 servings

Per serving: *272 calories, 18 g protein, 33 g carbohydrate, 8 g fat, 52 mg cholesterol, 579 mg sodium, 6 g dietary fiber*

Diet Exchanges: *0 milk, 3 vegetable, 0 fruit, 1 carbohydrate, 2 meat, ½ fat*

2 Carb Choices

Lemon-Rosemary Swordfish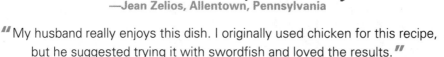

—Jean Zelios, Allentown, Pennsylvania

"My husband really enjoys this dish. I originally used chicken for this recipe, but he suggested trying it with swordfish and loved the results."

Prep time: 15 minutes; Marinate time: 1 hour;
Cook time: 12 minutes

1 large lemon
2 tablespoons olive oil
2 tablespoons chopped fresh rosemary
2 teaspoons minced garlic
½ teaspoon salt
½ teaspoon ground black pepper
4 swordfish steaks (4 ounces each)
Lemon slices, for garnish (optional)

Grate 2 tablespoons peel from the lemon into a small bowl. Squeeze the juice from the lemon into the cup. Add the oil, rosemary, garlic, salt, and pepper and stir to combine. Rub over the fish and place the fish in a large zip-top plastic bag. Seal the bag and refrigerate for 1 hour.

Preheat the oven to 450°F.

Coat a 13" × 9" baking pan with cooking spray. Place the fish in the pan. Pour any remaining marinade over the fish. Cover with foil.

Bake for 12 minutes, or until the fish flakes easily. Garnish with the lemon slices, if using.

Makes 4 servings

Per serving: *198 calories, 21 g protein, 3 g carbohydrate, 11 g fat, 41 mg cholesterol, 388 mg sodium, 1 g dietary fiber*

Diet Exchanges: *0 milk, 0 vegetable, 0 fruit, 0 carbohydrate, 3 meat, 2 fat*

0 Carb Choices

It Worked for Me!

Barbara Braley

VITAL STATS

Weight lost: 62 pounds

Time to goal: 1 year

Unique secret to success: Set small goals and don't worry about the long-term; you'll get there bit by bit.

Affirmation: *"My goal is to stay healthy."*

Barbara weighed 198 pounds when her doctor gave her the news that her health was in jeopardy. Heart problems and diabetes (both weight-related conditions) run in her family, so even though Barbara was only 28, she knew this warning was nothing to shrug off.

"I take after my dad. His side of the family is big-boned, and that is what everyone always said about me. At 28, my 'big bones' weren't getting any smaller. I worked part-time at a gym and watched 70-year-old people working out, while I couldn't even make it up a flight of stairs. After my doctor warned me about my cholesterol and high blood pressure, I finally thought to myself, 'This is ridiculous. It's time to change things.'

"I went home and literally emptied my re-frigerator. I threw everything fattening or unhealthy right in the trash, even if it was an unopened package. Then I took the trash bag and brought it out to the Dumpster. I also started exercising, but very slowly. I couldn't push myself because of a knee injury.

"When I started, I was a size 18. My first goal was to get down to a size 12. I didn't worry about pounds, just body size. Well, after cutting out all the junk food, I found I could fit into a 12 so fast, it hardly felt like trying. I thought, I've gotten this far, now I'll shoot for an 8. The next thing I knew, I was there. I wasn't really focusing on dropping pounds; I was simply eating right and exercising more. I went down to a 6, and now, believe it or not, I wear a 4. Setting small goals was the secret that took me all the way to achieving a big goal."

Stuffed Flounder

—Judith Ferina, Copiague, New York

" This is tasty and rich, therefore tricking me into believing that I am eating something other than bland diet food! *"*

Prep time: 15 minutes; Cook time: 22 minutes

1 tablespoon olive oil

½ pound peeled and deveined shrimp, cut up

½ teaspoon minced garlic

⅓–½ cup unseasoned dried bread crumbs

2 tablespoons grated Parmesan cheese

1 pound flounder fillets

¼ cup white wine or nonalcoholic white wine

½ tablespoon parsley

Preheat the oven to 350°F.

Heat the oil in a large skillet over medium-high heat. Add the shrimp and garlic and cook, stirring frequently, for 5 minutes, or until the shrimp is opaque. Remove to a large bowl. Add the bread crumbs and cheese and stir to combine.

Place the flounder on a work surface. Evenly divide the shrimp mixture among the fillets, spreading almost to the edge. Roll the fillets from a short end to enclose the filling. Secure with wooden picks. Place the rolls in a 13" × 9" baking dish. Pour the wine into the dish. Sprinkle with the parsley.

Bake for 15 minutes, or until the fish flakes easily.

Makes 4 servings

Per serving: *250 calories, 35 g protein, 7 g carbohydrate, 7 g fat, 143 mg cholesterol, 300 mg sodium, 0 g dietary fiber*

Diet Exchanges: *0 milk, 0 vegetable, 0 fruit, ½ carbohydrate, 5 meat, 1 fat*

½ Carb Choice

Hot Crab Oriental

—Rosalie Coponi, Emmaus, Pennsylvania

"This dish is easy, and has often been a Friday-night meal for our family."

Prep time: 10 minutes; Cook time: 35 minutes

8 ounces rotini

1 can (10¾ ounces) reduced-fat cream of celery or mushroom soup

½ cup fat-free mayonnaise

2 tablespoons light soy sauce

2 tablespoons lemon juice

2 cups lump crabmeat

1 can (8 ounces) water chestnuts, drained

3 ribs celery, chopped

2–3 scallions, chopped

Preheat the oven to 375°F.

Prepare the pasta according to package directions.

In an 11" × 7" baking dish, combine the soup, mayonnaise, soy sauce, and lemon juice. Stir in the crabmeat, water chestnuts, celery, and scallions. Add the pasta and stir to coat.

Bake for 20 minutes, or until hot and bubbly.

Makes 8 servings

Per serving: *290 calories, 14 g protein, 39 g carbohydrate, 8 g fat, 40 mg cholesterol, 800 mg sodium, 4 g dietary fiber*

Diet Exchanges: *0 milk, 2 vegetable, 0 fruit, 2 carbohydrate, 1 meat, 1½ fat*

3 Carb Choices

300-CALORIE DINNERS

Calories at dinnertime can easily reach the 800-calorie mark, which will really pack on the pounds. Imagine the weight-loss benefits of substituting with a 300-calorie dinner. Here are a few to try:

- Lean Cuisine Herb Roasted Chicken and 1 cup 1% milk
- Fantastic Foods Spicy Jamaican Rice and Beans, and 1 steamed broccoli stalk
- Boca Burger (Vegan original) on a bun with 2 pieces leaf lettuce, 1 slice tomato, and 2 teaspoons ketchup, and 1 cup steamed spinach with 1 teaspoon butter
- 3 ounces broiled salmon fillet, 1 cup garden salad with 2 tablespoons low-fat Caesar dressing, and small oat bran dinner roll
- 6 large shrimp with 2 tablespoons cocktail sauce, 2 cups salad with 2 tablespoons low-fat Italian dressing, and iced tea with 1 sugar cube

Greek Beef Stew

—Anne Roy, Ellicott City, Maryland

"It is a full meal and has all the flavor of a robust pasta meal without the calories."

Prep time: 25 minutes; Cook time: 1 hour

- 2 tablespoons canola oil
- 4–6 cloves garlic, minced
- 1 pound beef cubes, trimmed
- 1 pound small white onions
- 1 can (6 ounces) tomato paste
- ⅓ cup currants
- ½ cup red-wine vinegar
- ½ cup red wine
- 2 tablespoons brown sugar
- 6–8 cloves
- ½ teaspoon ground cumin
  Pinch of salt
- 1 bay leaf
- 1 stick cinnamon
  Ground black pepper, to taste

Heat the oil in a Dutch oven or deep pot over medium-high heat. Add the garlic and cook, stirring occasionally, for 3 minutes, or until softened. Add the beef, stirring to coat. Reduce the heat. Add the onions; do not stir.

In a small bowl, combine the tomato paste, currants, vinegar, wine, brown sugar, cloves, cumin, and salt. Pour over the beef mixture. Place the bay leaf and cinnamon stick on top. Cover and simmer for 1 hour; do not stir.

Sprinkle with pepper just before serving. Remove and discard the bay leaf and cinnamon stick.

Makes 4 servings

Per serving: *369 calories, 27 g protein, 38 g carbohydrate, 12 g fat, 68 mg cholesterol, 467 mg sodium, 5 g dietary fiber*

Diet Exchanges: *0 milk, 3½ vegetable, 1 fruit, ½ carbohydrate, 0 meat, 2 fat*

2½ Carb Choices

Kitchen Tip

Anne suggests serving this delicious stew with a fresh green salad, along with pita or garlic bread and a nice red wine.

Stir-Fry Beef

—Marlene Unruh, Chilliwack, British Columbia, Canada

*" I have lost 25 pounds in the past few months. This is a favorite supper.
It keeps me full, so I don't have any before-bedtime snacks. "*

Prep time: 25 minutes; Marinate time: 1 hour;
Cook time: 30 minutes

- 1 **cup brown or white rice**
- 2 **low-sodium beef bouillon cubes**
- 1¾ **cups water**
- ¼ **cup light soy sauce**
- ¼ **cup red wine (optional)**
- ½ **teaspoon minced garlic**
- 2 **teaspoons Montreal steak spice**
- 1 **sirloin steak, trimmed of visible fat
  and sliced in 1" pieces**
- 1 **green bell pepper, sliced**
- 1 **orange or red bell pepper, sliced**
- 1 **onion, sliced**
- 4 **ounces mushrooms, sliced**
- 2 **teaspoons cornstarch**

Prepare the rice according to package directions.

In a large bowl, combine the bouillon cubes and water. Stir to dissolve. Add the soy sauce, wine (if using), garlic, and steak spice. Stir to combine. Add the steak and stir to coat. Cover and refrigerate for 1 hour.

Meanwhile, heat a large nonstick skillet over medium-high heat. Remove the steak from the marinade and add to the skillet; reserve 1 cup of the marinade. Cook, stirring constantly, for 5 minutes, or until lightly browned. Add the bell peppers, onion, and mushrooms and cook, stirring constantly, for 5 minutes, or until the steak is no longer pink and vegetables are tender-crisp. Add the cornstarch to the reserved 1 cup marinade and stir into the pan. Cook for 5 minutes, or until the sauce is thickened. Serve over the rice.

Makes 4 servings

Per serving: *380 calories, 28 g protein, 45 g carbohydrate, 7 g fat, 70 mg cholesterol, 730 mg sodium, 3 g dietary fiber*

Diet Exchanges: *0 milk, 1 vegetable, 0 fruit, 2½ carbohydrate, 3½ meat, 1 fat*

3 Carb Choices

Fast Beef Stroganoff

332 Calories

—Lisa Rothwell, Virginia Beach, Virginia

"This is a very tasty way for me to enjoy cooking again, and because it's so fast and easy, I can have a home-cooked meal almost as quickly as I could have a Big Mac!"

Prep time: 15 minutes; Cook time: 15 minutes

- 12 **ounces no-yolk egg noodles**
- 1 **cup fat-free sour cream**
- 1 **cup 2% milk**
- 1 **package (20 ounces) roast beef with gravy**
- 1 **can (10¾ ounces) reduced-fat cream of mushroom soup**
- ½ **teaspoon salt**
- ¼–½ **teaspoon ground black pepper**

Prepare the noodles according to package directions. Drain and return to the pot.

Meanwhile, in a large bowl, combine the sour cream, milk, roast beef, soup, salt, and pepper. Add to the pot with the pasta and cook, stirring occasionally, over medium-high heat for 5 minutes, or until heated through.

Makes 8 servings

Per serving: *332 calories, 19 g protein, 30 g carbohydrate, 5 g fat, 38 mg cholesterol, 754 mg sodium, 1 g dietary fiber*

Diet Exchanges: *½ milk, 0 vegetable, 0 fruit, 1½ carbohydrate, 2 meat, ½ fat*

2 Carb Choices

Kitchen Tip

While the stroganoff is simmering, Lisa suggests using that time to whip up a quick and easy green salad.

MARINATING MAGIC

Marinades are typically blends of an acid—such as vinegar—plus oil, salt, and seasonings. They are a terrific way to boost the flavor of meats and fish. Follow the tips below for success.

Avoid aluminum containers. Marinate in a nonreactive container, such as one made of glass, ceramic, or even plastic.

Keep 'em cold. Always refrigerate foods while they marinate.

Keep it clean. Place cooked meat, fish, or poultry on a clean platter; don't return cooked food to the dish that held the uncooked item.

Set some aside. If using the marinade for basting, set aside a small amount of marinade *before* adding any raw meat, poultry, or fish to it. If you forget, be sure to boil any used marinade for at least 5 minutes before using it for basting or if serving it as a sauce.

Make cleanup easy. Mix the marinade in a zip-top plastic bag, then marinate right in the bag by adding the food, squeezing out air, and sealing. Turn the bag to coat the food completely, place in a dish, and refrigerate, turning occasionally. This works great for cookouts because you can throw the bag away when you're done.

Give it a stick. To help marinades penetrate more deeply, prick the food with a skewer before adding to the marinade.

Make it tender. Some ingredients contain enzymes that have a tenderizing effect. Yogurt, papaya, and pineapple are natural meat tenderizers. Add ¼ cup yogurt or pureed fruit or juice for every 1 pound meat; marinate for at least 3 hours. Buttermilk or sour cream also can help tenderize.

Avoid mushiness. Limit the marinating time to prevent a mushy texture. Marinate fish and seafood for less than 45 minutes; bone-in chicken breasts for 1 hour; skinless breasts less. Chicken thighs and wings can marinate for 2 hours. Marinate beef, pork, and lamb for 4 to 8 hours, and large pieces of meat for up to 24 hours.

Avoid toughness. To avoid tough marinated foods, go easy on the acid (lemon juice, vinegar, or wine) in the marinade. Tender meats such as chicken breasts will toughen fairly quickly in an overly acidic marinade and acid will "cook" raw seafood. Marinades for fish should use no more than 2 tablespoons acidic ingredients per ¼ cup oil.

Mexican Pie

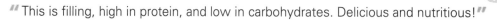

340 Calories

—Marylinn Albert, Feura Bush, New York

" This is filling, high in protein, and low in carbohydrates. Delicious and nutritious! "

Prep time: 12 minutes; Cook time: 24 minutes

- 8 ounces lean ground beef
- ½ small onion, finely chopped
- ½ packet taco seasoning
- 1 teaspoon olive oil
- 2 flatbreads (11" × 7" each)
- 1 cup fat-free refried beans
- 1 cup (4 ounces) Mexican cheese blend
- 1 tomato, finely chopped
- ¼ cup finely chopped black olives
- 2 tablespoons taco sauce
- 2 tablespoons sour cream (optional)
  Chopped fresh basil (optional)

Cook the beef and onion in a large skillet over medium-high heat for 10 minutes, or until the beef is no longer pink. Drain and return to the pan. Stir in the taco seasoning.

Heat the oil in a medium skillet over medium-high heat. Add the flatbread and cook for 2 minutes on each side, or until toasted. Remove to a plate.

Warm the refried beans in a small saucepan over medium heat. Stir in ½ cup of the cheese and cook for 10 minutes, or until the beans are heated through and the cheese is melted. Spoon the bean mixture onto the toasted flatbread. Top with the beef and sprinkle with the remaining ½ cup cheese. Top that with the tomato, olives, taco sauce, and sour cream, if using. Garnish with the basil, if using.

Makes 4 servings

Per serving: 340 calories, 20 g protein, 20 g carbohydrate, 19 g fat, 63 mg cholesterol, 779 mg sodium, 4 g dietary fiber

Diet Exchanges: 0 milk, ½ vegetable, 0 fruit, 1 carbohydrate, 2½ meat, 3 fat

1 Carb Choice

Weight-Loss Goulash

—Donna Heiser, Higley, Arizona

"This is very delicious, nourishing, and filling, and by eating this three or four times a week at lunch with fruit, I have a very good lunch without many calories"

Prep time: 5 minutes; Cook time: 15 minutes

¼ **pound lean ground beef**
½ **teaspoon garlic salt**
½ **teaspoon onion flakes**
1 **can (15 ounces) French beans**
1 **can (15 ounces) peas**
1 **can (15 ounces) bean sprouts**
1 **can (11½ ounces) tomato juice**
1 **can (4 ounces) mushrooms**

In a large skillet over medium-high heat, combine the beef, garlic salt, and onion flakes. Cook, stirring occasionally, for 5 minutes, or until the beef is no longer pink. Add the beans, peas, bean sprouts, tomato juice, and mushrooms. Reduce the heat to low and simmer for 10 minutes, or until the liquid is absorbed.

Makes 4 servings

Per serving: *199 calories, 14 g protein, 23 g carbohydrate, 5 g fat, 20 mg cholesterol, 688 mg sodium, 8 g dietary fiber*

Diet Exchanges: *0 milk, 2 vegetable, 0 fruit, 1 carbohydrate, 1½ meat, ½ fat*

1½ Carb Choices

SECRETS OF WEIGHT-LOSS WINNERS

• I took *Prevention*'s advice and started wearing nine bracelets, one each for the nine servings of fruits and vegetables. I don't move the bracelets from one arm to the other until I have also had an 8-ounce glass of water per bracelet. This keeps track of both the fruits and veggies, and my water. Plus, the water helps fill me up.

—**Angela Ghigliazza, Santa Rosa, California**

• Frozen grapes are a great snack!

—**Darlene Wright, Boone, North Carolina**

• Drink at least 20 ounces of water a half-hour before eating a meal—you won't be hungry when the meal arrives!

—**Christine Pierce, Lemon Grove, California**

Pork Medallions with Black Olives

—Kathy Osborne, Fort Wayne, Indiana

"This dish tastes great, and it's low in calories."

Prep time: 8 minutes; Cook time: 12 minutes

- 1 **pound pork tenderloin, trimmed, cut into 8 pieces, and pounded to ¼" thickness**
- ½ **teaspoon ground black pepper**
- ¼–½ **teaspoon salt**
- ¼ **cup unbleached or all-purpose flour**
- 1 **tablespoon olive oil**
- ½ **cup dry white wine or nonalcoholic wine**
- ½ **cup reduced-sodium chicken broth**
- 1 **tablespoon parsley**
- 2 **tablespoons sliced black olives, drained**

Sprinkle the pork with the pepper and salt. Place the flour in a shallow dish. Dredge the pork in the flour, turning to coat. Shake off any excess flour.

Heat 1½ teaspoons of the oil in a large nonstick skillet over medium-high heat. Add half of the pork and cook for 2 minutes on each side, or until no longer pink. Remove to a plate and keep warm. Repeat to use the remaining oil and pork.

Return the reserved pork to the pan. Add the wine, broth, and parsley and bring to a boil. Stir in the olives and cook for 4 minutes.

Makes 4 servings

Per serving: *226 calories, 25 g protein, 7 g carbohydrate, 8 g fat, 74 mg cholesterol, 263 mg sodium, 0 g dietary fiber*

Diet Exchanges: *0 milk, 0 vegetable, 0 fruit, ½ carbohydrate, 3 meat, 1½ fat*

½ Carb Choice

Lemony Pork Chops

284 Calories

—Laura Manspeaker, Finksburg, Maryland

Prep time: 10 minutes; Cook time: 14 minutes

⅓ cup unbleached or all-purpose flour

1 egg

¼ cup seasoned dried bread crumbs

1 tablespoon crab boil seasoning, such as Old Bay

4 boneless pork chops, trimmed of all visible fat and pounded to ¼" thickness

1 tablespoon olive oil

Lemon slices, for garnish

Place the flour in a shallow dish. Beat the egg in another shallow dish. Combine the bread crumbs and crab boil seasoning in a third dish. Dredge the pork in the flour, shaking off any excess. Coat with egg, then with bread crumb mixture, coating both sides thoroughly.

Heat the oil in a large nonstick skillet over medium heat. Add the pork chops and cook for 7 minutes on each side, or until a thermometer inserted in the center of a chop registers 160°F and the juices run clear. Serve topped with lemon slices.

Makes 4 servings

Per serving: *284 calories, 29 g protein, 18 g carbohydrate, 10 g fat, 124 mg cholesterol, 711 mg sodium, 1 g dietary fiber*

Diet Exchanges: *0 milk, 0 vegetable, 0 fruit, 1 carbohydrate, 4 meat, 1½ fat*

1 Carb Choice

Orange-Glazed Pork Tenderloin

—Betty Brader, Allentown, Pennsylvania

Prep time: 5 minutes; Cook time: 26 minutes

1 pound pork tenderloin, cut into 8 pieces
¾ cup orange juice
3 tablespoons brown sugar
3 tablespoons orange marmalade
2 tablespoons vinegar

Heat a large skillet coated with cooking spray over medium-high heat. Add the pork and cook for 3 minutes per side, or until browned and no longer pink in the center.

In a cup, combine the orange juice, brown sugar, marmalade, and vinegar. Pour over the pork. Cover and simmer for 20 minutes, or until the sauce thickens.

Makes 8 servings

Per serving: *200 calories, 24 g protein, 17 g carbohydrate, 4 g fat, 75 mg cholesterol, 65 mg sodium, 0 g dietary fiber*

Diet Exchanges: *0 milk, 0 vegetable, 0 fruit, 1 carbohydrate, 3 meat, ½ fat*

1 Carb Choice

THREE-INGREDIENT MARINADES

Each of these quick and easy marinades makes enough for 1½ to 2 pounds of meat or fish. Marinate fish up to 45 minutes; chicken about 1 hour; pork and beef, 4 to 8 hours.

Orange Fennel. Mix 1 cup orange juice, 2 teaspoons fennel seeds (crush with the bottom of a heavy pot), and ½ to 1 teaspoon crushed red-pepper flakes. Lovely with pork, chicken, or catfish.

Balsamic-Dijon. Mix ¼ cup olive oil, 2 tablespoons balsamic vinegar, and 1 tablespoon Dijon mustard. Use with chicken, pork, or beef tenderloin strips.

Asian-Ginger. Mix ¼ cup ketchup, 2 tablespoons lite soy sauce, and 1 tablespoon finely grated fresh ginger. Try with pork, top round steak, salmon, shrimp, and swordfish. Limit marinating time, or the food will get too salty.

Lemon-Pepper. Mix finely grated zest and juice of 1 large lemon, 3 tablespoons extra-virgin olive oil, and 1½ teaspoons coarse-ground black pepper. Very nice with salmon, fresh tuna, chicken, and pork.

Honey-Lime. Mix finely grated zest and juice of 1 large lime, 2 tablespoons extra-virgin olive oil, and 2 tablespoons honey. Use with shrimp, swordfish, chicken, and pork.

Rolled Swiss Chicken

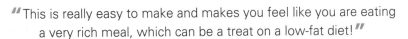

—Laura Goodson, Allen, Texas

" This is really easy to make and makes you feel like you are eating a very rich meal, which can be a treat on a low-fat diet!"

Prep time: 15 minutes; Cook time: 20 minutes

- **4 boneless, skinless chicken breast halves, pounded to ¼" thickness**
- **2 thin slices (about 2 ounces) reduced-fat Swiss cheese, cut in half**
- **2 roasted red pepper strips, halved (optional)**
- **8 leaves fresh basil (optional)**
- **2 tablespoons unbleached or all-purpose flour**
- **½ teaspoon ground black pepper**
- **1 tablespoon olive oil**
- **¾ cup reduced-sodium chicken broth**
- **¼ teaspoon dried oregano**

Place the chicken on a work surface. Top each piece with half a slice of the cheese, a pepper strip (if using), and 2 basil leaves (if using). Starting from the short ends, tightly roll up the chicken. Tie securely with kitchen string or secure with a wooden pick.

On waxed paper, combine the flour and black pepper. Dredge the chicken rolls in the flour mixture to coat.

Heat the oil in a large nonstick skillet over medium heat. Add the chicken rolls and cook, turning frequently, for 5 minutes, or until golden. Add the broth and oregano and bring to a boil over medium-high heat. Reduce the heat to low and simmer for 15 minutes, or until a thermometer inserted in the thickest portion registers 160°F and the juices run clear. The sauce should be slightly thickened. Remove and discard the string before serving.

Makes 4 servings

Per serving: *201 calories, 31 g protein, 4 g carbohydrate, 6 g fat, 71 mg cholesterol, 131 mg sodium, 0 g dietary fiber*

Diet Exchanges: *0 milk, 0 vegetable, 0 fruit, 0 carbohydrate, 4 meat, 1 fat*

0 Carb Choices

Chicken in Gravy

—Teresa Wargo, Pulaski, Wisconsin

"This recipe uses all low-fat ingredients."

Prep time: 5 minutes; Cook time: 15 minutes

- **1 tablespoon canola oil**
- **4 boneless, skinless chicken breast halves**
- **1 can (10¾ ounces) reduced-fat, reduced-sodium condensed cream of chicken soup**
- **¼ cup fat-free milk**
- **2 teaspoons lemon juice**
- **⅛ teaspoon ground black pepper**
- **4 lemon slices**

Heat the oil in a large nonstick skillet over medium heat. Add the chicken and cook for 10 minutes, or until both sides are browned. Drain if necessary.

In a bowl, combine the soup, milk, lemon juice, and pepper. Pour over the chicken in the pan. Top each chicken breast with a lemon slice. Reduce the heat, cover, and simmer for 5 minutes, or until a thermometer inserted in the thickest portion registers 160°F and the juices run clear.

Makes 4 servings

Per serving: *219 calories, 28 g protein, 10 g carbohydrate, 6 g fat, 73 mg cholesterol, 404 mg sodium, 0 g dietary fiber*

Diet Exchanges: *0 milk, 0 vegetable, 0 fruit, 1 carbohydrate, 4 meat, 1 fat*

1 Carb Choice

My Best Friend's Curry

—Laura Debassige, Yellowknife, Northwest Territories, Canada

"This recipe is quick, simple, and pleases even the most picky eaters! You can easily control portion size, and it helps in getting the daily requirement of vegetables and fruits."

Prep time: 20 minutes; Cook time: 6 minutes

- 1 **tablespoon olive oil**
- 1 **teaspoon curry powder, or to taste**
- 4 **boneless, skinless chicken breast halves, cut into bite-size pieces**
- 4 **ribs celery, finely chopped**
- 3 **tomatoes, finely chopped**
- 2 **apples, finely chopped**
- 2 **bananas, chopped**
- 1 **cucumber, finely chopped**
- 1 **can (8 ounces) pineapple chunks, drained**
- ½ **cup chopped cashews**
- ½ **teaspoon salt**

Heat the oil in a large skillet over medium heat. Add the curry powder and chicken and cook, stirring frequently, for 6 minutes, or until the chicken is no longer pink. Remove to a serving bowl. Add the celery, tomatoes, apples, bananas, cucumber, pineapple, cashews, and salt. Toss to combine.

Makes 6 servings

Per serving: *274 calories, 21 g protein, 31 g carbohydrate, 9 g fat, 44 mg cholesterol, 287 mg sodium, 6 g dietary fiber*

Diet Exchanges: *0 milk, 1 vegetable, 1½ fruit, 0 carbohydrate, 3 meat, 1½ fat*

2 Carb Choices

Kitchen Tip

Laura notes that you can prepare this dish using any combination of your favorite fruits and vegetables. A great reason to add this versatile recipe to your repertoire! Also, try serving it over cooked brown rice.

Chinese Spaghetti

—Rebecca Foley, Sherman Oaks, California

"The vegetables and chicken are very healthy. The spaghetti is whole wheat—also healthy, plus very filling. You leave the meal with a happy, full stomach."

Prep time: 15 minutes; Cook time: 12 minutes

16 ounces whole wheat spaghetti
1 head broccoli, cut into florets
1 small bunch bok choy, coarsely chopped
1 pound boneless, skinless chicken breasts, cut into thin strips
¼ cup stir-fry sauce
1 teaspoon sesame oil
1 teaspoon minced ginger
   Pinch of ground black pepper

Prepare the spaghetti according to package directions.

Meanwhile, heat a large wok or nonstick skillet coated with cooking spray over medium-high heat. Add the broccoli and bok choy and cook, stirring, constantly, for 4 minutes, or until tender-crisp. Remove to a bowl.

Add the chicken to the pan and cook, stirring constantly, for 4 minutes, or until no longer pink. Add the vegetables and spaghetti.

In a cup, combine the stir-fry sauce, oil, ginger, and pepper. Stir into the pan and cook, stirring constantly, for 2 minutes, or until heated through.

Makes 6 servings

Per serving: *435 calories, 36 g protein, 70 g carbohydrate, 5 g fat, 44 mg cholesterol, 292 mg sodium, 16 g dietary fiber*

Diet Exchanges: *0 milk, 2 vegetable, 0 fruit, 4 carbohydrate, 3 meat, ½ fat*

4½ Carb Choices

Island Rice with Turkey Kielbasa

—Joanne Burke, Panorama City, California

" This recipe has helped me lose weight because it is satisfying and calorie-sensible. It is also nutritious!"

Prep time: 5 minutes; Cook time: 45 minutes

- **1 cup white or brown rice**
- **½ cup liquid egg substitute**
- **8 ounces turkey kielbasa, cut into bite-size pieces**
- **1 can (8 ounces) pineapple chunks, drained**
- **2 tablespoons parsley**
  Shredded coconut, for garnish

Prepare the rice according to package directions.

In a medium nonstick skillet over medium heat, cook the egg substitute for 4 minutes, stirring frequently, until scrambled.

Heat a large nonstick skillet coated with cooking spray over medium-high heat. Add the kielbasa and cook, stirring occasionally, for 5 minutes, or until lightly browned. Add the rice, eggs, and pineapple and cook, stirring occasionally, for 5 minutes, or until heated through. Remove from the heat and stir in the parsley. Garnish with the coconut.

Makes 4 servings

Per serving: *292 calories, 14 g protein, 50 g carbohydrate, 3 g fat, 20 mg cholesterol, 543 mg sodium, 1 g dietary fiber*

Diet Exchanges: *0 milk, 0 vegetable, ½ fruit, 2½ carbohydrate, 1½ meat, ½ fat*

3 Carb Choices

Broccoli and Smokies

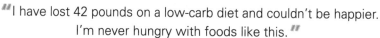

—Teresa Cosper, Burleson, Texas

"I have lost 42 pounds on a low-carb diet and couldn't be happier. I'm never hungry with foods like this. **"**

Prep time: 5 minutes; Cook time: 15 minutes

- **8 ounces smoked turkey sausage or Cheddar smoked sausage**
- **1 box (10 ounces) frozen broccoli**
- **1 small onion, finely chopped**
- **¼ cup (1 ounce) reduced-fat Cheddar or Monterey Jack cheese**

Cook the sausage in a large nonstick skillet over medium heat for 4 minutes, or until just beginning to brown. Add the broccoli and onion and cook, stirring frequently, for 8 minutes, or until the broccoli is tender-crisp and the sausage is no longer pink. Add the cheese and cook, stirring occasionally, for 3 minutes, or until the cheese is melted.

Makes 4 servings

Per serving: *139 calories, 13 g protein, 10 g carbohydrate, 6 g fat, 38 mg cholesterol, 578 mg sodium, 3 g dietary fiber*

Diet Exchanges: *0 milk, 2 vegetable, 0 fruit, 0 carbohydrate, 1½ meat, ½ fat*

1 Carb Choice

SECRETS OF WEIGHT-LOSS WINNERS

• Remember, moderation is the key. Try not to deny yourself any food that you may be craving. It is not always what you eat, but how much of it you have.

—**DiAnne Evans, Lawton, Oklahoma**

• Plan for events where you commonly find yourself overeating. At staff meetings, for example, I always know there will be rich treats that I will regret eating later. So, when I know I will be attending a meeting, I bring fruit to work and ensure I'm sitting far away from the treats so I neither feel tempted to indulge nor do I feel deprived!

—**Suzi Hushen, Palmerston, Ontario, Canada**

Salmon Hash

—Kevin Cunningham, Deer Park, New York

"This is nutritious, low in calories, easy and quick
to prepare, economical, and heart healthy!"

Prep time: 30 minutes; Cook time: 15 minutes

2 potatoes, chopped

1 large onion, finely chopped,
 with 1 tablespoon reserved for garnish

1 green bell pepper, finely chopped

1 can (15 ounces) red salmon, drained
 (do not use fresh)

 Creole spice, to taste

½ teaspoon freshly ground black pepper

3–4 scallions, chopped

1 tablespoon grated Parmesan cheese

¼ cup parsley, minced, with
 2 tablespoons reserved for garnish

1 teaspoon lemon rind

Place the potatoes in a microwaveable bowl.
Cover with plastic wrap and microwave on
high power for 3½ minutes. Let cool while
preparing the other ingredients.

Heat a large nonstick skillet coated with
cooking spray over medium heat. Add the
onion and bell pepper and cook, stirring frequently, for 5 minutes, or until the onion is
soft. Stir in the potatoes, salmon, Creole
spice, and black pepper. Cook, stirring, for 5
minutes, or until the potatoes are tender and
browned. Add the scallions, cheese, and
parsley. Mix thoroughly. Garnish with the remaining 1 tablespoon onion, 2 tablespoons
parsley, and the lemon rind.

Makes 4 servings

Per serving: *239 calories, 23 g protein, 23 g carbohydrate, 7 g fat, 42 mg cholesterol, 528 mg
sodium, 4 g dietary fiber*

Diet Exchanges: *0 milk, 2 vegetable, 0 fruit,
1 carbohydrate, 3 meat, 0 fat*

1½ Carb Choices

Tomato and Dill Fish

—Mary Kerin, Rockaway, New Jersey

356 Calories

*" This dish has plenty of vitamins and is tasty and filling.
I always have enough left for my lunch."*

Prep time: 15 minutes; Cook time: 45 minutes

1 cup brown rice

1 teaspoon unbleached or all-purpose flour

1 teaspoon cornmeal

1 pound halibut or whiting fillet or steak

1 tablespoon butter or butter substitute

4 medium tomatoes, peeled and chopped

1 small onion, chopped

6 sprigs fresh dill, chopped

4 sprigs fresh parsley, chopped

1 lemon, cut into 8 slices

Prepare the rice according to package directions.

Meanwhile, in a shallow dish or on waxed paper, combine the flour and cornmeal. Dredge the fish in the flour mixture to coat both sides.

Heat a large skillet coated with cooking spray over medium heat. Add the butter. When the butter is melted and sizzling, add the fish and cook for 3 minutes per side, or until browned on both sides. Add the tomatoes, onion, and dill. Cook for 20 minutes, or until the fish flakes easily.

Spoon the rice onto a warm serving platter and top with the fish and any juices. Garnish each fillet with parsley and lemon slices.

Makes 4 servings

Per serving: *356 calories, 29 g protein, 44 g carbohydrate, 7 g fat, 44 mg cholesterol, 107 mg sodium, 3 g dietary fiber*

Diet Exchanges: *0 milk, 1 vegetable, 0 fruit, 2½ carbohydrate, 3½ meat, 1 fat*

3 Carb Choices

Chili Lime Snapper

—Carolann Alexander, Houston, Texas

"I cannot cook! I knew I had to eat more fish, but could not figure out how to make it. This recipe is quick and easy enough (requiring just a few ingredients) that I actually make it about once a week. Because it has a little kick to it, it never gets dull, and it's very satisfying "

Prep time: 5 minutes; Cook time: 10 minutes

- 2 tablespoons olive oil
- 1 bunch fresh basil, coarsely chopped
- 1 Thai or serrano chile pepper, finely chopped (wear plastic gloves when handling)
- 1 pound red snapper fillets
- 1 lime
  Salt, to taste
  Ground black pepper, to taste

Heat the oil in a large skillet over medium heat. Add the basil and chile pepper and cook for 1 minute. Remove from the pan and set aside. Add the fish to the pan. Squeeze the juice from the lime over the fish and sprinkle with salt and black pepper. Cover and cook for 5 minutes. Turn the fish and season with additional black pepper. Cover and cook for 3 minutes longer, or until the fish flakes easily.

Makes 4 servings

Per serving: *181 calories, 23 g protein, 2 g carbohydrate, 8 g fat, 42 mg cholesterol, 73 mg sodium, 1 g dietary fiber*

Diet Exchanges: *0 milk, 0 vegetable, 0 fruit, 0 carbohydrate, 3 meat, 1½ fat*

0 Carb Choices

Kitchen Tip

Carolann likes to serve this spicy fish over a bed of rice, with vegetables on the side.

FIVE EASY TOPPINGS FOR FISH

Looking for some new and easy toppings for tasty fish? Here are five quick and delicious suggestions. Each of the following recipes will top off 1 pound of cooked fish.

Lemon-Caper Topping. Combine 2 tablespoons *each* lemon juice and capers, 1 tablespoon olive oil, 8 slivered oil-cured or calamata olives, and 2 teaspoons chopped fresh oregano or parsley.

Fresh Pepper and Tomato Topping. In a medium skillet over medium heat, sauté ½ cup chopped green bell pepper and ½ chopped red onion in 2 teaspoons olive oil for 2 minutes. Add 2 chopped tomatoes, 2 tablespoons lemon juice, 1 teaspoon paprika, ½ teaspoon dried thyme, and ⅛ teaspoon hot-pepper sauce. Cook for 5 minutes, or until the vegetables are tender.

Ginger-Sesame Sauce. In a small saucepan over medium-low heat, combine 2 teaspoons toasted sesame oil, 1 tablespoon *each* lite soy sauce and dry sherry, 1 chopped scallion, 1 teaspoon *each* grated fresh ginger and honey, and a pinch of ground red pepper. Cook just until hot but not boiling.

Tomato-Fennel Sauce. In a small saucepan over medium-low heat, combine ¼ cup white wine, 1 tablespoon olive oil, and ¾ teaspoon crushed fennel seeds. Bring to a simmer. Remove from the heat and let steep for 15 minutes. Stir in 2 chopped plum tomatoes, ¼ cup torn basil leaves, and ¼ teaspoon salt.

Creamy Curry Sauce. Place ½ teaspoon curry powder in a small skillet over medium-low heat. Toast, shaking the pan, until fragrant. Place in a small bowl and stir in ⅓ cup low-fat plain yogurt, 3 tablespoons reduced-fat mayonnaise, 2 tablespoons chopped fresh cilantro, and ¼ teaspoon *each* sugar and salt.

Shrimp and Feta Spinach Fettuccine

—Meghan Hamill, Bakersfield, California

"This dish increases my vegetable intake and has many different flavors to satisfy my hunger."

Prep time: 10 minutes; Cook time: 8 minutes

- 16 ounces spinach fettuccine
- 1 pound frozen cooked shrimp
- ¼ cup white wine
- 1 jar (6 ounces) marinated artichoke hearts
- 4 ounces oil-packed sun-dried tomatoes, sliced
- ½ cup (2 ounces) tomato-basil feta cheese
- 3 tablespoons Parmesan cheese
- ½ teaspoon garlic powder or garlic salt

Prepare the pasta according to package directions. Place the shrimp in a strainer under cool running water to thaw. When the pasta is done, pour into the strainer with the shrimp. Rinse with hot water and drain. Add the wine, tossing to coat as the wine drains.

In a large bowl, combine the artichoke hearts, tomatoes, and feta. Add the pasta mixture to the artichoke mixture and toss to combine. Sprinkle with the Parmesan and season with the garlic powder or garlic salt.

Makes 6 servings

Per serving: *440 calories, 31 g protein, 61 g carbohydrate, 9 g fat, 153 mg cholesterol, 515 mg sodium, 5 g dietary fiber*

Diet Exchanges: *0 milk, 1½ vegetable, 0 fruit, 3½ carbohydrate, 3 meat, 1 fat*

4 Carb Choices

QUICK AND EASY SPAGHETTI SAUCE STIR-INS

Stir any of the following into 2 cups (a 16-ounce jar) of marinara or plain tomato pasta sauce for a quick and slimming dinner. Serve over 12 ounces of the pasta of your choice. Makes 4 servings.

Mushrooms and Zucchini. Heat 1 tablespoon olive oil in a large nonstick skillet over medium-high heat. Add 8 ounces sliced cremini or baby portobello mushrooms; season to taste with dried Italian herb seasoning and salt and pepper. Sauté until tender. Add 1 thinly sliced medium zucchini and 1 tablespoon water; sauté until tender.

Sausage and Peppers. On an oiled broiler pan, arrange 8 ounces sliced Italian-style turkey sausage and 1 *each* sliced red and yellow bell peppers. Broil, turning once or twice, until the peppers are tender and the sausage is cooked through, about 10 minutes.

Broccoli, Basil, and Ricotta. Add 2 cups hot, cooked fresh or frozen broccoli florets and ¼ cup slivered fresh basil to pasta sauce. Mix with pasta. Top each serving with 2 tablespoons part-skim ricotta cheese.

Peperoncini and Ham. Heat 1 tablespoon olive oil in a large nonstick skillet over medium-high heat. Sauté 1 chopped onion, 1 chopped red bell pepper, 1 diced rib celery, and ¼ cup sliced peperoncini (Tuscan pickled peppers) until tender. Add ½ cup diced cooked ham; warm through. Season with crushed red pepper flakes to taste.

Beans and Cheese. Add a 15-ounce can drained and rinsed cannellini beans to pasta sauce; warm through. Stir in ½ cup chopped fresh Italian parsley and 6 chopped pitted kalamata olives. Mix sauce with pasta; top with ½ cup cubed part-skim mozzarella cheese.

Spicy Shrimp. Toss 10 to 12 ounces peeled and deveined large shrimp with 1 tablespoon olive oil, 2 minced garlic cloves, dried oregano, salt, and crushed red pepper flakes to taste. Broil until just cooked through.

Ocean Garden Fettuccine

—Amanda Parr, Mandeville, Louisiana

Prep time: 15 minutes; Cook time: 17 minutes

12 ounces whole wheat fettuccine

2 tablespoons olive oil

1 medium crookneck squash, finely chopped

1 can (10 ounces) diced tomatoes, drained

3 scallions, sliced

6 ounces mushrooms, sliced

2 cloves garlic, minced

½ cup fat-free milk

1 tablespoon flour

1 pound medium shrimp, peeled and deveined

5–8 leaves fresh basil, finely chopped, or ½ teaspoon dried

¼ cup (1 ounce) grated Parmesan cheese

Prepare the fettuccine according to package directions. Drain and place in a serving bowl.

Meanwhile, heat the oil in a large saucepan over medium-high heat. Add the squash, tomatoes, scallions, mushrooms, and garlic and cook, stirring frequently, for 8 minutes, or until the vegetables are tender.

In a cup, combine the milk and flour. Add to the skillet and cook, stirring, for 2 minutes, or until the sauce thickens. Add the shrimp and cook, stirring frequently, for 7 minutes, or until the shrimp are opaque. Stir in the basil. Add the shrimp mixture to the bowl with the pasta and toss to combine. Sprinkle with the cheese.

Makes 6 servings

Per serving: *402 calories, 29 g protein, 56 g carbohydrate, 9 g fat, 119 mg cholesterol, 280 mg sodium, 12 g dietary fiber*

Diet Exchanges: *0 milk, 1½ vegetable, 0 fruit, 3 carbohydrate, 3 meat, 1½ fat*

4 Carb Choices

Spicy 'n' Light Shrimp Curry

—Linda Stretch, Pittsburgh, Pennsylvania

"I was craving shrimp curry, the kind with coconut milk. I just tried to think of how to replicate the curry sauce I love so much, and tried this one night. This is an amazing substitute, really close to the real thing and very low in fat. My husband and I both love it."

Prep time: 20 minutes; Cook time: 15 minutes

12 ounces angel hair pasta or 1½ cups white rice
½ cup fat-free evaporated milk
½ cup fat-free sour cream
½–1 tablespoon curry powder
1 tablespoon finely chopped fresh basil
½ teaspoon red chili paste
2 teaspoons olive oil
1 pound medium shrimp, peeled and deveined
1 onion, finely chopped
1 red bell pepper, finely chopped
½ pound snow peas, trimmed
½ pound mushrooms, sliced

Prepare the pasta or rice according to package directions.

In a small bowl, combine the milk, sour cream, curry powder, basil, and chili paste. Set aside.

Heat 1 teaspoon of the oil in a large wok or nonstick skillet over medium-high heat. Add the shrimp and cook, stirring constantly, for 5 minutes, or until the shrimp are opaque. Remove to a bowl; set aside.

Heat the remaining 1 teaspoon oil in the wok. Add the onion, pepper, snow peas and mushrooms and cook, stirring constantly, for 3 minutes, or until tender-crisp. Stir in the shrimp and reserved milk mixture and cook, stirring constantly, for 2 minutes, or until heated through. Serve in bowls over the rice or pasta.

Makes 6 servings

Per serving: *375 calories, 28 g protein, 56 g carbohydrate, 4 g fat, 115 mg cholesterol, 177 mg sodium, 4 g dietary fiber*

Diet Exchanges: *½ milk, 1 vegetable, 0 fruit, 3 carbohydrate, 2½ meat, ½ fat*

4 Carb Choices

scallop sauté

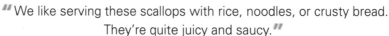

—Marge and Ed Wester, Thornton, New Hampshire

" We like serving these scallops with rice, noodles, or crusty bread.
They're quite juicy and saucy. *"*

Prep time: 15 minutes; Cook time: 10 minutes

- 1 **pound sea or bay scallops, washed and dried thoroughly**
- ½ **teaspoon salt**
- ¼ **teaspoon paprika**
- ⅛ **teaspoon freshly ground black pepper**
- 1 **clove garlic**
- 1 **tablespoon finely chopped fresh parsley**
- 3 **tablespoons lemon juice**
- 2 **tablespoons reduced-fat butter**

If using sea scallops, cut them into thirds or quarters.

Heat a large skillet generously coated with cooking spray over medium-high heat. Add the scallops and cook, stirring frequently, for 8 minutes, or until golden brown. Remove to a serving platter and keep warm.

In the same skillet, combine the lemon juice, butter, parsley, salt, paprika, pepper, and garlic. Cook, stirring, until the butter is melted. Pour over the scallops.

Makes 4 servings

Per serving: *130 calories, 20 g protein, 4 g carbohydrate, 4 g fat, 45 mg cholesterol, 510 mg sodium, 0 g dietary fiber*

Diet Exchanges: *0 milk, 0 vegetable, 0 fruit, 0 carbohydrate, 3 meat, 1 fat*

0 Carb Choices

Dirty Rice

—Rebecca Weathersbee, Belzoni, Mississippi

231 Calories

"Use margarine instead of butter for a lower-fat dish."

Prep time: 5 minutes; Cook time: 55 minutes

- ¾ **cup long-grain rice**
- 1 **can (10¾ ounces) reduced-fat beef broth**
- 3 **tablespoons butter**
- 1 **can (8 ounces) sliced mushrooms, drained**
- ½ **small onion, finely chopped**

Preheat the oven to 400°F.

In a 2-quart baking dish, combine the rice, broth, butter, mushrooms, and onion. Bake for 55 minutes, or until the rice is tender.

Makes 4 servings

Per serving: *231 calories, 5 g protein, 32 g carbohydrate, 10 g fat, 23 mg cholesterol, 606 mg sodium, 3 g dietary fiber*

Diet Exchanges: *0 milk, 1 vegetable, 0 fruit, 2 carbohydrate, 0 meat, 2 fat*

2 Carb Choices

Photo on page 99.

THREE QUICK WAYS WITH SWEET POTATOES

Though they're most often served with Thanksgiving dinner, sweet potatoes are terrific anytime. They're filled with nutrients, and unless they're swimming in butter, they can be a delicious part of a weight-loss plan. Here are three easy ways to enjoy sweets.

Baked Sweets. Scrub 1 small sweet potato for each person or 1 large per 2 people. Place in a baking pan. Bake at 425°F for 1 hour, or until very soft.

Oven-Fried Chili Sweets. Peel 2 medium sweet potatoes and cut into spears. Toss with 2 teaspoons olive oil, ½ to 1 teaspoon chili powder, and salt and pepper to taste. Place the potato spears on a baking sheet coated with cooking spray. Bake at 425°F for 40 minutes, or until browned and tender. Makes 4 servings.

Rosemary-Baked Sweets. Scrub 2 medium sweet potatoes and cut into chunks. Place in a pie plate and toss with 1 tablespoon chopped fresh rosemary, 2 teaspoons olive oil, and salt and crushed red pepper flakes to taste. Bake at 425°F, stirring twice, for 35 minutes, or until tender. Makes 4 servings.

Easy Tasty Cottage Fries

—Lesley Sawhook, Maineville, Ohio

"Whenever I have a craving for french fries or a salty snack, I whip up a bunch of these cottage fries instead of reaching for a bag of chips or running out for french fries. The pounds fell off, and I didn't feel like I was missing out on anything. They are delicious!"

Prep time: 10 minutes; Cook time: 10 minutes

3–4 large Idaho potatoes, sliced into half-dollar size pieces
½ teaspoon seasoned pepper
½ teaspoon garlic salt
½ teaspoon paprika
Fat-free spray butter

Preheat the oven to 375°F.

Place the potatoes in a single layer on a baking sheet. Sprinkle with the pepper, garlic salt, and paprika. Coat with the spray butter.

Bake for 10 minutes, or until tender and lightly browned.

Makes 4 servings

Per serving: *102 calories, 4 g protein, 26 g carbohydrate, 0 g fat, 0 mg cholesterol, 120 mg sodium, 3 g dietary fiber*

Diet Exchanges: *0 milk, 0 vegetable, 0 fruit, 1½ carbohydrate, 0 meat, 0 fat*

1½ Carb Choices

SECRETS OF WEIGHT-LOSS WINNERS

• Whenever I feel the need to snack late at night, I grab a piece of tooth-whitening gum and chew, chew, chew. Not only do I save my figure, but I also improve my appearance!

    —**Heather Cowley, Lake Dallas, Texas**

• Eat any sweets or carbs before 2:00 P.M. Eat only lean protein, fruits, and vegetables after 2:00 P.M. That way you don't feel you're missing anything, and tomorrow isn't that far away to wait for another carb or sweet treat.

    —**Karen Finnegan, Carson City, Nevada**

• To enjoy salad without calorie-laden dressings, make a salad and use your favorite pickles, chopped with some of the juice poured over the salad, for the salty/sour taste of dressing with far fewer calories.

—**Teresa Decker, Bellefonte, Pennsylvania**

Comfort Food Mashed Potatoes

—Shirley Slager, Edmonton, Alberta, Canada

Prep time: 10 minutes; Cook time: 25 minutes

- **2 pounds potatoes, peeled and cut into 1" cubes**
- **4 slices fat-free Cheddar cheese, torn into pieces**
- **1–2 tablespoons 1% milk**
- **1 teaspoon dried dill**

Place a vegetable steamer in a large saucepan. Fill with water to just below the steamer. Place the potatoes in the steamer. Cover and bring to a boil over high heat. Reduce the heat to medium-high. Cook for 20 to 25 minutes, or until tender.

Remove the potatoes to a large bowl. Beat with an electric mixer on medium speed until completely mashed. Gradually add the cheese and milk. Mix until the cheese is incorporated. Stir in the dill.

Makes 4 servings

Per serving: *270 calories, 13 g protein, 39 g carbohydrate, 9 g fat, 30 mg cholesterol, 179 mg sodium, 5 g dietary fiber*

Diet Exchanges: *0 milk, 0 vegetable, 0 fruit, 2½ carbohydrate, 1 meat, 1½ fat*

2½ Carb Choices

Potato Casserole

—Joni Goeders, Fort Worth, Texas

"This is delicious and comforting. The cauliflower extends the potato dish without adding calories."

217 Calories

Prep time: 15 minutes; Cook time: 35 minutes

- **3 large potatoes, peeled and sliced**
- **½ small head cauliflower, coarsely chopped**
- **1 teaspoon olive oil**
- **1 medium onion, chopped**
- **2 ounces turkey bacon, chopped**
- **1 cup (4 ounces) shredded reduced-fat Cheddar cheese**

Preheat the oven to 350°F.

Bring a large saucepan of water to a boil over medium-high heat. Add the potatoes and boil for 15 minutes, or until fork-tender. Remove to a bowl; do not drain the water from the pot. Add the cauliflower to the pot and boil for 5 minutes, or until fork-tender. Place in the bowl with the potatoes. Mash with a potato masher or an electric mixer on medium speed.

Heat the oil in a small skillet over medium-high heat. Add the onion and bacon and cook, stirring, for 5 minutes, or until soft.

Spoon half of the potato mixture into a baking dish. Sprinkle with half of the cheese and half of the bacon. Repeat layering to use the remaining ingredients, ending with bacon.

Bake for 10 minutes, or until heated through and the cheese has melted.

Makes 4 servings

Per serving: *217 calories, 14 g protein, 32 g carbohydrate, 6 g fat, 19 mg cholesterol, 371 mg sodium, 5 g dietary fiber*

Diet Exchanges: *0 milk, 1 vegetable, 0 fruit, 1½ carbohydrate, 1½ meat, 1 fat*

2 Carb Choices

spaghetti squash

—Roni Sharp, Thornhill, Ontario, Canada

"Not only does squash taste good, but it has lots of nutrition and is easy to make. It's great cold for lunch at work the next day and is not fattening."

Prep time: 15 minutes; Cook time: 40 minutes

1 **spaghetti squash (2 pounds), halved lengthwise and seeded**

¼ **cup water**

1 **tablespoon butter, melted**

1 **tablespoon grated Parmesan cheese**

¼ **teaspoon ground black pepper**

Preheat the oven to 400°F. Coat a 13" × 9" baking dish with cooking spray.

Place the squash, cut side down, in the prepared baking dish. Add the water.

Bake for 40 minutes, or until tender when pierced with a sharp knife. With a fork, scrape the squash strands into a large bowl. Add the butter, Parmesan, and pepper and toss to coat.

Makes 6 servings

Per serving: *68 calories, 1 g protein, 11 g carbohydrate, 3 g fat, 6 mg cholesterol, 61 mg sodium, 2 g dietary fiber*

Diet Exchanges: *0 milk, 2 vegetable, 0 fruit, 0 carbohydrate, 0 meat, ½ fat*

1 Carb Choice

Kitchen Tip

Roni also likes to serve this spaghetti squash with frozen veggies, no-salt diced tomatoes, or a bit of salsa stirred in. Sometimes she adds beans, tofu, lentils, or a grain such as kasha or bulgur and freshly ground black pepper or spicy seasoning to taste.

Joan's Delicious Veggies

—Joan Ormes, Philadelphia, Pennsylvania

" I make these veggies at least three times a week. If you have a large appetite, you can eat a heaping plate of these veggies and not gain an ounce."

Prep time: 20 minutes; Cook time: 17 minutes

1   large onion, sliced
1   red bell pepper, finely chopped
½   eggplant, cubed
½   head cauliflower, cut into florets
1   large zucchini, sliced
1   cup sliced mushrooms
1   cup salsa
¼   cup balsamic vinegar
1   head broccoli, cut into florets
¼ –½   teaspoon dried oregano
¼ –½   teaspoon dried basil
     Pinch of ground red pepper

Heat a large skillet coated with cooking spray over medium heat. Add the onion and bell pepper and cook for 2 minutes. Add the eggplant, cauliflower, zucchini, and mushrooms and cook for 3 minutes. Stir in the salsa, vinegar, oregano, basil, and red pepper. Stir in the broccoli and cover. Cook for 12 minutes, or until the vegetables are tender. Season with additional oregano and basil, if desired.

Makes 8 servings

Per serving: *64 calories, 3 g protein, 14 g carbohydrate, 0 g fat, 0 mg cholesterol, 163 mg sodium, 4 g dietary fiber*

Diet Exchanges: *0 milk, 2½ vegetable, 0 fruit, 0 carbohydrate, 0 meat, 0 fat*

1 Carb Choice

Kitchen Tip

Joan likes to serve these veggies with 3-ounce broiled salmon fillets.

Zucchini and Tomatoes

—Carol Lewis, Upland, California

*"This tastes really yummy and has lots of vegetables.
You can even make it without the oil or cheese."*

Prep time: 20 minutes; Cook time: 13 minutes

1 teaspoon olive oil
4 tomatoes, chopped
3 zucchini, sliced
1 onion, finely chopped
1 green bell pepper, chopped
2 cloves garlic, minced
2 teaspoons dried Italian seasoning
¼ teaspoon salt
⅛ teaspoon ground black pepper
2 tablespoons grated Parmesan cheese
   or crumbled feta cheese
3 leaves fresh basil, thinly sliced

Heat the oil in a medium saucepan over medium heat. Add the tomatoes, zucchini, onion, bell pepper, garlic, Italian seasoning, salt, and black pepper and stir to combine. Cover and cook for 10 minutes, or until the vegetables are tender. Top with the cheese, cover, and cook for 3 minutes longer, or until the cheese is melted. Sprinkle with the basil.

Makes 6 servings

Per serving: *62 calories, 3 g protein, 11 g carbohydrate, 1 g fat, 1 mg cholesterol, 246 mg sodium, 3 g dietary fiber*

Diet Exchanges: *0 milk, 1 vegetable, 0 fruit, ½ carbohydrate, 0 meat, 0 fat*

1 Carb Choice

Photo on page 245

Mushrooms and Broccoli

—Carol Kepple, McKees Rocks, Pennsylvania

Prep time: 10 minutes; Cook time: 9 minutes

2 tablespoons olive oil
1 clove garlic, minced
2 cups broccoli florets
1 cup mushrooms, sliced
1 carrot, thinly sliced

Heat the oil in a large skillet over medium-high heat. Add the garlic and cook, stirring occasionally, for 1 minute, or until fragrant. Add the broccoli, mushrooms, and carrot and cook, stirring frequently, for 8 minutes, or until the vegetables are tender-crisp.

Makes 4 servings

Per serving: *85 calories, 2 g protein, 5 g carbohydrate, 7 g fat, 0 mg cholesterol, 21 mg sodium, 2 g dietary fiber*

Diet Exchanges: *0 milk, 1 vegetable, 0 fruit, 0 carbohydrate, 0 meat, 1½ fat*

0 Carb Choices

Kitchen Tip

If you don't have time to chop fresh vegetables, you can use a 12-ounce bag of frozen mixed stir-fry vegetables instead.

Quick Spinach Sauté

—Suzanne Aycock, Annapolis, Maryland

"Voilá! A quick, healthy dish."

Prep time: 8 minutes; Cook time: 8 minutes

1–2 tablespoons olive oil

2 cloves garlic, crushed

1 cup sliced mushrooms

1 package (10 ounces) frozen chopped spinach, thawed and squeezed dry

½ cup grape tomatoes, halved

Place the oil and garlic in a cold skillet over medium heat for 2 minutes, or until the garlic is soft. Add the mushrooms and cook, stirring occasionally, for 5 minutes, or until the mushrooms release their liquid. Stir in the spinach and tomatoes and heat through.

Makes 4 servings

Per serving: *59 calories, 3 g protein, 5 g carbohydrate, 4 g fat, 0 mg cholesterol, 55 mg sodium, 3 g dietary fiber*

Diet Exchanges: *0 milk, 1 vegetable, 0 fruit, 0 carbohydrate, 0 meat, 1 fat*

0 Carb Choices

QUICK FIXES FOR FROZEN VEGGIES

If you'd like to add some zip to ordinary frozen vegetables, give these mini recipes a try. Each uses 2 cups of hot, cooked frozen vegetables, and makes 4 servings.

Amandine. Mix peas or peas and carrots with 2 teaspoons butter. Sprinkle with 2 tablespoons toasted slivered or sliced natural almonds.

Lemon-Dill. Mix chopped broccoli or Italian-style green beans with 1 tablespoon snipped fresh dill, 1 teaspoon extra-virgin olive oil, ½ teaspoon grated lemon zest, and 2 teaspoons lemon juice.

Green-Chili. Sauté 1 bunch sliced scallions in 2 teaspoons olive oil. Stir in 1 teaspoon chili powder and 2 to 3 tablespoons canned chopped mild green chile peppers. Mix with corn, wax beans, or sliced carrots.

Stir-fry. Sauté 2 sliced garlic cloves and 2 thin slices ginger in 2 teaspoons olive oil until fragrant. Mix with stir-fry vegetables and season with soy sauce.

Garlic and Butter. Sauté 3 minced garlic cloves in 2 teaspoons butter. Mix with broccoli, spinach, cauliflower, or a mixture. Top with grated Parmesan.

Beans Romano. Cook cut green beans. Before draining, add 15-ounce can rinsed and drained small white beans and ½ cup roasted red pepper strips; heat through. Drain. Mix with 1 tablespoon low-fat pesto and 2 tablespoons grated Parmesan.

Ginger-Orange. Heat 2 tablespoons orange juice, 2 teaspoons butter, 1½ teaspoons honey, 1 teaspoon lemon juice, ⅛ teaspoon ground ginger, and ground black pepper to taste. Toss with carrots, carrots and peas, or cauliflower.

Hot Roasted Vegetables

—Barbra Clark, River Falls, Wisconsin

"With all of the vegetables, I am not hungry for sweets. It is working great!"

Prep time: 15 minutes; Cook time: 35 minutes

- **2 tablespoons olive oil**
- **4 cloves garlic, minced**
- **1½ teaspoons dried rosemary**
- **½ teaspoon salt**
- **8 cups cut mixed vegetables, such as onions, potatoes, red bell pepper, tomatoes, carrots, and zucchini**
- **½ cup (2 ounces) shredded reduced-fat mozzarella cheese (optional)**

Preheat the oven to 450°F.

In a 13" × 9" baking pan, combine the oil, garlic, rosemary, and salt. Place in the oven for 5 minutes. Remove from the oven and add the vegetables, tossing to coat. Bake for 25 minutes, or until the vegetables are tender. Sprinkle with the cheese, if using. Bake for 5 minutes longer, or until the cheese is melted.

Makes 6 servings

Per serving: *132 calories, 3 g protein, 21 g carbohydrate, 5 g fat, 0 mg cholesterol, 218 mg sodium, 4 g dietary fiber*

Diet Exchanges: *0 milk, 2½ vegetable, 0 fruit, ½ carbohydrate, 0 meat, 1 fat*

1½ Carb Choices

Desserts

(shown with Chilly Hot Chocolate, page 221)

Whoopie Pies

—Gail Hillyer, St. Martin, Manitoba, Canada

"These are something everyone loves, and they're easy to make."

Prep time: 10 minutes; Cook time: 5 minutes

1 cup unbleached or all-purpose flour

¼ cup unsweetened cocoa powder

1 teaspoon baking soda

¼ teaspoon salt

½ cup sugar

¼ cup butter

1 egg white

½ cup 1% milk

¾ cup marshmallow creme

Preheat the oven to 425°F.

In a medium bowl, combine the flour, cocoa powder, baking soda, and salt.

In a large bowl, combine the sugar, butter, and egg white. With an electric mixer on medium speed, beat for 2 minutes, or until fluffy. Stir in the flour mixture, then the milk, until just blended.

Drop the dough by rounded tablespoons onto large, ungreased baking sheets to make 32 cookies. Bake for 5 minutes, or until the tops spring back when lightly touched.

Place the baking sheets on a rack to cool completely. Spoon about 2 teaspoons marshmallow on the bottoms of 16 of the cookies. Top with the remaining 16 cookies.

Makes 16 whoopie pies

Per serving: *97 calories, 2 g protein, 16 g carbohydrate, 3 g fat, 10 mg cholesterol, 160 mg sodium, 1 g dietary fiber*

Diet Exchanges: *0 milk, 0 vegetable, 0 fruit, 1 carbohydrate, 0 meat, ½ fat*

1 Carb Choice

Kitchen Tip

Gail notes that the whoopie pies will keep in an airtight container for up to 3 days.

Flax-Cinnamon Chip Cookies

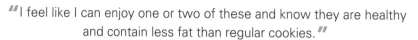

—Marcia Wych, Des Moines, Iowa

"I feel like I can enjoy one or two of these and know they are healthy and contain less fat than regular cookies."

Prep time: 10 minutes; Cook time: 10 minutes

½ **cup butter**
¼ **cup plain applesauce**
¼ **cup ground flaxseed**
1 **cup packed brown sugar**
2 **eggs or 4 egg whites**
1½ **teaspoons vanilla extract**
⅔ **cup soy flour**
⅔ **cup oat bran flour**
1 **teaspoon baking soda**
2½ **cups rolled oats**
½ **cup cinnamon chips**
½ **cup raisins or other dried fruit or chopped nuts**

Preheat the oven to 350°F. Coat 2 baking sheets with cooking spray.

In a large bowl, combine the butter, applesauce, and flaxseed. Add the brown sugar and beat well with an electric mixer on medium speed. Add the eggs or egg whites and vanilla extract and beat to incorporate.

In a medium bowl, combine the soy flour, oat bran flour, and baking soda. Add to the butter mixture and stir to combine. Gradually stir in the oats. Fold in the cinnamon chips and raisins. Drop the dough by rounded teaspoons onto the prepared baking sheet.

Bake for 10 minutes, or until golden. Remove to a rack to cool.

Makes about 56 cookies

Per cookie: *65 calories, 2 g protein, 9 g carbohydrate, 3 g fat, 10 mg cholesterol, 45 mg sodium, 1 g dietary fiber*

Diet Exchanges: *0 milk, 0 vegetable, 0 fruit, ½ carbohydrate, 0 meat, ½ fat*

1 Carb Choice

Kitchen Tip

Marcia suggests keeping a close eye on these cookies as they bake, as the flaxseed will make them brown quickly. Remove them from the oven when they reach the desired color.

Healthy Brownie Cookies

—Cary Sutherland, Christmas, Michigan

"This recipe is great for chocoholics. It has really helped me stay with my weight-loss program. I still feel like I can have something sweet without any guilt."

Prep time: 10 minutes; Cook time: 12 minutes

1 box (21 ounces) low-fat brownie mix
2½ cups unprocessed bran
¾ cup orange juice
½ teaspoon coconut extract
   Confectioners' sugar (optional)

Preheat the oven to 350°F. Coat 2 baking sheets with cooking spray.

In a large bowl, combine the brownie mix and bran. Add the orange juice and coconut extract and stir to combine. Drop the dough by rounded teaspoons onto the prepared baking sheets.

Bake for 12 minutes. Remove to a rack to cool. Lightly dust with confectioners' sugar, if using.

Makes about 40 cookies

Per cookie: *83 calories, 2 g protein, 16 g carbohydrate, 3 g fat, 0 mg cholesterol, 45 mg sodium, 1 g dietary fiber*

Diet Exchanges: *0 milk, 0 vegetable, 0 fruit, 1 carbohydrate, 0 meat, ½ fat*

1 Carb Choice

Kitchen Tip

Cary notes that these cookies will firm up as they cool, and that they keep very well in the freezer. Just place them in a zip-top freezer bag.

Unprocessed bran is available in the cereal aisle of supermarkets.

Oatmeal-Raisin Cookies

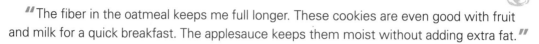

—**Lorelle Boxler, Salina, Kansas**

"The fiber in the oatmeal keeps me full longer. These cookies are even good with fruit and milk for a quick breakfast. The applesauce keeps them moist without adding extra fat."

Prep time: 20 minutes; Cook time: 8 minutes

- ¾ **cup all-purpose flour**
- 1 **teaspoon ground cinnamon**
- ½ **teaspoon baking soda**
- ¼ **teaspoon baking powder**
- ¼ **teaspoon salt**
- ¼ **cup packed brown sugar**
- ¼ **cup granulated sugar**
- ⅓ **cup unsweetened applesauce**
- ¼ **cup butter**
- 1 **egg white**
- 1 **teaspoon vanilla extract**
- 1⅓ **cups quick-cooking oats**
- ¾ **cup raisins or craisins**

Preheat the oven to 375°F. Coat 2 baking sheets with cooking spray.

Sift the flour, cinnamon, baking soda, baking powder, and salt together in a large bowl.

In a medium bowl, with an electric mixer on medium speed, combine the brown sugar, granulated sugar, applesauce, butter, egg white, and vanilla extract. Add to the flour mixture and stir to combine. Stir in the oats and raisins or craisins. Drop the dough by rounded teaspoons onto the prepared baking sheets.

Bake for 8 minutes, or until golden.

Makes about 40 cookies

Per cookie: *48 calories, 1 g protein, 9 g carbohydrate, 1 g fat, 5 mg cholesterol, 50 mg sodium, 1 g dietary fiber*

Diet Exchanges: *0 milk, 0 vegetable, 0 fruit, ½ carbohydrate, 0 meat, 0 fat*

½ **Carb Choice**

Kitchen Tip

When baking cookies on 2 separate baking sheets, switch their rack position halfway through the baking time to ensure even doneness.

Soy Bars

—Miran Sedlacek, Port Charlotte, Florida

" I have used these bars as a substitute for one meal a day. They have helped me lose weight and lower my cholesterol. They taste good! "

Prep time: 20 minutes; Cook time: 35 minutes

1 **cup whole grain pastry flour**

½ **cup soy flour**

½ **cup rolled oats**

1 **tablespoon baking powder**

4 **packets sugar substitute or 4 teaspoons sugar**

½ **teaspoon salt**

2 **cups club soda**

2 **eggs**

1 **tablespoon oil**

½ **cup sugar-free carob chips**

6 **dates or apricots, chopped**

6 **figs, chopped**

¼ **cup chopped walnuts**

Preheat the oven to 350°F. Coat a 9" × 9" baking pan with cooking spray.

In a large bowl, combine the pastry flour, soy flour, oats, baking powder, sugar substitute or sugar, and salt.

In a medium bowl, combine the club soda, eggs, and oil. Add to the flour mixture and stir to combine. Stir in the carob chips, dates or apricots, and figs. Pour the batter into the prepared pan. Sprinkle with the walnuts.

Bake for 35 minutes, or until a wooden pick inserted in the center comes out almost clean. Cool in the pan on a rack.

Makes 16 bars

Per bar: *123 calories, 4 g protein, 17 g carbohydrate, 5 g fat, 25 mg cholesterol, 200 mg sodium, 3 g dietary fiber*

Diet Exchanges: *0 milk, 0 vegetable, ½ fruit, ½ carbohydrate, 0 meat, 1 fat*

1 Carb Choice

Kitchen Tip

Use kitchen shears coated with cooking spray to chop the dried fruit in this recipe. It makes chopping easier, and the fruit won't stick to the shears.

Chocolate-Marshmallow Fudge

99 Calories

—Judy Parsons, Surrey, British Columbia, Canada

"I cannot seem to do without chocolate, and this seems like a good alternative to my old fudge recipe."

Prep time: 20 minutes; Cook time: 5 minutes; Stand time: 3 hours

1⅔ cups sugar

⅔ cup fat-free evaporated milk

2 tablespoons butter or reduced-calorie margarine

2 cups loosely packed mini marshmallows

12 ounces semisweet chocolate chips

Coat an 8" × 8" baking pan with cooking spray.

Bring the sugar, evaporated milk, and butter or margarine to a boil in a medium saucepan over medium heat. Reduce the heat to medium-low and cook, stirring constantly, for 3 minutes. Stir in the marshmallows and chocolate chips. Remove from the heat and stir until smooth. Pour into the prepared pan. Let stand at room temperature for 3 hours, or until set. Store, covered, in the refrigerator.

Makes 36 squares

Per square: *99 calories, 1 g protein, 18 g carbohydrate, 3 g fat, 0 mg cholesterol, 15 mg sodium, 1 g dietary fiber*

Diet Exchanges: *0 milk, 0 vegetable, 0 fruit, 1 carbohydrate, 0 meat, ½ fat*

1 Carb Choice

Kitchen Tip

If you like, you can sprinkle the top of the fudge with a small amount of chopped walnuts after pouring the fudge into the pan.

It Worked for Me!

Donna Marrin

VITAL STATS

Weight lost: 45 pounds

Time to goal: 1 year

Unique secret to success:
Learning to love being outdoors, making walking a perfectly easy, always-available form of exercise.

Affirmation: *"Exercise will keep me young."*

Donna gained weight with her first pregnancy—and it just never came off. In her mind, the weight became a thyroid-related issue that seemed simply impossible to beat. Embarking on a weight-loss program that delivered amazing results, Donna discovered that the control was in her hands all the time.

"I couldn't understand why, as the years passed, I continued to gain weight, while people who ate much more than I did never seemed to gain an ounce. I was convinced that I had a thyroid problem. I pointed to my constant exhaustion as evidence—and also used my tiredness as an excuse not to exercise at all.

"Not one day passed that I didn't feel upset with myself. In addition to my low self-esteem, I was well aware of the health risks that go along with excess weight. I just felt helpless to change anything.

"A coworker joined Weight Watchers, and I dismissed the group as just another diet scam. Soon, though, I saw her and others losing weight. I took the leap, visited a local meeting, and reluctantly paid the required fees, all the while thinking, 'But aren't I worth this much?'

"I learned to control my portion sizes and keep a food journal. No matter how little you think you are eating, you don't realize the reality of it until you write it all down. This trick has taught me to be aware of every bite, and it's so easy—I keep a small date book in my purse and jot down quick notes.

"Losing the weight made a big difference in my ability and desire to be physically active. I am not the kind of person to join a gym, but 4 months into the program, I felt motivated to begin walking outdoors a couple evenings a week, both for the exercise and for the fresh air. Amazingly, this former couch potato is now running 5K several nights a week.

"I feel fabulous and have energy to burn. Shopping for clothes is fun for the first time in my life, and I wear shirts tucked in. Imagine!"

Very Cherry Dessert

—Jean Adam, Orefield, Pennsylvania

"*This is a very tasty substitute for cherry pie.*"

Prep time: 15 minutes; Cook time: 25 minutes

16 ounces fresh sour cherries, pitted

½ cup + 2 tablespoons sugar

1 teaspoon lemon juice

3 tablespoons cornstarch

½ cup water

½ cup unbleached or all-purpose flour

1 tablespoon butter substitute

Preheat the oven to 375°F.

In a large saucepan over medium heat, combine the cherries, ½ cup of the sugar, and lemon juice.

In a cup, combine the cornstarch and water and stir until smooth. Stir into the cherry mixture and cook for 5 minutes, or until the sauce thickens and looks clear. Evenly divide the cherry mixture among 4 ramekins or custard cups.

In a small bowl, combine the flour, the remaining 2 tablespoons sugar, and the butter substitute. Form into a crumb mixture. Sprinkle over the cherries in the ramekins. Place the ramekins on a baking sheet.

Bake for 20 minutes, or until slightly brown. Cool on a rack.

Makes 4 servings

Per serving: *251 calories, 2 g protein, 60 g carbohydrate, 1 g fat, 1 mg cholesterol, 24 mg sodium, 1 g dietary fiber*

Diet Exchanges: *0 milk, 0 vegetable, 1 fruit, 3 carbohydrate, 0 meat, 0 fat*

4 Carb Choices

Kitchen Tip

For best results, Jean and her husband, David, use sour cherries that they pick and freeze themselves when they're in season. The fresh taste really shines through!

Easy Baked Apples

—Stephanie Rothschild, New York City

"I also like this snack with kefir or crème fraîche."

Prep time: 5 minutes; Cook time: 5 minutes

2 apples, cored
2 tablespoons brown sugar
¼ teaspoon ground cinnamon
2 tablespoons low-fat plain yogurt

Place a drop of water on a microwaveable plate. Place the apples on the plate and coat with butter-flavored cooking spray. Sprinkle with the brown sugar and cinnamon. Microwave for 5 minutes, or until fork-tender. Serve topped with the yogurt.

Makes 2 servings

Per serving: *141 calories, 1 g protein, 37 g carbohydrate, 0 g fat, 0 mg cholesterol, 15 mg sodium, 5 g dietary fiber*

Diet Exchanges: *0 milk, 0 vegetable, 1½ fruit, 1 carbohydrate, 0 meat, 0 fat*

2½ Carb Choices

Kitchen Tip

Instead of yogurt, try serving these tasty apples with either kefir or crème fraîche, as Stephanie suggests. Kefir is made from fermented milk and has a slightly sour taste and texture, similar to yogurt. It's available in natural food stores. Crème fraîche is a richly textured thickened cream available in specialty and gourmet stores.

Tasty Apple Dessert

—Jean Adam, Orefield, Pennsylvania

"This is a dessert for one, and it certainly satisfies the desire for a high-calorie piece of apple pie."

Prep time: 5 minutes; Cook time: 3 minutes

1 **apple, peeled and sliced**
½ **teaspoon brown sugar**
¼ **teaspoon ground cinnamon**
1 **teaspoon butter substitute**

Place the apple slices in a microwaveable dessert dish. Sprinkle with the brown sugar, cinnamon, and butter substitute. Cover with plastic wrap and microwave for 3 minutes, or until the apples are tender and the butter is melted.

Makes 1 serving

Per serving: *103 calories, 0 g protein, 27 g carbohydrate, 0 g fat, 0 mg cholesterol, 20 mg sodium, 5 g dietary fiber*

Diet Exchanges: *0 milk, 0 vegetable, 1½ fruit, ½ carbohydrate, 0 meat, 0 fat*

2 Carb Choices

Kitchen Tip

To cook the apples, Jean uses the "fresh vegetable soft" setting on the microwave.

Sautéed Bananas with Praline Sauce

—Sarah Ballweg, Middleton, Wisconsin

"This is a great treat and a reward for a good day's work. I enjoy every last bit, and I do not have to feel guilty. And if I can enjoy a recipe this sweet and tasty and not feel guilty, that in turn does not make me feel bad and send me to the refrigerator for the night."

Prep time: 3 minutes; Cook time: 12 minutes

¼ **cup + 1½ tablespoons maple syrup**

3 **tablespoons fat-free milk**

3 **tablespoons chopped pecans**

4 **large bananas, peeled, halved lengthwise, and sliced**

Bring the maple syrup, milk, and pecans to a boil in a small saucepan over medium-high heat. Reduce the heat to medium-low and simmer for 10 minutes, or until the mixture thickens and reduces to about ⅓ cup.

Meanwhile, heat a large nonstick skillet coated with cooking spray over medium-high heat. Add the bananas and cook, stirring frequently, for 2 minutes.

Place the bananas in a serving dish and top with the praline sauce.

Makes 4 servings

Per serving: *253 calories, 2 g protein, 56 g carbohydrate, 4 g fat, 0 mg cholesterol, 20 mg sodium, 6 g dietary fiber*

Diet Exchanges: *0 milk, 0 vegetable, 2½ fruit, 1 carbohydrate, 0 meat, ½ fat*

4 Carb Choices

Kitchen Tip

To keep the bananas from turning brown, Sarah suggests waiting to slice them until just before you're ready to cook them.

Cool Snacking

—Cynthia Hildebrand, Lubbock, Texas

125 Calories

"When the urge for ice cream kicks in, this has a lot fewer calories and no fat. The frozen topping tastes as good as ice cream, maybe better!"

Prep time: 10 minutes; Freeze time: 2 hours

8 ounces fat-free frozen whipped topping, thawed

2 sheets reduced-fat cinnamon graham crackers, coarsely crumbled

1 cup strawberries, sliced

1 tablespoon chocolate syrup

Kitchen Tip

This recipe also works nicely with fat-free frozen yogurt in place of the whipped topping. Allow the frozen yogurt to soften slightly, then layer and freeze as directed.

Divide one-third of the whipped topping among 4 dessert bowls. Sprinkle one-third of the graham crackers, one-third of the strawberries, and 1 teaspoon of the chocolate syrup evenly among the 4 bowls. Repeat layering 2 more times to use the remaining ingredients. Freeze for 2 hours, or until hardened. Serve frozen or allow to thaw slightly.

Makes 4 servings

Per serving: *125 calories, 1 g protein, 26 g carbohydrate, 0 g fat, 0 mg cholesterol, 35 mg sodium, 1 g dietary fiber*

Diet Exchanges: *0 milk, 0 vegetable, ½ fruit, 1½ carbohydrate, 0 meat, 0 fat*

2 Carb Choices

SECRETS OF WEIGHT-LOSS WINNERS

• Whenever I make large dishes that I know will produce many leftovers, I freeze individual meal-sized portions for quick meals later in the month.

—Heather Cowley, Lake Dallas, Texas

• I buy healthy snacks in bigger packages and then fill snack-size plastic bags with premeasured portions. By doing it this way, I save money and I know exactly how many calories I'm consuming.

—Shonna Macaulay, San Antonio, Texas

Heavenly Berries

—Stephanie Rothschild, New York City

"This recipe makes you feel as if you're indulging in a rich, delicious dessert. I eat it after dinner while my family is eating ice cream, and I don't feel like I'm being deprived."

Prep time: 10 minutes; Freeze time: 15 minutes

- ¼ **cup nonfat dry milk powder**
- ¼ **cup cold water**
- 2 **teaspoons sugar**
- ⅛ **teaspoon vanilla extract**
- 1 **cup fresh mixed berries, such as raspberries and blueberries**

In a medium bowl, combine the milk powder, water, sugar, and vanilla extract. Cover and place in the freezer for 15 minutes. Beat with an electric mixer on medium speed for 5 minutes, or until a creamy texture forms.

Place the berries in dessert bowls and top with the milk mixture.

Makes 2 servings

Per serving: *77 calories, 4 g protein, 16 g carbohydrate, 0 g fat, 0 mg cholesterol, 45 mg sodium, 4 g dietary fiber*

Diet Exchanges: *½ milk, 0 vegetable, ½ fruit, 0 carbohydrate, 0 meat, 0 fat*

1 Carb Choice

SHOPPING SAVVY

It Measures Up

This clever, restyled measuring cup will become a favorite kitchen tool. You can read the numbers from the side or when looking down into the cup, without having to bend over. A smart, red, snug-fitting lid is handy for storing foods in the fridge or to eliminate splattering in the microwave. Turn the lid to get different settings. The open setting enables you to pour without drips; other settings

are for straining and sprinkling. Sold in cookware shops and supermarkets, Pyrex Measuring Cups are available in 1-cup, 2-cup, 4-cup, and 8-cup sizes.

Photo courtesy of Pyrex

Fresh Fruit Fantasy

—Pamela Curtis, Dayton, Ohio

"I eat this instead of salty snacks or fattening ice cream, pies, or cakes."

Prep time: 15 minutes; Chill time: 1 hour

2 **Jonathan apples, peeled, cored, and sliced**

2 **bananas, sliced**

1 **clementine orange, peeled and segmented**

1 **cup seedless grapes**

1 **cup fresh sliced strawberries**

2 **cups light frozen whipped topping, thawed**

In a medium bowl, combine the apples, bananas, orange, grapes, and strawberries. Gently fold in the whipped topping. Refrigerate for 1 hour before serving.

Makes 8 servings

Per serving: *114 calories, 1 g protein, 24 g carbohydrate, 2 g fat, 0 mg cholesterol, 0 mg sodium, 3 g dietary fiber*

Diet Exchanges: *0 milk, 0 vegetable, 1½ fruit, ½ carbohydrate, 0 meat, ½ fat*

2 Carb Choices

FAST FRUIT DESSERTS

To add some variety to your daily fruit servings, try some of these tasty ideas. Each mini-recipe makes 4 servings.

Strawberry Soup with Angel Croutons. Toast 1 cup cubed angel food cake under the broiler; let cool. Mix 1 pound hulled and sliced strawberries and 3 tablespoons sugar and let stand for 20 minutes. Puree in a food processor with ½ cup apple juice until smooth. Serve with the croutons.

Gingered Cantaloupe. Mix ½ teaspoon finely grated peeled fresh ginger with 1 tablespoon sugar. Mix with 2 cups cantaloupe chunks.

Watermelon with Mint. Mix 2 cups watermelon chunks (or mixed watermelon and honeydew) with 1 tablespoon slivered fresh mint leaves.

Pears with Chocolate. Slice 2 ripe Bartlett pears or firm-ripe Bosc pears in half; remove the cores with a melon baller, and slice thinly. Arrange on plates. With a vegetable peeler, shave a little semisweet or bittersweet chocolate from a small bar over each.

Maple Apple Wedges. Choose 4 crisp medium McIntosh or Empire apples. Core and slice into wedges and place in 4 bowls. Drizzle 1 tablespoon pure maple syrup over each and sprinkle lightly with ground cinnamon.

Fruit Trifle

—Phillip Vickery, Southaven, Mississippi

"I love dessert, and since I'm dieting, I have to really watch my fat and calorie intake. This is a dessert that feels and tastes luxurious but does not make me feel guilty or blow my diet!"

Prep time: 20 minutes; Chill time: 1 hour

- **5 bananas, sliced**
- **1 pint (2 cups) strawberries, hulled and sliced**
- **1 large bunch seedless red grapes**
- **1 can (11 ounces) mandarin oranges, drained**
- **1 prepared angel food cake, cut into bite-size pieces**
- **8 ounces fat-free frozen whipped topping, thawed**

In a medium bowl, combine the bananas, strawberries, grapes, and oranges.

Place one-third of the cake cubes in the bottom of a trifle bowl or deep glass bowl. Spoon one-third of the fruit mixture over the top, then one-third of the whipped topping. Repeat layering 2 more times to use the remaining cake cubes, fruit, and whipped topping. Cover and chill for 1 hour before serving.

Makes 16 servings

Per serving: *177 calories, 3 g protein, 41 g carbohydrate, 0 g fat, 0 mg cholesterol, 200 mg sodium, 2 g dietary fiber*

Diet Exchanges: *0 milk, 0 vegetable, 1 fruit, 2 carbohydrate, 0 meat, 0 fat*

3 Carb Choices

Kitchen Tip

This bright and fruity trifle is also yummy with fat-free or reduced-fat vanilla yogurt in place of the whipped topping.

Sinfully Good Yogurt and Fruit Delight

228 Calories

—Diane Nelson, Waleska, Georgia

"I divide this dish into 2 servings and have one for breakfast and the remainder as a snack or dessert later in the day. It has never been so easy to get my daily fruit allowance. Best of all, my husband and grandchildren love it just as much as I do."

Prep time: 8 minutes; Chill time: 6 hours

- 1 **medium red-skinned apple, cut into bite-size chunks**
- 1 **can (8 ounces) juice-packed unsweetened pineapple chunks or tidbits**
- ¼ **cup mini marshmallows**
- 6 **ounces fat-free vanilla yogurt**
- 1 **tablespoon chopped nuts, such as pecans or almonds**

In a large bowl, combine the apple, pineapple (with juice), and marshmallows. Stir well. Chill for at least 6 hours to blend the flavors.

Drain excess juice. Top with the yogurt and sprinkle with the nuts.

Makes 2 servings

Per serving: *228 calories, 5 g protein, 47 g carbohydrate, 3 g fat, 1 mg cholesterol, 70 mg sodium, 4 g dietary fiber*

Diet Exchanges: *0 milk, 0 vegetable, 1½ fruit, 1½ carbohydrate, 0 meat, ½ fat*

3 Carb Choices

Kitchen Tip

When draining the excess juice from the fruit and marshmallow mixture, Diane suggests saving it instead of spilling it out. It makes a delicious, sweet-tasting drink.

Layered Ambrosia

—Elisa Forman, Brockton, Massachusetts

"I take this dessert with me as my 'what can I bring for dessert' idea. It tastes great, and I can have a large portion without doing much damage."

Prep time: 10 minutes; Chill time: 1 hour

- 1 can (20 ounces) unsweetened crushed pineapple, drained
- 1 can (11 ounces) mandarin oranges, drained
- 8 ounces light frozen whipped topping, thawed
- 1 bag colored or plain mini marshmallows
- 2 packages (12 per package) ladyfingers

In a large bowl, combine the pineapple, oranges, and whipped topping.

Place a layer of 8 of the ladyfingers in the bottom of a trifle dish. Cover with one-third of the pineapple mixture. Sprinkle with one-third of the marshmallows. Repeat layering to use the remaining ingredients, ending with marshmallows. Chill for at least 1 hour before serving.

Makes 16 servings

Per serving: *146 calories, 2 g protein, 26 g carbohydrate, 3 g fat, 60 mg cholesterol, 30 mg sodium, 0 g dietary fiber*

Diet Exchanges: *0 milk, 0 vegetable, ½ fruit, 1½ carbohydrate, 0 meat, ½ fat*

2 Carb Choices

Banana Cream "Pie"

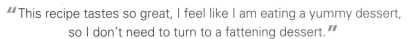

—JoAnn Tremel, Mint Spring, Virginia

*"*This recipe tastes so great, I feel like I am eating a yummy dessert,
so I don't need to turn to a fattening dessert.*"*

Prep time: 5 minutes

- **8 ounces fat-free banana or vanilla yogurt**
- **½ cup quick-cooking rolled oats**
- **1 small banana, sliced**
- **1 tablespoon fat-free frozen whipped topping, thawed**
- **2 teaspoons wheat germ (optional)**

In a small bowl, combine the yogurt and oats. Spoon into 2 dessert dishes. Top with the banana and whipped topping. Sprinkle with the wheat germ, if using.

Makes 2 servings

Per serving: *239 calories, 9 g protein, 48 g carbohydrate, 2 g fat, 0 mg cholesterol, 80 mg sodium, 4 g dietary fiber*

Diet Exchanges: *0 milk, 0 vegetable, 1 fruit, 2 carbohydrate, 0 meat, ½ fat*

3 Carb Choices

Kitchen Tip

If you like, you can substitute fat-free vanilla frozen yogurt for the frozen whipped topping.

Yogurt Pops

—Eileen Locke, Lubec, Maine

70 Calories

" This satisfies any craving you might have, especially in the evening. You'll think you're having a high-calorie goodie! **"**

Prep time: 8 minutes; Freeze time: 5 hours

8 ounces low-fat plain or flavored yogurt

6 ounces concentrated unsweetened fruit juice, such as mixed berry flavor

Dash of vanilla extract or honey

Kitchen Tip

If you like, you can stir ½ cup blueberries and ½ cup chopped strawberries into the yogurt mixture before filling the paper cups. With the added volume, you'll make 6 pops instead of 4.

In a medium bowl, combine the yogurt, juice, and vanilla extract or honey. Pour into four 3-ounce paper cups and partially freeze for 1 hour. Insert wooden sticks into each cup and freeze for 4 hours, or until solid.

Makes 4 pops

Per pop: *70 calories, 4 g protein, 14 g carbohydrate, 0 g fat, 0 mg cholesterol, 45 mg sodium, 0 g dietary fiber*

Diet Exchanges: *½ milk, 0 vegetable, ½ fruit, 0 carbohydrate, 0 meat, 0 fat*

1 Carb Choice

QUICK WAYS WITH FROZEN YOGURT

A little frozen yogurt after dinner can really hit the spot and satisfy your sweet craving. Add any of the following to a pint of softened frozen fat-free vanilla yogurt. Each mini-recipe makes 4 servings. If you're the only one having dessert, reduce the recipe or freeze the other 3 servings.

Georgia Peach. Mix 2 chopped or mashed ripe fresh peaches or 4 canned peach halves and 1 tablespoon brown sugar. Add softened yogurt and mash until blended. Freeze at least 15 minutes before serving.

Piña Colada. Mix 1 well-drained 8-ounce can crushed pineapple packed in juice, 1 tablespoon brown sugar, ½ teaspoon rum extract, and ⅛ teaspoon coconut extract. Add softened yogurt and mash until blended. Freeze at least 15 minutes before serving.

Strawberry Swirl. Mix 2 cups thinly sliced strawberries with 2 tablespoons strawberry pourable fruit. Let stand for 10 minutes. Add softened yogurt and mash until blended. Freeze at least 15 minutes before serving.

Ice Cream Sandwich

—Paula Towery, Hopkinsville, Kentucky

"This makes a good snack that the kids love, too."

Prep time: 5 minutes; Freeze time: 30 minutes

4 low-fat graham crackers, any flavor

¼ cup + 2 tablespoons fat-free frozen yogurt, any flavor, softened

1 teaspoon semisweet chocolate chips, melted

Place the graham crackers on a work surface and spoon the yogurt evenly onto 2 of the crackers. Drizzle with the melted chocolate and top with the remaining crackers. Wrap in plastic wrap and freeze for 30 minutes, or until set.

Makes 2 sandwiches

Per sandwich: *69 calories, 3 g protein, 14 g carbohydrate, 1 g fat, 0 mg cholesterol, 30 mg sodium, 1 g dietary fiber*

Diet Exchanges: *0 milk, 0 vegetable, 0 fruit, 1 carbohydrate, 0 meat, 0 fat*

1 Carb Choice

Kitchen Tip

Try different combinations of fat-free frozen yogurt and graham cracker flavors, such as mint chocolate chip with chocolate grahams or butter pecan with cinnamon grahams.

Pumpkin Treats

—Alberta Mobley, Jefferson City, Missouri

"This recipe is a nice treat."

Prep time: 5 minutes

1 can (15 ounces) pumpkin

1 package (4-serving size) fat-free, sugar-free instant vanilla pudding mix

1 cup fat-free or light frozen whipped topping, thawed

2 teaspoons pumpkin pie spice

32 low-fat cinnamon graham cracker squares

In a medium bowl, thoroughly combine the pumpkin, pudding mix, whipped topping, and pumpkin pie spice. Serve with the graham crackers.

Makes 32 servings

Per serving: *43 calories, 1 g protein, 10 g carbohydrate, 0 g fat, 0 mg cholesterol, 75 mg sodium, 2 g dietary fiber*

Diet Exchanges: *0 milk, 0 vegetable, 0 fruit, 1 carbohydrate, 0 meat, 0 fat*

1 Carb Choice

Pudding Cup with Bananas

274 Calories

—Tracey Pintell, Valley Lee, Maryland

"This dessert is easy to make in a single serving, so I'm not worried about overestimating serving sizes. Plus, it's a great dessert for dinners with my calorie-conscious friends."

Prep time: 5 minutes

3 low-fat graham crackers

4 teaspoons water

1 cup prepared fat-free vanilla or banana pudding

1 banana, sliced

¼ cup fat-free whipped cream

2 tablespoons ground flaxseeds
   Fresh mint leaves, for garnish

Place the graham crackers in a zip-top plastic bag. Seal the bag and use a rolling pin to crush into crumbs. Evenly divide the crumbs between 2 individual serving dishes. Moisten the crumbs with the water and loosely pack the crumbs around the sides and bottom of the dishes.

Top each with about 1 tablespoon of the pudding, then add all but 2 slices of the banana. Add the remaining pudding. Place the last banana slices on top of the pudding and top with the whipped cream. Sprinkle with the flaxseeds. Garnish each serving with mint leaves.

Makes 2 servings

Per serving: *274 calories, 9 g protein, 36 g carbohydrate, 11 g fat, 25 mg cholesterol, 320 mg sodium, 7 g dietary fiber*

Diet Exchanges: *0 milk, 0 vegetable, 1 fruit, 1½ carbohydrate, 0 meat, 2 fat*

2½ Carb Choices

Kitchen Tip

Tracey notes that the flaxseeds add fiber and a nutty flavor, but you can leave them out if you want a nearly fat-free dessert.

Rice Pudding

—Wanda Beeken, Goldsboro, North Carolina

*"*This pudding kept me from munching on candy bars!*"*

Prep time: 5 minutes; Cook time: 50 minutes

1½ cups cooked white rice

 2 cups fat-free milk

 5 eggs

¼ cup packed brown sugar

¼ cup granulated sugar

 1 teaspoon vanilla extract

Preheat the oven to 375°F. Coat an 8" × 8" baking dish with cooking spray.

In a large bowl, combine the rice, milk, eggs, brown sugar, granulated sugar, and vanilla extract. Spread evenly in the prepared pan.

Bake for 50 minutes, or until set.

Makes 6 servings

Per serving: *225 calories, 9 g protein, 35 g carbohydrate, 5 g fat, 180 mg cholesterol, 97 mg sodium, 0 g dietary fiber*

Diet Exchanges: *½ milk, 0 vegetable, 0 fruit, 2 carbohydrate, 1 meat, ½ fat*

2 Carb Choices

Kitchen Tip

If you're not using leftover cooked rice for this recipe, you'll need about ½ cup uncooked rice. Prepare according to the package directions.

No-Bake Strawberry Dessert

145 Calories

—Teresa Wargo, Pulaski, Wisconsin

"This recipe uses all low-fat ingredients, yet it is a wonderfully sweet dessert.**"**

Prep time: 20 minutes; Chill time: 1 hour

1 **prepared angel food cake, cut into 1" cubes**

2 **packages (0.3 ounces each) sugar-free strawberry gelatin**

2 **cups boiling water**

1 **package (16–20 ounces) frozen unsweetened whole strawberries, thawed**

2 **cups 1% milk**

1 **package (1 ounce) sugar-free instant vanilla pudding mix**

8 **ounces reduced-fat frozen whipped topping, thawed**

Place the cake cubes in a 13" × 9" baking dish.

In a medium bowl, combine the gelatin and water and stir to dissolve. Stir in the strawberries. Pour over the cake cubes in the pan and gently press cake down. Cover and refrigerate for 1 hour, or until set.

In another medium bowl, whisk together the milk and pudding mix for 2 minutes, or until slightly thickened. Spoon over the cake. Spread the whipped topping over the top. Cover and refrigerate until serving.

Makes 16 servings

Per serving: *145 calories, 4 g protein, 31 g carbohydrate, 0 g fat, 0 mg cholesterol, 240 mg sodium, 1 g dietary fiber*

Diet Exchanges: *0 milk, 0 vegetable, 0 fruit, 2 carbohydrate, 0 meat, 0 fat*

2 Carb Choices

Apple Cake

—Faye Canape, Englishtown, New Jersey

Prep time: 35 minutes; Cook time: 1 hour 30 minutes

3 cups whole grain pastry flour
1 cup + 5 tablespoons sugar
3 teaspoons baking powder
1 cup olive oil
¾ cup egg whites
½ cup orange juice
2½ teaspoons vanilla extract
¼ cup chopped walnuts
¼ cup semisweet chocolate chips
4 Granny Smith apples, peeled and sliced
1 tablespoon ground cinnamon

Preheat the oven to 350°F. Coat a 10" tube pan with cooking spray and lightly dust with flour.

In a large bowl, combine the flour, 1 cup of the sugar, and the baking powder. In a medium bowl, combine the oil, egg whites, orange juice, and vanilla extract. Gradually stir the oil mixture into the flour mixture. Stir in the walnuts and chocolate chips.

Place the apples in another large bowl and top with the remaining 5 tablespoons sugar and the cinnamon. Stir to combine.

Pour a layer of the batter into the prepared pan. Top with a layer of apples. Repeat layering, ending with batter.

Bake for 1 hour 30 minutes, or until a wooden pick inserted in the center comes out almost clean.

Makes 20 servings

Per serving: *237 calories, 3 g protein, 30 g carbohydrate, 12 g fat, 0 mg cholesterol, 88 mg sodium, 3 g dietary fiber*

Diet Exchanges: *0 milk, 0 vegetable, ½ fruit, 1½ carbohydrate, 0 meat, 2½ fat*

2 Carb Choices

Berry Cake

—Huguette English, Beaverbrook, New Brunswick, Canada

" Most cakes are high in fat, but I've tried different ways and this is
the best way I can have it and stay in control of the calories and fat grams. *"*

Prep time: 25 minutes; Cook time: 40 minutes

1 egg white
¾ cup sugar
⅓ cup butter or margarine
1 teaspoon vanilla extract
¼ teaspoon salt
1 egg, separated
1½ cups + 1 tablespoon all-purpose flour
1 teaspoon baking powder
⅓ cup fat-free milk
2 cups mixed berries, such as raspberries,
strawberries, and/or blueberries

Preheat the oven to 350°F. Coat a 9" × 9"
baking pan with cooking spray.

In a large bowl, with an electric mixer on
medium speed, beat the egg white until stiff.
Add ¼ cup of the sugar and beat until
smooth.

In another bowl, with the mixer on
medium speed, beat the butter or margarine,
vanilla extract, salt, and the remaining ½ cup
sugar until creamy. Add the egg yolk and
beat to incorporate. Add 1½ cups of the
flour, the baking powder, milk, and egg
white. Beat until thoroughly combined.

Coat the berries with the remaining
1 tablespoon flour and add to the batter.
Pour into the prepared pan.

Bake for 40 minutes, or until a wooden
pick inserted in the center comes out clean.

Makes 12 servings

Per serving: *228 calories, 4 g protein, 36 g carbohydrate, 7 g fat, 40 mg cholesterol, 210 mg sodium,
1 g dietary fiber*

Diet Exchanges: *0 milk, 0 vegetable, ½ fruit,
2 carbohydrate, 0 meat, 1½ fat*

2½ Carb Choices

Upside Down Peach Cake

210 Calories

—Andrea Collins, Geneva, Florida

"This is so good, it keeps me from eating the more fatty cakes and pies."

Prep time: 30 minutes; Cook time: 30 minutes

- 3 tablespoons maple syrup
- 1 tablespoon butter or light margarine, melted
- 2 peaches, peeled and thinly sliced
- ½ cup dried cranberries
- ½ cup whole wheat flour
- ½ cup all-purpose flour
- 1½ teaspoons baking powder
- 1 teaspoon ground cinnamon
- ¼ cup fat-free evaporated milk
- ¼ cup liquid egg substitute
- ¼ cup fat-free plain yogurt
- ¼ cup honey
- 2½ tablespoons canola oil
- 1 teaspoon vanilla extract
- ¼ teaspoon almond extract

Preheat the oven to 350°F. Coat a 9" round baking pan with cooking spray. Line the bottom with a circle of waxed paper and coat with spray.

In a cup, combine the maple syrup and butter or margarine. Pour into the prepared pan and swirl over the bottom. Arrange the peaches and cranberries in a decorative pattern over the syrup mixture.

In a large bowl, combine the whole wheat flour, all-purpose flour, baking powder, and cinnamon.

In a medium bowl, combine the evaporated milk, egg substitute, yogurt, honey, oil, vanilla extract, and almond extract. Add to the flour mixture and stir to combine. Pour the batter over the fruit in the pie pan and smooth the top.

Bake for 30 minutes, or until light brown and puffy. Cool in the pan on a rack for 10 minutes. Carefully invert the cake onto a serving plate and remove the waxed paper.

Makes 8 servings

Per serving: *210 calories, 4 g protein, 35 g carbohydrate, 6 g fat, 5 mg cholesterol, 135 mg sodium, 2 g dietary fiber*

Diet Exchanges: *0 milk, 0 vegetable, ½ fruit, 1½ carbohydrate, 0 meat, 1 fat*

2 Carb Choices

Piña Colada Cake

—**Annette Boswell, Meadville, Pennsylvania**

Prep time: 8 minutes; Cook time: 20 minutes

- 1 **package (14½ ounces) angel food cake mix**
- 1 **can (8 ounces) unsweetened crushed pineapple**
- 8 **ounces fat-free frozen whipped topping, thawed**
- ½ **cup (2 ounces) toasted coconut**

Preheat the oven to 350°F. Coat a 13" × 9" baking dish with cooking spray.

In a large bowl, combine the cake mix and pineapple. Pour into the prepared baking dish.

Bake for 20 minutes, or until a wooden pick inserted in the center comes out almost clean. Cool completely on a rack.

Evenly spread the whipped topping over the cake. Sprinkle with the coconut. Cover and refrigerate until ready to serve.

Makes 16 servings

Per serving: *149 calories, 2 g protein, 30 g carbo-hydrate, 2 g fat, 0 mg cholesterol, 200 mg sodium, 0 g dietary fiber*

Diet Exchanges: *0 milk, 0 vegetable, 0 fruit, 2 carbohydrate, 0 meat, ½ fat*

2 Carb Choices

SHOPPING SAVVY

A Better Brownie

Craving a little something sweet but don't want the fat? Why not whip up a batch of No Pudge! Fudge Brownie Mix. Simply add fat-free yogurt (and maybe a little vanilla extract), and in no time, you'll have rich, fudgy brownies without all the guilt. Choose your flavor: Original, Cappuccino, Mint, or Raspberry. One 2" square brownie weighs in at about 110 calories, and no fat. Look for No Pudge! Fudge Brownie mixes in supermarkets or online at www.nopudge.com.

Photo courtesy of No Pudge

Orange Gelatin Cake

—Joan Harvey, Rockland, Maine

"This cake keeps well in an airtight container. Watch it disappear, just like your pounds will!"

Prep time: 25 minutes; Cook time: 1 hour

1 **package (18½ ounces) yellow cake mix (no pudding in mix)**

1 **package (3 ounces) sugar-free low-calorie orange gelatin**

⅔ **cup orange juice**

½ **cup vegetable oil**

4 **large or 5 medium eggs**

   Zest of 1 orange

   Confectioners' sugar

Preheat the oven to 350°F. Coat a 10" tube pan with cooking spray.

In a large bowl, combine the cake mix and gelatin. In a medium bowl, combine the orange juice, oil, eggs, and orange zest. Add to the cake mixture and beat with an electric mixer on medium speed for 3 minutes, or until thoroughly combined. Pour into the prepared pan.

Bake for 1 hour, or until a wooden pick inserted in the center comes out clean. Cool in the pan on a rack. When cool, invert onto a serving plate and dust lightly with confectioners' sugar.

Makes 16 servings

Per serving: *248 calories, 5 g protein, 27 g carbohydrate, 12 g fat, 55 mg cholesterol, 370 mg sodium, 0 g dietary fiber*

Diet Exchanges: *0 milk, 0 vegetable, 0 fruit, 2 carbohydrate, 0 meat, 2 fat*

2 Carb Choices

Kitchen Tip

For an extra-special touch, Joan suggests placing a large, clean paper doily on top of the cake before sprinkling with the confectioners' sugar, to create a lovely patterned effect.

Reduced-Fat Chocolate Cake

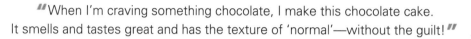

213 Calories

—Rita Schwass, Kirkwood, Illinois

"When I'm craving something chocolate, I make this chocolate cake. It smells and tastes great and has the texture of 'normal'—without the guilt!"

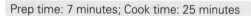

Prep time: 7 minutes; Cook time: 25 minutes

- 1 box (1 lb., 2.25 ounces) chocolate cake mix
- 1 cup water
- ¾ cup liquid egg substitute
- ½ cup applesauce
- ⅓ cup fat-free half-and-half

Preheat the oven to 350°F. Coat a 13" × 9" baking pan with cooking spray and dust lightly with flour.

In a large bowl, combine the cake mix, water, egg substitute, applesauce, and half-and-half. Beat with an electric mixer on low speed for 30 seconds. Increase the speed to medium and beat for 2 minutes. Pour into the prepared pan.

Bake for 25 minutes, or until a wooden pick inserted in the center comes out clean. Cool on a rack.

Makes 12 servings

Per serving: *213 calories, 5 g protein, 33 g carbohydrate, 7 g fat, 5 mg cholesterol, 390 mg sodium, 1 g dietary fiber*

Diet Exchanges: *0 milk, 0 vegetable, 0 fruit, 2 carbohydrate, 0 meat, 1 fat*

2 Carb Choices

Heather's First Cake

—Heather Balentine, Emory, Texas

*"*This recipe helped me a lot!*"*

Prep time: 15 minutes; Cook time: 25 minutes

2 **cups all-purpose flour**

1½ **cups sugar**

¼ **cup + 2 tablespoons unsweetened cocoa powder**

1 **teaspoon baking soda**

Pinch of salt

1 **cup buttermilk**

⅓ **cup oil**

3 **eggs**

1 **teaspoon vanilla extract**

1 **tablespoon confectioners' sugar (optional)**

Preheat the oven to 375°F. Coat a 13" × 9" baking pan with cooking spray.

In a large bowl, combine the flour, sugar, cocoa powder, baking soda, and salt.

In a medium bowl, combine the buttermilk, oil, eggs, and vanilla extract. Add to the flour mixture and stir to combine. Pour into the prepared pan.

Bake for 25 minutes, or until a wooden pick inserted in the center comes out clean. Cool completely in the pan on a rack. Tap the confectioners' sugar over the top, if using.

16 servings

Per serving: *196 calories, 4 g protein, 33 g carbohydrate, 6 g fat, 40 mg cholesterol, 105 mg sodium, 1 g dietary fiber*

Diet Exchanges: *0 milk, 0 vegetable, 0 fruit, 2 carbohydrate, 0 meat, 1 fat*

2 Carb Choices

Chocolate-Walnut Cake

—Huguette English, Beaverbrook, New Brunswick, Canada

" I love having dessert after my supper, and this cake leaves me satisfied. *"*

Prep time: 10 minutes; Cook time: 20 minutes

1¼ cups all-purpose flour

¾ cup sugar

¼ cup unsweetened cocoa powder

1 teaspoon baking powder

1 teaspoon baking soda

1 cup hot water

¼ cup butter or margarine

1 large egg

1 teaspoon vanilla extract

⅓ cup fat-free caramel sundae sauce

⅓ cup chopped walnuts

Preheat the oven to 350°F. Coat a 9" × 9" baking pan with cooking spray.

In a large bowl, combine the flour, sugar, cocoa powder, baking powder, and baking soda.

In a medium bowl, combine the water, butter or margarine, egg, and vanilla extract. Add to the flour mixture and stir to combine thoroughly. Pour into the prepared pan.

Bake for 20 minutes, or until a wooden pick inserted in the center comes out clean. Cool in the pan on a rack. When cool, slice into servings, place on dessert plates, drizzle with the sauce, and sprinkle with the walnuts.

Makes 16 servings

Per serving: *140 calories, 2 g protein, 23 g carbohydrate, 5 g fat, 20 mg cholesterol, 85 mg sodium, 1 g dietary fiber*

Diet Exchanges: *0 milk, 0 vegetable, 0 fruit, 1½ carbohydrate, 0 meat, 1 fat*

1½ Carb Choices

Strawberry Pie

—Ashley Wondra, Charlotte, North Carolina

*" My husband and I love this treat! It is a good, healthy dessert.
We don't feel guilty eating it because it is mostly fruit. "*

Prep time: 10 minutes; Chill time: 1 hour

- **1 prepared graham cracker pie crust**
- **1 can (20 ounces) strawberry pie filling**
- **1 pint fresh or thawed frozen strawberries, hulled and sliced, with some reserved for garnish**
- **8 ounces fat-free frozen whipped topping, thawed**

Kitchen Tip

Ashley notes that this pie tastes the best when it's served chilled. Chilling the pie gives the flavors a chance to blend.

Alternately layer the pie filling and strawberries in the prepared crust. Top with the whipped topping. Garnish with any remaining strawberry slices. Refrigerate for at least 1 hour before serving.

Makes 8 servings

Per serving: *273 calories, 1 g protein, 47 g carbohydrate, 7 g fat, 0 mg cholesterol, 190 mg sodium, 2 g dietary fiber*

Diet Exchanges: *0 milk, 0 vegetable, 0 fruit, 3 carbohydrate, 0 meat, 1 fat*

3 Carb Choices

SHOPPING SAVVY

Cute Fruit

Getting enough fruit servings just got easier and a lot more fun. You'll love Melissa's Pixie Tangerines; they're sweet, petite, and easy to peel and eat (no seeds). Weighing in at about 3 ounces each, they're also easy to tote—tuck a couple into a lunchbox or purse for a quick, nutritious snack. Their short season runs from March to May, and one Pixie

Tangerine has about 50 calories. They're available in most supermarkets. For a store locator, go to www.melissas.com.

Photo courtesy of Melissa's

No-Bake Cheese Pie

—Janet Label, Laval, Quebec, Canada

300 Calories

*"*This is one of my family's favorite desserts, which I save
for special occasions instead of baking a cake.*"*

Prep time: 5 minutes; Chill time: 2 hours

6 ounces reduced-fat cream cheese

1 cup fat-free sour cream

¼ cup fat-free milk

1 package (4-serving size) sugar-free instant vanilla pudding mix

1 reduced-fat prepared graham cracker pie crust (9")

1 can (20 ounces) light cherry pie filling

In a blender, combine the cream cheese, sour cream, and milk. Process to mix thoroughly. Place in a large bowl. Stir in the pudding mix. Pour the mixture into the prepared crust and smooth the top. Top with the pie filling. Cover and refrigerate for at least 2 hours before serving.

Makes 8 servings

Per serving: *300 calories, 6 g protein, 51 g carbohydrate, 9 g fat, 5 mg cholesterol, 500 mg sodium, 0 g dietary fiber*

Diet Exchanges: *½ milk, 0 vegetable, 1 fruit, 2 carbohydrate, 0 meat, 1½ fat*

3½ Carb Choices

SECRETS OF WEIGHT-LOSS WINNERS

• Replace oil with applesauce in muffins and other baked goods.

—**Heidi Kraemer, Vancouver, British Columbia, Canada**

• I find that looking for vegetarian recipes from other countries offers a variety of tastes and textures that satisfy without meat.

—**Linda Nichols, Seattle, Washington**

• In the evenings when you want something sweet, like chocolate, have a cup of low-fat hot chocolate or a cup of coffee with some chocolate creamer. It is low in calories and fat.

—**Sandra Myers, Bradenton, Florida**

Chocolate Peanut Butter Pie

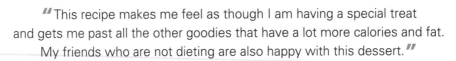

265 Calories

—Andrea King, Eaton Rapids, Michigan

*"This recipe makes me feel as though I am having a special treat
and gets me past all the other goodies that have a lot more calories and fat.
My friends who are not dieting are also happy with this dessert."*

Prep time: 10 minutes; Cook time: 3 minutes;
Chill time: overnight

1¾ cups fat-free milk

⅓ cup reduced-fat peanut butter
(not fat-free as it won't set up)

1 package (2.1 ounces) sugar-free instant
chocolate pudding mix

1 cup light frozen whipped topping,
thawed

1 prepared reduced-fat graham cracker
or chocolate cookie pie crust (9")

Chocolate shavings (optional)

In a large microwaveable bowl, combine the milk and peanut butter. Cover with plastic wrap and microwave at 50% power for 3 minutes, or until the peanut butter is melted. Stir until smooth. Add the pudding mix and stir until thickened. Gently fold in the whipped topping. Spoon the mixture into the pie crust and smooth the top. Cover and refrigerate overnight.

Top each serving with chocolate shavings (if using). Serve chilled.

Makes 8 servings

Per serving: *265 calories, 8 g protein, 34 g carbohydrate, 9 g fat, 2 mg cholesterol, 275 mg sodium, 2 g dietary fiber*

Diet Exchanges: *½ milk, 0 vegetable, 0 fruit, 1½ carbohydrate, ½ meat, 1½ fat*

2 Carb Choices

Kitchen Tip

For an easy flavor variation, Andrea suggests substituting sugar-free instant vanilla pudding mix for the chocolate.

It Worked for Me!

Jean Adam

VITAL STATS

Weight lost: 65 pounds

Time to goal: 3 years

Unique secret to success:
Walking away from unhealthy desserts and snacks; just because there are doughnuts on a plate does not mean I have to eat one.

Affirmation: *"I want to live a long and healthy life."*

Jean had been heavy since childhood. When she developed heart failure 3 years ago, she felt that she had no choice but to lose weight. Her success has changed—and literally saved—her life.

"I never had a problem with fast food or junk snacks—a weakness for home-baked things was what kept the pounds on me for years. If I baked a cake for any reason, I would have to have a slice.

"When I was diagnosed with heart failure, I got really scared. I knew things had to change, but I wasn't sure what I was going to do about it. I was hospitalized for a week and lost 13 pounds, which both surprised and inspired me.

"A hospital nutritionist taught me about portion sizes. I still use the palm of my hand to gauge a serving of meat. After I went home, I didn't join any special weight-loss programs, and I really didn't think about dropping pounds. I focused more on becoming healthier in general and cutting down on salt in particular.

"I eat a lot of vegetables and fruit now, and I avoid sauces and gravies. My health has improved; I still take medicine for my heart, but I can move so much better than I used to. I notice that I don't get winded as easily. I also do some toning exercises every morning, including simple leg lifts and sit-ups. I feel a bit stronger now, and I definitely think it's because of my morning routine.

"What surprised me most is that losing weight was not a hardship. It's just changing your way of thinking about food in order to have a better life. After my health scare, I really wanted to be able to participate in my life again—and now I can. My husband and I even go dancing every other week or so, allowing me to get in some fun, romantic exercise that we both enjoy."

Peanut Butter Pie

288 Calories

—Brookie Matheos, Ayden, North Carolina

"When I just have to have something sweet, this is it, and it's not too fattening."

Prep time: 15 minutes; Chill time: 4 hours

- ½ cup reduced-fat peanut butter
- 4 ounces fat-free cream cheese
- 4 ounces reduced-fat cream cheese
- ½ cup fat-free sweetened condensed milk
- 2 tablespoons lemon juice
- 1 cup light frozen whipped topping, thawed
- 5 tablespoons mini chocolate chips
- 1 prepared reduced-fat chocolate cookie pie crust (9")

In a large bowl, combine the peanut butter, fat-free cream cheese, and reduced-fat cream cheese. Beat with an electric mixer on medium speed until smooth. Gradually beat in the milk and lemon juice.

Gently fold in the whipped topping and 4 tablespoons of the chocolate chips. Spoon into the pie crust and smooth the top. Sprinkle the remaining 1 tablespoon chocolate chips over the top. Cover and refrigerate for at least 4 hours.

Makes 10 servings

Per serving: *288 calories, 9 g protein, 42 g carbohydrate, 11 g fat, 8 mg cholesterol, 330 mg sodium, 1 g dietary fiber*

Diet Exchanges: *0 milk, 0 vegetable, 0 fruit, 3 carbohydrate, 1 meat, 2 fat*

3 Carb Choices

Kitchen Tip

If you prefer a firmer texture, Brookie suggests letting the pie chill overnight.

Easy Entertaining

Shakes and Smoothies

Appetizers, Pizzas, Tortillas, and Sandwiches

Grills, Casseroles, and Chilis

Mixed Fruit Slushes

—**Mildred Kihn, Sacramento, California**

"I have this for breakfast every morning. It gives me my morning start and helps carry me over until lunch."

Prep time: 2 minutes

1 can (20 ounces) pineapple chunks
1 can (15 ounces) mixed fruit
1 cup frozen strawberries
1 medium banana

In a blender, combine the pineapple (with juice), mixed fruit (with juice), strawberries, and banana. Blend until smooth.

Makes 8 servings

Per serving: *62 calories, 1 g protein, 16 g carbohydrate, 0 g fat, 0 mg cholesterol, 7 mg sodium, 2 g dietary fiber*

Diet Exchanges: *0 milk, 0 vegetable, 1 fruit, 0 carbohydrate, 0 meat, 0 fat*

1 Carb Choice

Berry Smoothies

—**Cindy Hochstrasser, Meridian, Idaho**

"I'm just starting a weight-loss regimen, and this drink is my choice for breakfast or an afternoon snack. My husband and best friend beg me to make them constantly!"

Prep time: 2 minutes

1 can (16 ounces) water- or juice-packed peaches
8 ounces raspberry yogurt
8 ounces frozen mixed berries, such as strawberries, blueberries, and blackberries
½ cup frozen blueberries
1½ cups apple juice

In a blender, combine the peaches (with juice), yogurt, mixed berries, blueberries, and apple juice. Blend on high speed until pureed.

Makes 8 servings

Per serving: *77 calories, 2 g protein, 18 g carbohydrate, 0 g fat, 1 mg cholesterol, 22 mg sodium, 2 g dietary fiber*

Diet Exchanges: *0 milk, 0 vegetable, 1 fruit, 0 carbohydrate, 0 meat, 0 fat*

1 Carb Choice

Mixed Fruit Slush (front) and Berry Smoothie (rear)

Banana Smoothies

119 Calories

—**Christine Obrien, Torrington, Connecticut**

"This has a fantastic taste, especially during the hot summer months."

Prep time: 1 minute

> **2 bananas**
> **2 cups 1% milk**
> **1–2 tablespoons chocolate or other flavor syrup**
> **½ cup ice cubes**

In a food processor or blender, combine the bananas, milk, chocolate syrup, and ice cubes. Process until frothy.

Makes 4 servings

Per serving: *119 calories, 5 g protein, 23 g carbohydrate, 1 g fat, 5 mg cholesterol, 65 mg sodium, 2 g dietary fiber*

Diet Exchanges: *½ milk, 0 vegetable, 1 fruit, 0 carbohydrate, 0 meat, 0 fat*

1½ Carb Choices

SHOPPING SAVVY

Soy Good!

If you're looking for a way to get more soy into your life or if you prefer not to drink dairy milk, check out Pacific Select Low Fat Soy Milk. Made from organic soybeans, it's sold in aseptic packs in plain and vanilla flavors. The company also produces a line

of nondairy nut and grain beverages. Choose from almond, hazelnut, rice, oat, and multigrain. Pacific Select Low Fat Soy Milk is sold in the natural foods sections of many supermarkets and at Whole Foods or Wild Oats. For a store locator, visit www.pacificfoods.com.

Photo courtesy of Pacific Foods

Chilly Hot Chocolate

—Laura Kendrick, Lawndale, North Carolina

" This tastes just like a chocolate milkshake. You can add more ice to help get your water in, which I have a problem with. It's also very filling. *"*

Prep time: 4 minutes

1 cup ice
½ cup fat-free milk
1 packet sugar-free instant hot cocoa mix
   Light whipped cream for topping (optional)

In a blender, combine the ice, milk, and hot cocoa mix. Process for 1 minute, or until blended. Top with the whipped cream, if using.

Makes 2 servings

Per serving: *45 calories, 4 g protein, 7 g carbohydrate, 0 g fat, 2 mg cholesterol, 119 mg sodium, 0 g dietary fiber*

Diet Exchanges: *½ milk, 0 vegetable, 0 fruit, 0 carbohydrate, 0 meat, 0 fat*

½ **Carb Choice**

Photo on page 162

Layered Bean Dip (front) and Sassy Salsa (rear)

Layered Bean Dip

—Jill Mondry, Grand Forks, North Dakota

"This is a great party dip. No one can guess it's low calorie!"

Prep time: 10 minutes; Cook time: 20 minutes

- 1 can (14–19 ounces) fat-free refried beans
- 1 can (14–19 ounces) black beans, rinsed and drained
- ½ cup reduced-fat sour cream
- 1 cup prepared salsa
- ½ cup (2 ounces) shredded reduced-fat Mexican blend or Cheddar cheese
- Chopped fresh cilantro (optional)

Preheat the oven to 375°F.

In an 8" baking dish, combine the refried beans and black beans. Spread to cover the bottom of the dish. Spread the sour cream over the beans. Top with the salsa and cheese.

Cover and bake for 20 minutes, or until hot and bubbly. Garnish with the cilantro, if using.

Makes 2½ cups

Per tablespoon: *24 calories, 1 g protein, 3 g carbohydrate, 1 g fat, 1 mg cholesterol, 104 mg sodium, 1 g dietary fiber*

Diet Exchanges: *0 milk, 0 vegetable, 0 fruit, ½ carbohydrate, 0 meat, 0 fat*

½ Carb Choice

Kitchen Tip

Jill suggests serving this dip with pita chips or baked tortilla chips.

Sassy Salsa

—Ronni Fox, Buffalo, New York

"I love to take this to parties so I am not tempted by unhealthy snacks."

Prep time: 20 minutes; Stand time: 15 minutes

- 5 ripe tomatoes, seeded and finely chopped
- 1 small red onion, finely chopped
- ½ cup mandarin orange segments
- ¼ cup thinly sliced celery
- 2 tablespoons chopped green olives
- 1 teaspoon olive oil
- Salt, to taste
- 1 lime, halved
- 1 or 2 small pickled jalapeño chile peppers

In a large bowl, combine the tomatoes, onion, oranges, celery, olives, oil, and salt. Squeeze the juice from the lime halves over the top. Add the chile peppers and stir to combine. Cover and let stand for 15 minutes.

Makes 4 cups

Per tablespoon: *5 calories, 0 g protein, 1 g carbohydrate, 0 g fat, 0 mg cholesterol, 9 mg sodium, 0 g dietary fiber*

Diet Exchanges: *0 milk, 0 vegetable, 0 fruit, 0 carbohydrate, 0 meat, 0 fat*

0 Carb Choices

Bacon Dip

—Huguette English, Beaverbrook, New Brunswick, Canada

"This recipe means I don't have to deny myself good food."

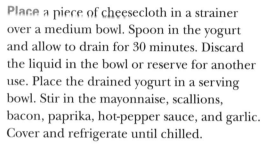

Prep time: 30 minutes

16 ounces fat-free plain yogurt

6 tablespoons low-fat mayonnaise

¼ cup finely chopped scallions

¼ cup cooked turkey bacon pieces

¼ teaspoon paprika

8 drops hot-pepper sauce, or to taste

2 cloves garlic, minced

Place a piece of cheesecloth in a strainer over a medium bowl. Spoon in the yogurt and allow to drain for 30 minutes. Discard the liquid in the bowl or reserve for another use. Place the drained yogurt in a serving bowl. Stir in the mayonnaise, scallions, bacon, paprika, hot-pepper sauce, and garlic. Cover and refrigerate until chilled.

Makes 1½ cups

Per tablespoon: *25 calories, 1 g protein, 2 g carbohydrate, 2 g fat, 3 mg cholesterol, 62 mg sodium, 0 g dietary fiber*

Diet Exchanges: *0 milk, 0 vegetable, 0 fruit, 0 carbohydrate, 0 meat, ½ fat*

0 Carb Choices

Kitchen Tip

Huguette likes to serve this dip with baked tortilla chips.

Bean Dip

—Patti Tan, Richmond, British Columbia, Canada

"I'm a big proponent of eating beans—they are a great source of protein, fiber, and folic acid. Unfortunately, many Americans cook beans with fat or meats. Try this lighter bean recipe with some whole wheat pita bread, flatbread, or rye crackers."

Prep time: 5 minutes

- 2 **cups cooked beans, such as cannellini, pinto, or great Northern**
- 2 **tablespoons extra-virgin olive oil**
- 2 **tablespoons prepared horseradish**
- ¼ **cup finely chopped onion**
- ¼ **teaspoon salt**
- 2 **scallions, trimmed and finely chopped**

In a blender or food processor, combine the beans, oil, horseradish, and onion. Process until smooth, adding a little water if necessary. Sprinkle with the salt. Garnish with the scallions.

Makes 1½ cups

Per tablespoon: *33 calories, 1 g protein, 4 g carbohydrate, 1 g fat, 0 mg cholesterol, 29 mg sodium, 1 g dietary fiber*

Diet Exchanges: *0 milk, 0 vegetable, 0 fruit, ½ carbohydrate, 0 meat, 0 fat*

½ **Carb Choice**

It Worked for Me!

Barbara Sloan

VITAL STATS

Weight lost: 50 pounds

Time to goal: 15 months

Unique secret to success: Vowing never to "diet", I changed my attitude instead.

Affirmation: *"Losing weight will be fun and easy for me."*

Barbara weighed 124 pounds as a teen, but was an adult and wore a size 16 when she started trying to lose weight. She was down to around 160 pounds at her son's wedding. That was when she had just had enough. She decided to get rid of the rest of the weight—for good.

"I was committed to the idea that if I just ate right, the pounds would come off naturally. I wanted to be able to stay on the same program when I finished, so that I would never regain the weight again.

"It was important to me to make this a fun process. For me, that meant focusing on learning new ways to build meals. I had already gone mostly vegetarian due to my high cholesterol levels, so I just continued on that path and cut out any remaining meat in my diet. Vegetarian cooking helped me cut my total cholesterol levels and triglycerides dramatically, while also raising my 'good' HDL levels. No cholesterol medicine for me!

"I've developed a class for our local adult education program where I'll be sharing all I've learned about weight loss—my doctor has even asked me for business cards so she can send her patients to my class!

"Even though I know how important it is, I really find exercise boring. I refuse to join a gym! Instead I follow an 8-minute resistance training program at home, using free weights and ankle weights. I can now open jars more easily and my calves look more toned. I also really enjoy walking. Thanks to my daily walks, I now wear a size 4–6! When I go out alone, I will often use a tape player and listen to a recorded book. I find that a juicy mystery story will get me motivated for my next walking session—I only listen to the tapes when I'm walking, so if I want to know what happened, I have to get out and exercise."

Bacon Asparagus Wraps

—Gregory Smith, Washington, D.C.

"This is low-calorie, fast, delicious, and visually appealing. One or two sheaves can be a meal or used at a dinner party as a stunning vegetable. "

Prep time: 7 minutes; Cook time: 7 minutes

24 spears asparagus
8 slices low-fat turkey bacon
3 tablespoons sesame seeds, lightly toasted
   Olive oil in spritzer
1 tablespoon soy sauce

Preheat the broiler.

Wrap 3 spears of asparagus around the middle with a strip of bacon. Secure with a wooden pick. Repeat to use the remaining asparagus and bacon.

Place the sesame seeds in a shallow dish. Spritz the asparagus wraps with olive oil and roll in the sesame seeds. Place on a baking sheet. Drizzle with soy sauce.

Broil on the top rack for 7 minutes, or until the bacon is cooked and the asparagus is tender-crisp and light green.

Makes 8 servings

Per serving: *73 calories, 4 g protein, 4 g carbohydrate, 4 g fat, 12 mg cholesterol, 348 mg sodium, 1 g dietary fiber*

Diet Exchanges: *0 milk, ½ vegetable, 0 fruit, 0 carbohydrate, ½ meat, ½ fat*

½ Carb Choice

Kitchen Tip

Gregory notes that this recipe can be spiced up with the addition of red-pepper flakes, ginger, or orange juice and zest for alternate flavors.

Toasted Vegetable Tacos

—Barbara Whysong, Concord, California

"This recipe is healthy, tasty, and takes only minutes to prepare. I use toasted flour tortillas frequently. Toasting them makes the outside crisp and the inside soft."

Prep time: 5 minutes; Cook time: 2 minutes

½–1 cup chopped fresh vegetables, such as broccoli, snap peas, green beans, and red bell pepper
1 flour tortilla (8" diameter)
1 teaspoon raspberry chipotle sauce
1 tablespoon shredded taco cheese mix

Place the vegetables in a microwaveable bowl. Cover with plastic wrap and microwave for 1 minute, or until tender-crisp.

Bend the tortilla until the edges meet, but do not fold. Carefully toast in a toaster (see Kitchen Tip).

Spread the chipotle sauce on the tortilla. Top with the vegetables and sprinkle with the cheese.

Makes 1 serving

Per serving: *181 calories, 7 g protein, 28 g carbohydrate, 5 g fat, 6 mg cholesterol, 341 mg sodium, 1 g dietary fiber*

Diet Exchanges: *0 milk, ½ vegetable, 0 fruit, 1½ carbohydrate, ½ meat, ½ fat*

1½ Carb Choices

Kitchen Tip

Before toasting the tortilla, be sure that it will safely fit into your toaster. If it should get stuck, unplug the toaster and allow it to cool before attempting to remove the tortilla.

Meatless Tacos

—Emily Bickell, Kitchener, Ontario, Canada

*"*With this and other vegetarian recipes, I have lost 10 pounds.*"*

Prep time: 10 minutes; Cook time: 15 minutes

1 tablespoon vegetable oil

4 large button mushrooms, finely chopped

1 small onion, finely chopped

1 cup canned black beans, rinsed and drained

¼ cup water

½ package (about 1½ tablespoons) taco seasoning

8 taco shells

⅓ cup shredded lettuce

⅓ cup chopped tomato

⅓ cup chopped green bell pepper

⅓ cup (1½ ounces) shredded reduced-fat Cheddar or Monterey Jack cheese

¼ cup sliced black olives (optional)

Salsa, to taste

Reduced-fat sour cream (optional)

Preheat the oven or a toaster oven to 350°F.

Heat the oil in a large skillet over medium heat. Add the mushrooms and onion and cook, stirring frequently, for 3 minutes, or until the onion is translucent. Add the beans and cook, stirring, for 1 minute. Add the water and taco seasoning. Reduce the heat to low and simmer for 5 to 10 minutes.

Place the taco shells on a baking sheet. Bake for 5 minutes, or until warmed. Remove to a serving plate. Evenly divide the bean mixture among the taco shells. Top with the lettuce, tomato, bell pepper, cheese, olives (if using), salsa, and sour cream (if using).

Makes 8 servings

Per serving: *122 calories, 4 g protein, 15 g carbohydrate, 5 g fat, 1 mg cholesterol, 280 mg sodium, 3 g dietary fiber*

Diet Exchanges: *0 milk, 0 vegetable, 0 fruit, 1 carbohydrate, ½ meat, 1 fat*

1 Carb Choice

Burritos

—Maureen Dye, Holmes Beach, Florida

"This is a very filling dinner, with a small amount of calories and fat. The whole wheat lavash bread really fills you totally."

Prep time: 10 minutes; Cook time: 11 minutes

- ½ **pound lean ground turkey**
- 2 **tablespoons taco seasoning**
- 1 **can fat-free refried beans**
- 1 **whole wheat lavash bread, warmed**
- ⅓ **cup chopped tomatoes**
- ¼ **cup salsa**
- ¼ **cup (1 ounce) shredded reduced-fat Cheddar or Monterey Jack cheese**
- ¼ **cup fat-free sour cream**

Heat a large skillet coated with cooking spray over medium heat. Add the turkey and taco seasoning, following the package directions, and cook, stirring occasionally, for 8 minutes, or until the turkey is no longer pink.

Place the beans in a microwaveable bowl. Cover with plastic wrap and microwave for 3 minutes, or until heated through. Add to the skillet with the turkey and stir to combine.

Place the lavash on a plate. Top with the turkey mixture, tomatoes, salsa, cheese, and sour cream. Cut into 4 slices and serve.

Makes 4 servings

Per serving: *253 calories, 19 g protein, 30 g carbohydrate, 6 g fat, 48 mg cholesterol, 874 mg sodium, 6 g dietary fiber*

Diet Exchanges: *0 milk, ½ vegetable, 0 fruit, 1½ carbohydrate, 2 meat, ½ fat*

2 Carb Choices

Kitchen Tip

Maureen notes that you can microwave the assembled burritos to heat them through before topping with the salsa and sour cream.

Light Spinach Roll-Ups

—Nancy Ballard, Johnson City, Tennessee

Prep time: 10 minutes; Chill time: 2 hours

1 cup light mayonnaise

1 cup fat-free sour cream

1 can (5½ ounces) sliced water chestnuts, drained

1 packet (1 ounce) ranch dip mix

4 scallions, finely chopped (white and green parts)

¼ cup crumbled cooked bacon

2 boxes (10 ounces each) frozen chopped spinach, thawed and squeezed dry

10 fat-free flour tortillas (12" in diameter)

In a medium bowl, combine the mayonnaise, sour cream, water chestnuts, dip mix, scallions, and bacon. Add the spinach and stir to combine. Evenly divide the spinach mixture among the tortillas, spreading to within 1" of edges. Roll the tortillas and place in a zip-top food storage bag. Refrigerate for at least 2 hours or overnight.

Slice into pinwheels just before serving.

Makes 10 servings

Per serving: *251 calories, 7 g protein, 34 g carbohydrate, 11 g fat, 13 mg cholesterol, 770 mg sodium, 4 g dietary fiber*

Diet Exchanges: *½ milk, 1 vegetable, 0 fruit, 1½ carbohydrate, 0 meat, 2 fat*

2 Carb Choices

SHOPPING SAVVY

A Zesty Spread

Wake up your sandwich with a luscious spread that's low in fat, but merits a high-five in taste—French's GourMayo Flavored Light Mayonnaise. It's available in three exciting flavors: Wasabi Horseradish, Chipotle Chili, and Sun Dried Tomato, each with half the fat of regular mayo. French's GourMayo is sold in handy plastic squeeze bottles in most supermarkets.

Photo courtesy of French's

Easy Pizza Lite

—Lisa Gregory, McDonald, Tennessee

"I have a strong craving for pizza, and with this recipe, I get the taste without all the fat and calories. Since June, I have lost 50 pounds. I still have a long way to go, but recipes like this make it easier."

Prep time: 5 minutes; Cook time: 10 minutes

1 **flour tortilla (8" diameter)**

2 **tablespoons pizza sauce**

¼ **cup (1 ounce) shredded reduced-fat mozzarella cheese**

4 **thin slices turkey pepperoni**

Preheat the oven or toaster oven to 350°F.

Place the tortilla on a baking sheet. Spread the sauce over the tortilla. Top with the cheese and pepperoni.

Bake for 10 minutes, or until the cheese is melted.

Makes 1 serving

Per serving: *375 calories, 31 g protein, 31 g carbohydrate, 14 g fat, 83 mg cholesterol, 1,664 mg sodium, 0 g dietary fiber*

Diet Exchanges: *0 milk, 0 vegetable, 0 fruit, 2 carbohydrate, 4 meat, ½ fat*

2 Carb Choices

Kitchen Tip

If you're watching your sodium intake, substitute chopped fresh bell pepper, broccoli, or other veggies for the turkey pepperoni.

SECRETS OF WEIGHT-LOSS WINNERS

• I've found that taking a photograph of myself and taping it to the refrigerator door is extremely helpful to keep me focused and reduce impulse eating.

—**Catherine Rome, Basking Ridge, New Jersey**

• Brush your teeth often; you won't want to put food in a fresh mouth.

—**Earlene Othling, Deshler, Nebraska**

Easy Pizza Lite (left) and Tortilla Broccoli Pizza, (page 236; right)

Tortilla Broccoli Pizza

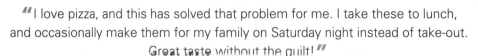

—Janet Ferree, Kutztown, Pennsylvania

"I love pizza, and this has solved that problem for me. I take these to lunch, and occasionally make them for my family on Saturday night instead of take-out. Great taste without the guilt!"

Prep time: 5 minutes; Cook time: 8 minutes

2 small flour tortillas (8" diameter)
½ cup marinara sauce
1 cup broccoli florets
¼ cup (1 ounce) shredded reduced-fat mozzarella cheese

Preheat the oven to 400°F.

Place the tortillas on a pizza pan or baking sheet. Spread ¼ cup of the sauce on each tortilla. Top each with ½ cup of the broccoli and 2 tablespoons of the cheese.

Bake for 8 minutes, or until the cheese is melted and the tortillas are slightly crisp.

Makes 2 servings

Per serving: *241 calories, 11 g protein, 35 g carbohydrate, 7 g fat, 7 mg cholesterol, 598 mg sodium, 4 g dietary fiber*

Diet Exchanges: *0 milk, ½ vegetable, 0 fruit, 2 carbohydrate, ½ meat, 1 fat*

2½ Carb Choices

Photo on page 235

Veggie Pizza

—Ellen Parodi, Philadelphia, Pennsylvania

"This is a filling snack or lunch that gives you the satisfaction of pizza without the fat. You can load as many veggies onto the muffin as it will hold, and you'll be surprised how much ⅛ cup shredded mozzarella really is when melted. It's a fairly healthy, guilt-free lunch. By the way, kids love it, too—at least mine always have!"

Prep time: 10 minutes; Cook time: 3 minutes

- **1 English muffin, split**
- **¼ cup tomato sauce**
- **¼ cup chopped mushrooms**
- **2 tablespoons chopped green bell pepper**
- **2 tablespoons chopped onion**
- **2 tablespoons shredded reduced-fat mozzarella cheese**

Preheat the oven or toaster oven to 350°F.

Toast the muffin halves. Evenly divide the sauce, mushrooms, bell pepper, onion, and cheese between the muffin halves.

Bake for 3 minutes, or until the cheese is melted.

Makes 1 serving

Per serving: *225 calories, 10 g protein, 41 g carbohydrate, 3 g fat, 6 mg cholesterol, 717 mg sodium, 4 g dietary fiber*

Diet Exchanges: *0 milk, 3 vegetable, 0 fruit, 2 carbohydrate, ½ meat, 0 fat*

3 Carb Choices

Tuna Patties

—Monica Richards, Pearland, Texas

"These tuna patties are a great alternative to the 'normal' cold tuna salad, but still healthy with omega 3's. They satisfy you with protein!"

Prep time: 8 minutes; Cook time: 7 minutes

1 **can (12 ounces) albacore tuna, drained**

2 **small scallions (green and white parts), finely chopped**

1 **egg**

1 **egg white**

¼ **teaspoon salt**

2 **slices low-fat Swiss or American cheese**

2 **whole wheat English muffins, split**

2 **large leaves lettuce**

4 **slices tomato**

In a medium bowl, combine the tuna, scallions, egg, egg white, and salt. Form into 2 patties.

Heat a medium skillet coated with cooking spray over medium heat. Add the patties and cook for 2 minutes on each side, or until lightly browned.

Meanwhile, place 1 slice of cheese on 2 of the muffin halves. Toast in the toaster oven until the cheese is melted. Top the other muffin halves with tuna patties. Top with the lettuce, tomato, and the remaining muffin halves.

Makes 2 servings

Per serving: *442 calories, 55 g protein, 32 g carbohydrate, 10 g fat, 183 mg cholesterol, 1,033 mg sodium, 5 g dietary fiber*

Diet Exchanges: *0 milk, ½ vegetable, 0 fruit, 2 carbohydrate, 8 meat, ½ fat*

2 Carb Choices

Soy Sloppy Joes

—June C. Clarks, Grove, Minnesota

"This is really good—tastes just like real sloppy Joes with meat!"

Prep time: 10 minutes; Cook time: 5 minutes

1 can (6 ounces) tomato paste

½ cup water

1 teaspoon dried oregano

1 teaspoon Worcestershire sauce

¼ teaspoon ground red pepper

1 teaspoon olive oil

2 cloves garlic, minced

1 onion, chopped

1 green bell pepper, chopped

2 cups soy crumbles

Salt, to taste (optional)

4 teaspoons prepared mustard (optional)

4 whole wheat rolls

4 leaves lettuce (optional)

In a small bowl, combine the tomato paste, water, oregano, Worcestershire sauce, and red pepper.

Heat the oil in a large skillet over medium-high heat. Add the garlic, onion, bell pepper, soy crumbles, and tomato paste mixture. Bring to a boil. Season with salt, if using. The sauce should be thick and spreadable. Add a little more water if a thinner consistency is desired.

Spread the mustard, if using, onto the bottoms of the rolls. Top with the soy-crumble mixture and lettuce, if using. Top with the roll tops.

Makes 6 servings

Per serving: *340 calories, 21 g protein, 35 g carbohydrate, 15 g fat, 0 mg cholesterol, 1,287 mg sodium, 9 g dietary fiber*

Diet Exchanges: *0 milk, 2 vegetable, 0 fruit, 1½ carbohydrate, 2 meat, 2½ fat*

2 Carb Choices

Kitchen Tip

June makes a batch of these sloppy Joes every 2 weeks. She wraps single servings and stores them in the freezer. At lunchtime, just microwave for 1 minute.

Vegetable Bagel

—Kristin King, Johnson City, Tennessee

" I love the taste of this, and since it is relatively low in calories and is very satisfying, I am not hungry for several hours. "

Prep time: 9 minutes; Cook time: 6 minutes

- **1 bagel, split**
- **1 tablespoon fat-free cream cheese**
- **⅓ cucumber, thinly sliced**
- **⅓ tomato, finely chopped**
- **1 portobello mushroom, thinly sliced**
- **2 slices reduced-fat or fat-free Swiss cheese**

Preheat the broiler.

Lightly toast the bagel in a toaster oven. Spread the cream cheese on each half of the bagel. Top each bagel half with cucumber, tomato, mushroom, and a slice of cheese. Place on a broiler-pan rack and broil for 4 minutes, or until the cheese is melted.

Makes 2 servings

Per serving: *119 calories, 9 g protein, 19 g carbohydrate, 1 g fat, 6 mg cholesterol, 207 mg sodium, 1 g dietary fiber*

Diet Exchanges: *0 milk, 1 vegetable, 0 fruit, 1 carbohydrate, 1 meat, 0 fat*

1 Carb Choice

SHOPPING SAVVY

Make Mine a Mini

Nothing beats the flavor and convenience of this adorable baby watermelon. Sold year-round, this is one

watermelon that will easily fit in the fridge or can travel to the beach. It's the ideal size for about four watermelon lovers, and it's seedless. The experts at Melissa's tell us to choose firm fruit that is heavy for its size and that yields slightly to pressure. Once cut, or if it's very ripe, store it in the fridge. Two cups of mini watermelon chunks (4 fruit servings) equals just 80 calories. Look for Melissa's Mini Watermelons in supermarkets. For a store locator, visit www.melissas.com.

Photo courtesy of Melissa's

It Worked for Me!

Wendy Oland

VITAL STATS

Weight lost: 42 pounds

Time to goal: 18 months

Unique secret to success: Taking weight loss very slowly—it's not a race!

Affirmation: *"Keeping busy is good for my body and my mind."*

Undergoing surgery and starting a new medication caused Wendy to gain weight—a not uncommon side effect of many medical treatments. Instead of letting the pounds pile on or neglecting her health, Wendy took control of her weight and her life.

"I just never wanted to weigh that much. The pounds were hard on my body, I could tell, and hard on my heart. I knew that I wanted to start eating better and get back in control. It just took some health warnings to give me the push I needed.

"I started having some stomach trouble and learned that I had gallstones. That was the excuse I needed to cut out most of the fat in my diet. I was a complete 'sweetaholic', so I also opted to stop eating sugar completely. I think this particular decision was harder on my friends and family than it was on me—my mother-in-law and even my friends just couldn't stand it when I would refuse a piece of cake or candy. It was difficult to explain to them, but I stayed strong and resisted persuasion. Since my weight loss, my husband has

actually apologized to me for bringing home tempting baked goods.

"Cutting out the sugar and the fat quickly made a big difference, and I never really had to count calories. I had tried it for a while, but it didn't seem to work for me. I just watched my portion sizes, cut back on the amount I was eating overall, and started walking for exercise. This was the magic combination for me.

"I had always walked, even at my heaviest, but when I decided to get serious about losing weight, I started using a walking program that you do in your house. I used an abdominal belt for resistance and a videotape, 5 or 6 days a week. I also added some weight training with hand-held weights. Now, I am not at the lowest weight of my life, but I am definitely at my most toned; my body is smaller than it's been before. I no longer weigh myself every day, but I make sure to step on the scale at least once a week to keep an eye on things. The fit of my clothes also helps keep me aware of maintaining my weight loss."

Savory Grilled Tomatoes

—Eileen Barringer, Leeds Point, New Jersey

"This is a nicer and more unique way to have a vegetable that's normally served cold and in a salad. The wonderful flavors make me feel less like I am dieting, and it's great to serve guests even if they are not watching their weight."

Prep time: 5 minutes; Cook time: 5 minutes

- **6 tomatoes, halved and seeded**
- **¾ teaspoon garlic powder**
- **12 leaves fresh basil**
- **¼ cup + 2 tablespoons reduced-fat crumbled blue cheese or feta cheese**

Preheat the grill to medium.

Pat the tomatoes dry with a paper towel. Coat with cooking spray. Top the cut sides of the tomato halves with garlic powder and basil leaves. Sprinkle with the cheese. Place on the grill rack and grill for 5 minutes, or until lightly browned, soft, and the cheese is bubbly.

Serve hot or at room temperature.

Makes 12 servings

Per serving: *22 calories, 2 g protein, 3 g carbohydrate, 1 g fat, 2 mg cholesterol, 64 mg sodium, 1 g dietary fiber*

Diet Exchanges: *0 milk, ½ vegetable, 0 fruit, 0 carbohydrate, 0 meat, 0 fat*

0 Carb Choices

Marinated Grilled Salmon

—Linda Crawford, Covington, Louisiana

"This recipe is very flavorful and imparts a feeling of satisfaction and fullness without being high in calories or fat. It is nutritionally valuable also."

Prep time: 5 minutes; Marinate time: 1 hour 30 minutes; Cook time: 10 minutes

¼ cup + 2 tablespoons low-sodium soy sauce

¼ cup + 2 tablespoons white Zinfandel wine

1 pound salmon steaks

1 teaspoon salt-free garlic and herb seasoning

In a shallow pan, combine the soy sauce and wine. Add the salmon and turn to coat both sides. Coat the top of the salmon with the garlic and herb seasoning. Cover and refrigerate for 45 minutes. Turn the salmon and coat the top with the seasoning. Cover and refrigerate for 45 minutes longer.

Coat a grill rack with cooking spray. Preheat the grill.

Turn the fish in the marinade, recoating both sides. Place on the grill and cook for 10 minutes, or until the fish flakes easily.

Makes 4 servings

Per serving: *180 calories, 23 g protein, 1 g carbohydrate, 7 g fat, 62 mg cholesterol, 664 mg sodium, 0 g dietary fiber*

Diet Exchanges: *0 milk, 0 vegetable, 0 fruit, 0 carbohydrate, 3 meat, ½ fat*

0 Carb Choices

COOKING FISH

Thin fillets like sole, haddock, catfish, and flounder are no more than ½" thick. They cook quickly, so keep a watchful eye. **Thick fillets** like cod, some snapper, center cuts of salmon, monkfish, orange roughy, and grouper average about 1½" thick. **Steaks,** including swordfish, tuna, mahi mahi, and salmon, are usually about 1" thick.

Times below vary according to the fat content and density of the fish used.

	Thin Fillets	Thick Fillets	Steaks
Broil	2–6 min, depending on thickness and proximity to broiler; place 4"–6" from broiler	10 min per 1" of thickness; place 4"–6" from broiler	10 min per 1" of thickness; place as close as possible to broiler
Grill	3–5 min; medium-hot fire	5–7 min; medium-hot fire	5–7 min; hot fire
Roast	About 6 min; 450°F	About 10 min per 1" of thickness: 450°F	About 10 min per 1" of thickness; 450°F

(shown with Zucchini and Tomatoes, page 154)

Caesar Kebabs

255 Calories

—Karen Preston, Stoney Creek, Ontario, Canada

" Grilled on the barbecue or broiled in the oven, these are very good! "

Prep time: 12 minutes; Cook time: 35–45 minutes

  4 **small potatoes, scrubbed and halved**
  1 **pound steak or boneless, skinless chicken breasts, cut into bite-size pieces**
  2 **medium red and/or green bell peppers, cut into chunks**
  1 **small onion, cut into chunks**
     Pinch of salt
     Pinch of ground black pepper
  ½ **cup light Caesar vinaigrette dressing**

Bring a medium pot of water to a boil over high heat. Add the potatoes and cook for 20 minutes, or until fork-tender.

Coat a grill rack or broiler-pan rack with cooking spray. Preheat the grill or broiler.

In a large bowl, combine the beef and/or chicken, potatoes, peppers, onion, salt, and pepper. Add the dressing and toss to coat. Alternately thread the meat and vegetables onto 4 metal skewers. Place on the prepared rack or pan and cook, turning occasionally, for 15 minutes for beef, 25 minutes for chicken, or until the meat is no longer pink.

Makes 4 servings

Per serving: *255 calories, 30 g protein, 30 g carbohydrate, 3 g fat, 66 mg cholesterol, 398 mg sodium, 4 g dietary fiber*

Diet Exchanges: *0 milk, 1 vegetable, 0 fruit, 1½ carbohydrate, 4 meat, 0 fat*

2 Carb Choices

Marinated Chicken

203 Calories

—Cindy Dupont, Shoreview, Minnesota

"This recipe helps me maintain a low-cal, high-protein diet. My family loves it!"

Prep time: 5 minutes; Marinate time: 30 minutes; Cook time: 20 minutes

4 **boneless, skinless chicken breast halves**
2 **tablespoons olive oil**
2 **tablespoons Worcestershire sauce**
2 **tablespoons balsamic vinegar**
1 **tablespoon minced garlic**
1 **tablespoon sugar**
2 **teaspoons dried basil**

Place the chicken in a 13" × 9" baking dish. Pierce the chicken in several places with a fork.

In a small bowl, combine the oil, Worcestershire sauce, vinegar, garlic, sugar, and basil. Pour over the chicken, turning the pieces to coat thoroughly. Cover and refrigerate for at least 30 minutes to blend the flavors.

Coat a grill rack with cooking spray. Preheat the grill.

Place the chicken on the grill and cook for 10 minutes per side, or until a thermometer inserted in the thickest portion registers 160°F and the juices run clear.

Makes 4 servings

Per serving: *203 calories, 26 g protein, 6 g carbohydrate, 7 g fat, 66 mg cholesterol, 149 mg sodium, 0 g dietary fiber*

Diet Exchanges: *0 milk, 0 vegetable, 0 fruit, ½ carbohydrate, 4 meat, 1 fat*

½ Carb Choice

--- Kitchen Tip ---

Cindy likes to serve this dish with roasted mixed vegetables.

Spinach-Mushroom Lasagna

214 Calories

—Barbara Sloan, Wallingford, Connecticut

*"*I have lost at least 30 pounds, without dieting, by making and eating great dishes like this.*"*

Prep time: 30 minutes; Cook time: 1 hour 15 minutes; Stand time: 10 minutes

1 pound fat-free ricotta cheese

2 packages (10 ounces each) frozen chopped spinach, thawed and squeezed dry

1 cup fat-free sour cream

1 egg

1 tablespoon Italian seasoning

1 sprig fresh rosemary, minced

¼ teaspoon salt

¼ teaspoon ground black pepper

1 onion, chopped

2 cloves garlic, minced

1 jar (28 ounces) spaghetti or pasta bake sauce

12 oven-ready lasagna noodles

10 ounces sliced mushrooms

1 cup (4 ounces) shredded low-fat mozzarella cheese

½ cup (2 ounces) grated Parmesan cheese

Preheat the oven to 425°F. Coat a 13" × 9" baking dish with cooking spray.

In a large bowl, combine the ricotta, spinach, sour cream, egg, Italian seasoning, rosemary, salt, and pepper.

Heat a small nonstick skillet coated with cooking spray over medium-high heat. Add the onion and garlic and cook, stirring frequently, for 5 minutes, or until the onion is soft. Stir into the ricotta mixture.

Spread a thin layer of the spaghetti sauce on the bottom of the prepared pan. Layer the noodles, mushrooms, and ricotta mixture, top with more sauce and repeat two more times, ending with sauce. Fill the sauce jar with water and pour over the top. Cover with foil.

Bake for 1 hour, adding more water, ¼ cup at a time, if needed. Remove the foil and sprinkle with the mozzarella and Parmesan. Bake for 10 minutes longer.

Let stand for 10 minutes before serving.

Makes 16 servings

Per serving: *214 calories, 13 g protein, 27 g carbohydrate, 6 g fat, 28 mg cholesterol, 442 mg sodium, 3 g dietary fiber*

Diet Exchanges: *0 milk, 1 vegetable, 0 fruit, 1½ carbohydrate, 1 meat, 1 fat*

2 Carb Choices

Kitchen Tip

Barbara wraps each piece of this lasagna individually, then freezes. That way, when she wants a good dinner in a hurry, she takes out one piece, adds salad and a veggie, and voilá! In 10 to 15 minutes, she has a great dinner with under 300 calories.

Ground Turkey Lasagna

267 Calories

—Jennifer Schuerer, Menasha, Wisconsin

"This recipe is a revised version of one of my favorite recipes of my mom's. Instead of using ground beef and other ingredients that contribute added fat, the low-fat substitutes still make it a tasty dish!"

Prep time: 30 minutes; Cook time: 45 minutes

1 pound ground turkey breast

1 can (14½ ounces) diced tomatoes

1 small onion, finely chopped

1 cup sliced mushrooms (fresh or canned)

1 clove garlic, minced

1 teaspoon dried oregano

1 teaspoon dried rosemary

1 jar (28 ounces) spaghetti sauce

9 lasagna noodles

2 cups (16 ounces) fat-free cottage cheese

2 cups (8 ounces) shredded reduced-fat mozzarella cheese

¼ cup grated Parmesan cheese

In a large nonstick skillet over medium heat, combine the turkey, tomatoes, onion, mushrooms, garlic, oregano, and rosemary. Cook for 10 minutes, or until the turkey is no longer pink. Add the sauce and simmer for 15 minutes.

Meanwhile, prepare the lasagna noodles according to package directions.

Preheat the oven to 350°F.

Coat a 13" × 9" baking pan with cooking spray. Place 3 noodles, side by side, in the bottom of the pan. Top with one-third of the cottage cheese, one-third of the turkey mixture, and one-third of the mozzarella. Continue layering two more times, ending with mozzarella. Sprinkle with the Parmesan.

Bake for 20 to 30 minutes, or until hot and bubbly.

Makes 12 servings

Per serving: *267 calories, 21 g protein, 27 g carbohydrate, 8 g fat, 42 mg cholesterol, 646 mg sodium, 3 g dietary fiber*

Diet Exchanges: *0 milk, ½ vegetable, 0 fruit, 1½ carbohydrate, 2½ meat, 1 fat*

2 Carb Choices

Kitchen Tip

Jennifer likes to serve this hearty lasagna with a side of garlic bread. You can also add a green salad or vegetable side dish. Or, slice up a large zucchini and layer it in the lasagna with the other ingredients to slip in a veggie serving!

Taco Casserole

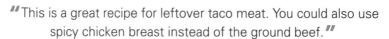

—Becky Conner, Houston, Texas

"This is a great recipe for leftover taco meat. You could also use spicy chicken breast instead of the ground beef."

Prep time: 10 minutes; Cook time: 37 minutes

1½ **pounds ground turkey breast or lean ground beef**

1 **packet (1¼ ounces) taco seasoning**

½ **bag (13 ounces) low-fat baked tortilla chips, crushed**

8 **ounces fat-free sour cream**

1 **can (14–19 ounces) pinto beans or white beans, rinsed and drained**

½ **cup salsa**

3 **tomatoes, chopped**

2 **cups shredded lettuce**

1 **cup (4 ounces) shredded reduced-fat Cheddar cheese**

2 **tablespoons chopped green or black olives**

Preheat the oven to 375°F.

In a large nonstick skillet over medium heat, cook the turkey or beef for 5 minutes, or until no longer pink. Drain. Add the taco seasoning and ½ cup water (per package directions) and cook, stirring occasionally, for 12 minutes, or until the liquid is absorbed. Place half of the crushed chips in the bottom of an 8" baking dish. Cover with the meat, sour cream, beans, salsa, and the remaining chips.

Bake for 20 to 25 minutes, or until hot and bubbly. Just before serving, top with the tomatoes, lettuce, cheese, and olives.

Makes 8 servings

Per serving: *417 calories, 26 g protein, 55 g carbohydrate, 11 g fat, 71 mg cholesterol, 1,044 mg sodium, 7 g dietary fiber*

Diet Exchanges: *½ milk, 1 vegetable, 0 fruit, 3 carbohydrate, 2½ meat, 1 fat*

4 Carb Choices

Round Steak Casserole

—Sandra Lehmann, Onarga, Illinois

304 Calories

" This is very filling, so you don't eat as much as you would normally. **"**

Prep time: 20 minutes; Cook time: 1 hour 40 minutes

1 **tablespoon canola oil**

1 **pound top round steak, cut into 1" pieces**

4 **medium potatoes, quartered**

2 **cans (28 ounces each) crushed tomatoes**

1 **can (12 ounces) green beans, drained**

1 **can (12 ounces) sliced carrots, drained**

1 **small head cabbage, chopped**

1 **onion, quartered**

1 **teaspoon salt**

1 **teaspoon dried thyme**

½ **teaspoon ground black pepper**

½ **teaspoon garlic powder**

Preheat the oven to 425°F.

Heat the oil in a large ovenproof Dutch oven over medium heat. Add the steak and cook for 10 minutes, or until browned. Add the potatoes, tomatoes, green beans, carrots, cabbage, onion, salt, thyme, pepper, and garlic powder. Cover and bake for 1 hour. Reduce the heat to 400°F. Uncover and bake for 30 minutes longer, or until no longer pink.

Makes 6 servings

Per serving: *304 calories, 25 g protein, 38 g carbohydrate, 9 g fat, 45 mg cholesterol, 796 mg sodium, 8 g dietary fiber*

Diet Exchanges: *0 milk, 4 vegetable, 0 fruit, 1 carbohydrate, 2½ meat, 1½ fat*

2½ Carb Choices

SECRETS OF WEIGHT-LOSS WINNERS

• Exercising at work with my coworkers has been beneficial to my well-being. We have been walking for 15 minutes in the morning and 15 minutes in the afternoon, three times a week. Short exercises help to tone your body, and it also helps to put a SMILE on your face!
—**Jean M. Potter, New Berlin, Wisconsin**

• Do some sort of activity every day, even if it's only for a short period of time. Better yet, incorporate the exercise into your daily routine, such as walking or biking to work.
—**Maryann Treffers, Vancouver, British Columbia, Canada**

• Close the door, put on your favorite music (rock and roll works for me), and just start moving your body. Remember, no one can see you—shake, wave, jump around, do whatever you want and burn some calories!
—**Sandy Thiessen, Winnipeg, Manitoba, Canada**

Artichoke Casserole

—**Carolyn Vega, New Orleans, Louisiana**

"I have substituted Triscuits (grated in a blender) for the bread crumbs, and added more artichoke juice and less olive oil. This is a very good dish for holidays when you're on a diet."

Prep time: 10 minutes; Cook time: 10 minutes

2 cans (14 ounces each) artichoke hearts, drained with ¾ cup juice reserved

¾ cup seasoned dried bread crumbs

1 can (6½ ounces) crabmeat, drained, or ½ pound fresh lump crabmeat

2 tablespoons extra-virgin olive oil

¼ cup grated Parmesan cheese

Juice of 1 lemon

1 teaspoon minced garlic

¼ teaspoon salt

⅛ teaspoon hot-pepper sauce, or to taste

Preheat the oven to 400°F. Coat an 11" × 7" baking dish with cooking spray.

Combine the artichokes, the reserved artichoke juice, ½ cup of the bread crumbs, the crabmeat, 1 tablespoon of the oil, the cheese, lemon juice, garlic, salt, and hot-pepper sauce in the prepared baking dish. Sprinkle with the remaining ¼ cup bread crumbs and drizzle with the remaining 1 tablespoon oil.

Bake for 10 minutes, or until hot and bubbly.

Makes 12 servings

Per serving: *101 calories, 7 g protein, 12 g carbohydrate, 3 g fat, 12 mg cholesterol, 681 mg sodium, 2 g dietary fiber*

Diet Exchanges: *0 milk, 1 vegetable, 0 fruit, ½ carbohydrate, ½ meat, ½ fat*

1 Carb Choice

Hearty Bean Chili

—Jaime Lynn Currie, Rockwood, Ontario, Canada

"This recipe is so filling, and the chili itself is very low-calorie and high in fiber. This is a fantastic meal that will leave you absolutely satisfied!"

Prep time: 10 minutes; Cook time: 45 minutes

- 3 cups brown rice
- 1 can (28 ounces) diced tomatoes
- 1 can (28 ounces) kidney beans, rinsed and drained
- 1 can (28 ounces) chickpeas, rinsed and drained
- 1 can (28 ounces) black beans, rinsed and drained
- 1 onion, finely chopped
- 1 green bell pepper, finely chopped
- 2 tablespoons chili powder
- 1 tablespoon dried oregano
- 2 teaspoons ground cumin
- ¼ teaspoon salt
- ¼ teaspoon ground black pepper

Prepare the rice according to package directions.

Meanwhile, in a large pot over medium-high heat, combine the tomatoes (with juice), kidney beans, chickpeas, black beans, onion, and bell pepper. Cook for 20 minutes, or until the peppers are tender. Stir in the chili powder, oregano, cumin, salt, and pepper. Reduce the heat to low and simmer for 20 minutes to blend the flavors.

Serve over the rice.

Makes 8 servings

Per serving: *298 calories, 16 g protein, 55 g carbohydrate, 2 g fat, 0 mg cholesterol, 922 mg sodium, 16 g dietary fiber*

Diet Exchanges: *0 milk, 2 vegetable, 0 fruit, 3 carbohydrate, ½ meat, 0 fat*

4 Carb Choices

Kitchen Tip

Jaime Lynn advises carefully measuring the rice so that you don't inadvertently use too much.

Turkey Chili

—Jodi Halverson, Ogden, Utah

"The nice thing about this chili is that it fills you up and satisfies like nothing else I have tried. I eat a cup and a half a day and feel great. Additionally, if you have a hard time getting all your vegetables in, this helps because it is loaded with veggies."

Prep time: 10 minutes; Cook time: 35 minutes

10 **ounces extra-lean ground turkey breast**

1 **medium onion, finely chopped**

2 **cans (28 ounces each) diced tomatoes**

2 **cans (15 ounces each) fat-free, reduced-sodium beef broth**

1 **can (14–19 ounces) black beans, rinsed and drained**

4 **ribs celery, finely chopped**

2 **medium zucchini, finely chopped**

2 **medium yellow squash, finely chopped**

2 **green bell peppers, finely chopped**

1 **packet (1¼ ounces) dry chili seasoning**

Heat a large pot coated with cooking spray over medium-high heat. Add the turkey and onion and cook, stirring frequently, for 5 minutes, or until the turkey is no longer pink. Add the tomatoes (with juice), broth, beans, celery, zucchini, squash, peppers, and chili seasoning. Reduce the heat to medium and simmer for 30 minutes, or until the vegetables are tender.

Makes 6 servings

Per serving: *229 calories, 19 g protein, 29 g carbohydrate, 3 g fat, 37 mg cholesterol, 884 mg sodium, 9 g dietary fiber*

Diet Exchanges: *0 milk, 3 vegetable, 0 fruit, 1 carbohydrate, 2 meat, 0 fat*

2 Carb Choices

Black Bean Chicken Chili

—Karla Hettinger, Livingston, Illinois

" This chili has a really good taste and is very satisfying. You can have quite a bit for little calories or fat and high fiber. "

Prep time: 10 minutes; Cook time: 4–5 hours

2 **boneless, skinless chicken breasts**

1 **can (15 ounces) gold hominy**

1 **can (15 ounces) white hominy**

1 **can (14–19 ounces) black beans, rinsed and drained**

1 **can (14–19 ounces) chili beans, rinsed and drained**

1 **can (14½ ounces) tomatoes with chile peppers (rotel)**

1 **can (10¾ ounces) fat-free reduced-sodium chicken broth**

1 **teaspoon ground cumin**

Place the chicken in a slow cooker, cover, and cook for 1 hour on the high heat setting, or until no longer pink. Remove to a cutting board and shred with a fork. Return the chicken to the slow cooker.

Add the gold hominy, white hominy, black beans, chili beans, tomatoes, broth, and cumin. Cover and simmer for 3 to 4 hours, or until cooked through.

Makes 4 servings

Per serving: *395 calories, 29 g protein, 60 g carbohydrate, 3 g fat, 33 mg cholesterol, 1,129 mg sodium, 15 g dietary fiber*

Diet Exchanges: *0 milk, 1 vegetable, 0 fruit, 3½ carbohydrate, 3 meat, 0 fat*

4 Carb Choices

Photography Credits

Front Cover

Mitch Mandel/Rodale Images

Back Cover

Courtesy of Barbara Sloan (before and after)

Mitch Mandel/Rodale Images (Caesar Kebabs, Piña Colada Cake, Turkey Chili)

Interior

Mitch Mandel/Rodale Images: pages iii, 6, 7, 25, 38, 40, 44, 47, 50, 53, 57, 65, 66, 69, 77, 82, 92, 94, 97, 99, 100, 103, 111, 114, 118, 123, 127, 131, 136, 141, 144, 150, 153, 159, 160, 162, 170, 174, 176, 181, 182, 187, 190, 195, 196, 199, 200, 202, 207, 209, 210, 212, 215, 216, 219, 222, 224, 227, 229, 232, 235, 237, 240, 245, 246, 250, 256

Kurt Wilson/Rodale Images: pages 2, 3, 4, 11, 13, 14, 20, 24, 32, 36, 37

Rodale Images: pages 9, 18, 22, 26

Brian Hagiwara: page 5

Robert Gerheart: page 16

Sally Ullman: page 21

Howard Puckett: page 27

Courtesy of Jeanie Callaghan: page 72

Courtesy of Lori Lefort: page 90

Courtesy of Jean Zelios: page 108

Courtesy of Barbara Braley: page 113

Courtesy of Donna Marrin: page 169

Courtesy of Jean Adam: page 213

Courtesy of Barbara Sloan: page 226

Courtesy of Wendy Oland: page 242

Index

Boldface references indicate photographs. <u>Underscored</u> references indicate sidebars and tables.

Conversion Chart

These equivalents have been slightly rounded to make measuring easier.

Volume Measurements

U.S.	Imperial	Metric
¼ tsp	–	1 ml
½ tsp	–	2 ml
1 tsp	–	5 ml
1 Tbsp	–	15 ml
2 Tbsp (1 oz)	1 fl oz	30 ml
¼ cup (2 oz)	2 fl oz	60 ml
⅓ cup (3 oz)	3 fl oz	80 ml
½ cup (4 oz)	4 fl oz	120 ml
⅔ cup (5 oz)	5 fl oz	160 ml
¾ cup (6 oz)	6 fl oz	180 ml
1 cup (8 oz)	8 fl oz	240 ml

Weight Measurements

U.S.	Metric
1 oz	30 g
2 oz	60 g
4 oz (¼ lb)	115 g
5 oz (⅓ lb)	145 g
6 oz	170 g
7 oz	200 g
8 oz (½ lb)	230 g
10 oz	285 g
12 oz (¾ lb)	340 g
14 oz	400 g
16 oz (1 lb)	455 g
2.2 lb	1 kg

Length Measurements

U.S.	Metric
¼"	0.6 cm
½"	1.25 cm
1"	2.5 cm
2"	5 cm
4"	11 cm
6"	15 cm
8"	20 cm
10"	25 cm
12" (1')	30 cm

Pan Sizes

U.S.	Metric
8" cake pan	20 × 4 cm sandwich or cake tin
9" cake pan	23 × 3.5 cm sandwich or cake tin
11" × 7" baking pan	28 × 18 cm baking tin
13" × 9" baking pan	32.5 × 23 cm baking tin
15" × 10" baking pan	38 × 25.5 cm baking tin (Swiss roll tin)
1½ qt baking dish	1.5 liter baking dish
2 qt baking dish	2 liter baking dish
2 qt rectangular baking dish	30 × 19 cm baking dish
9" pie plate	22 × 4 or 23 × 4 cm pie plate
7" or 8" springform pan	18 or 20 cm springform or loose-bottom cake tin
9" × 5" loaf pan	23 × 13 cm or 2 lb narrow loaf tin or pâté tin

Temperatures

Fahrenheit	Centigrade	Gas
140°	60°	–
160°	70°	–
180°	80°	–
225°	105°	¼
250°	120°	½
275°	135°	1
300°	150°	2
325°	160°	3
350°	180°	4
375°	190°	5
400°	200°	6
425°	220°	7
450°	230°	8
475°	245°	9
500°	260°	–

A SIMPLE TABLE

RECIPES AND RITUALS
FOR A LIFE IN BALANCE

CHI-SAN WAN
AND NATALI STAJCIC

introduction

We met many years ago and formed a bond over our mutual love of food. We discovered that the modern-day dilemma we all face is trying to find a connection between 'natural living' and integrating that with the society and culture in which we live. With this in mind, we started our company The Pressery — creating fresh, natural, wholesome almond milk — with the aim of offering a simple measure towards leading a healthy and balanced lifestyle.

CHI

Growing up with a family in the restaurant business, I have always found myself surrounded by food and drink, and developed a huge appreciation for it from when I was a child. Every occasion would be marked with a feast of some kind – at my birthday in June it was traditional to have a barbecue for the whole family, any other cause for celebration would involve a banquet of many dishes. It was always very important to sit down together and eat at mealtimes, and this ethos has been instilled in me since those early days of feasting. My favourite thing to this day is to gather loved ones around a table and while away time together.

Somewhere, in between the meals and gatherings growing up, I turned my head to studying fashion design. During my first year in halls of residence, I honed my cooking skills. Living in halls and having a shared kitchen meant I could cook the way I wanted. Things never got too experimental; I was (and still am) in awe of the simplicity of beautiful produce. I went on to living in a house with six other girls and, strangely, we all loved to cook. Even if we came home late after a long day in class, we'd end it in the kitchen — chopping and chatting; I've always found this side to cooking very therapeutic.

Upon graduating, I jumped from job to job in fashion trying to find my forte, eventually settling as a stylist. I worked in London and internationally but after eight years I wanted to cut my teeth on something new, something that resonated more with me. I had become more fascinated by what we put in our bodies in terms of food and drink, rather than what we put on our bodies in terms of clothes and accessories. Through the stress of working in the fashion industry, I had started noticing my eating habits and how tweaking them could change the course of my day. I'd never considered myself as somebody who ate badly, but when I began to pay attention more, to listen to my body and mind, things seemed a lot clearer. Fashion became less important, and food took centre stage in my life, more than ever before.

I thought long and hard about how I could integrate my skill set from fashion into the food industry; what I could do that was missing and what would make a difference. I'd been making almond milk at home for some time, after discovering the ones I was buying in the shops, thinking I was making a 'healthier' choice, were actually full of ingredients I didn't recognise and only 1–3 per cent almonds. On my birthday one summer's evening, surrounded by good friends and good food as usual, I told Natali what I'd been thinking and what I wanted to do. She said she felt exactly the same and we began to plot.

NATALI

I grew up in London where I spent the first part of my childhood living just off the culturally diverse Uxbridge Road. We were surrounded by so many different kinds of cuisine and my mum really made the most of this, cooking something new most evenings. We lived on a tight budget but our food was always prepared with love.

My relationship with food when I was a child was uncomplicated; I was happy eating most things. I did a lot of ballet and dancing so food really acted as fuel. My pasta portions increased as my dancing schedule became more rigorous but I remained a twig in spite of them and it was only when I injured myself aged 16 that my relationship with food changed. My injury, although not incredibly serious, came at the wrong time. It was during the auditions period for dance college and although I managed to gain a place at two good schools, I did not achieve the scholarship I needed to fulfil my dancing dreams and they came to an abrupt halt.

My early 20s were spent working at music festivals. I learned so much and enjoyed it immensely but it is safe to say I burned the candle at both ends. My behaviour was put on pause when I had a phone call that changed the course of my life forever. I was walking home one evening and my mum called me to say that my littlest brother Samuel had been diagnosed with a brain tumour. I collapsed and two strangers helped me up and walked me home. My brother died a month later at the age of 12. When something like this stops you in your tracks things cannot

continue as they did before. I certainly tried to carry on living the way
I had but my perspective on life had been changed. I was 24.

Just over a year later I gave birth to my daughter Frankie-Mae. However,
I suffered severe post-partum psychosis and it was a very tough time for me.
This suffering forced me to look at my diet and lifestyle in more detail and
question whether I was supporting myself as best I could. I didn't like taking
medication, as it hadn't agreed with me, so I was ready to try anything else
that might help. I realised that while I loved to cook, at that point most of
my meals really weren't nourishing so I set about changing this. I knew it
would be a long journey, but after a couple of years I began to feel as though
I was helping myself with my food choices and I started to feel stronger. It
took a while to establish these food habits but they are permanent, they are
my passion and they constantly develop. Today I still feel the consequences
of my brother's death and I am on a constant quest to keep my mind strong.
Balance is something that is very important to me.

It was around this time that Chi and I began talking about our desire to start
a business. I was trying to juggle full-time employment with motherhood —
poorly — and wanted to be part of something exciting and innovative. We
developed the idea quickly and launched into it without too much thought.
I don't think we could have done it any other way; it was a leap of faith.

THE PRESSERY

The Pressery officially launched in March 2014 from Natali's kitchen. The first
six months were a labour of love — we worked so hard. The physical aspect
was draining; we were making all of the almond milk by hand ourselves — and
delivering it — along with running the new business. Evenings would be spent
labelling our bottles; mornings would start at 5am to make the milk before the
city woke up. Initially we sold the milk at our local market — no more than
20 litres per week — but by June we had major stockists, such as Selfridges and
Daylesford Organic. A year into the business, we were producing much more
than we could manage so at this point we outsourced production to a local East
London company so that we could concentrate on growing the brand. Because
it was not pasteurised in any way, our almond milk had a very short shelf life,

which limited how much we could produce as we didn't want to produce too much and have it turn bad, so we crowdsourced investment so that we could make the almond milk more widely available. We launched our long-life version in March 2016.

Beyond the milk itself, The Pressery has allowed us to have a platform where we are able to share more about the ethos behind the brand and the lifestyle that we embrace. We can explore and discuss the pursuit of happiness in this crazy, modern world of ours. The challenges surrounding the day-to-day running of our company encouraged us to come up with coping methods. These coping methods quickly became our tools for life and they have become the foundation of this book — this is the food that we eat, the food that we share, the lotions and potions we concoct and the rituals we try to follow. We wanted to empower ourselves and others with the wisdom of mindfulness, food, drink, rituals and slow living.

OUR FOOD PHILOSOPHY

How we eat, what we eat and what we don't eat has never been so divisive. We seem compelled to label ourselves; perhaps it makes us feel more in control, sure of our choices. Unfortunately, through obsessive labelling and restrictive diets people can lose the very best thing about cooking and eating – both should bring you pleasure. We can't always spend hours making supper but we can and should take 15 minutes away from a screen to sit down and eat well. Cooking can be meditative, all you need is an organised kitchen with a few of the right tools and a collection of recipes. Eating can be a moment alone to reflect on the day you've had or the day you are about to have. It can be a time to sit together as a family and reconnect or it can be on a table packed with your closest friends and some good wine. Taking time to eat will satisfy you completely. There should be no guilt and no shovelling. Just mindful enjoyment.

We don't subscribe to any diet camp. We enjoy everything about food. It is one of the things that we have full control over. Advertising tries to pull us in various directions but we are now fuelled with the resources to make educated choices when it comes to what we put in our bodies. It is so important to remember that we are each very different and the food that works for your friend may not be right for you. Take time to try things out and find out what feels good for you. *A Simple Table* is not a book of shoulds or musts, it is merely an account of what we have found works for us to make us feel well and at our best, and this is still an evolving journey packed with new discoveries as we continue to learn and move deeper into optimal living.

THIS BOOK

A Simple Table is a book for you to pick up any day of the week and find a simple recipe you wish to cook, or a piece of advice or ritual you might like to adopt in your life. We're not trying to reinvent the wheel with all of our recipes. Some of them might be classic dishes you recognise, or include elements that are borrowed from them. But whatever mood you are in, we hope you will find a recipe to inspire you and leave you satisfied. There are meals that can suit families, alongside options for solo dining. We have included very healthy and light choices but also warming, indulgent food. This is how we eat. You'll see the same ingredients popping up in a lot of the recipes; this is intentional. We don't expect you to buy tons of new stuff you will use only once. Cooking and eating has to be sustainable in order for you to continue discovering what works for you and your body.

A LIFE IN BALANCE

This is more than a recipe book. In the chapter we've called 'Rituals' you will find a few suggestions to build balance in areas of your life outside food. For example, we present our thoughts on how to exercise regularly, start your day or make some of your own beauty basics. Some of these ideas may be new to you but we encourage you to explore. They are things that we like to do in our daily lives, but by no means are they to be followed rigidly — we simply hope that there is something here that might appeal and that you find something that benefits you in your day-to-day life. Bite off a little at a time; find out what works for you. And if nothing else, we hope that the following five tips might help you to pause and find a bit of balance and simplicity among the mayhem as you go about your day.

1. ACCEPTANCE
Think of life in balance as a bendable line; accept that things will be ever changing and that balance is how you perceive it. If you can include a few

consistent elements in your day you will find the inevitable changes that life
brings about easier to handle. Think of these daily rituals as your anchor. Take
time off them when you need to but always come back to them.

2. SMALL CHANGES

Don't attempt to change everything overnight. Prioritise and make small changes.
You have a much greater chance of creating good lifelong habits if you move
slowly. True progress takes time. We are always making small changes, our
personal development never stops.

3. MOVE

Always. Find the movement that you enjoy, mix it up if that suits you or keep a
constant if you prefer to. Movement is the key to a healthy body and mind. Walk
with your friends or family, have running races or crawl around with a toddler.
Just keep on moving.

4. STAY CURIOUS

Keep learning, go to galleries, jump off rocks into the sea, try new foods, meet
new people. Just stay curious in every area of your life.

5. GENTLENESS

Be gentle with yourself. Do not scold yourself. If you break a good habit just
begin again. Talk to yourself as you would a most treasured friend. Be kind and
supportive to yourself.

FINALLY...

We hope this book will be well-thumbed, well-loved, well-shared but, above all,
we want it to be functional. Our aim is that you can come back to it regularly,
and use it as an anchor which can add grounding elements to your life. We hope
you find inspiration in the advice offered. We are not suggesting a life overhaul.
Instead, you should be able to dip in and out of this book on any given day of the
week and find what you are looking for, be it a recipe or some lifestyle inspiration.
Take what you want from it. There is nothing too complicated or unfamiliar
because for something to really make a difference, it has to be sustainable. Only
over time can we see real change.

our store cupboard essentials

ALMOND MILK

For those wishing to consume less dairy or who are dairy intolerant, almond milk is a great plant-based milk alternative due to its nutty flavour and creamy texture. Almonds contain magnesium, calcium, vitamin E and protein which make them a nutritious addition to the kitchen. Making your own almond milk is easy and most delicious (you'll find our recipe on page 158) but you can now find a plethora of almond milks on the supermarket shelves. Make sure you check that it has a high percentage of almonds, as some have as little as 1 per cent and bulk out the milk with lots of other ingredients that your body won't recognise. We may be biased, but we like The Pressery.

AMINO ACID / LIQUID AMINOS

An all-purpose seasoning, made from soy protein, this is an alternative to soya sauce. It's not fermented, is gluten-free and contains 16 essential and non-essential amino acids in natural occurring amounts from soy protein. It's perfect to add to salad dressings, soups, roast vegetables or marinades. We like to use Bragg.

APPLE CIDER VINEGAR

Made from fermented apple cider, this vinegar should always be bought organic, raw, unfiltered and with the 'mother' (that's the cloudy strands at the bottom of the bottle which is evidence of natural fermentation). Rich in enzymes, it aids digestion, supports your immune system and alkalises the body. It's great used in dressings and sauces, or have a tablespoon of it in some water if you're suffereing from indigestion. We like using the one by Biona.

BUCKWHEAT FLOUR

Despite what the name suggests, buckwheat is in fact not part of the wheat family. It's not even a grain, but a seed from a plant that is closely related to rhubarb. High in protein and minerals, buckwheat is a great wheat-free alternative and, therefore, lighter on the stomach.

CACAO BUTTER

Made from cold-pressing the oil from the cacao bean, cacao butter is the base ingredient for chocolate and is also used a lot in skincare products. It also smells wonderful.

CACAO NIBS

Cacao nibs are cacao beans that have been separated from their husks and broken into very small pieces. Bitter in taste, yet with that beautiful chocolatey hit, they are the most raw form of chocolate, high in magnesium and antioxidants. Enjoy them like dark chocolate but with all the nutritional benefits – they're great thrown into baked goods in place of chocolate chips.

CACAO POWDER

This is the rawest form of cocoa powder but it still has the nutrients of the cacao bean. Use as a replacement for cocoa or chocolate powder for a boost in antioxidants and minerals. Cacao powder is great for baked goods, cooking or throwing into smoothies to give them a velvety chocolate taste.

CHAGA

Even though the chaga mushroom has existed for hundreds of years, it's only recently that it has come to the surface as a 'superfood'. Mostly harvested from the colder northern hemispheres, this powerful funghi survives the harshest of climates, which makes it full of extraordinary antioxidants.

CHIA SEEDS

High in omega-3 fatty acids, chia seeds come from the chia plant, part of the mint family. Though very small in size, when soaked in a liquid, the seeds swell so that they bulk out and roughly triple in size. They will satisfy due to their fatty acids, protein and fibre. You can make a chia seed pudding by adding one or two tablespoons of chia seeds to 240ml of almond milk (see page 158 if you want to make your own), giving it a good stir, and letting it sit for at least 20 minutes to allow the seeds to absorb the milk. Add honey to taste and top it with fruit. Chia seeds can be used to 'thicken' recipes.

COCONUT OIL

With a higher smoking point than many other oils, coconut oil is great to use for cooking and most of our recipes call for it. Although its flavour is mild, some might find it off-putting, so if that is the case, you can also buy coconut oil that has been lightly steamed – this makes it odourless while retaining most of its nutrient profile. Coconut oil has other benefits outside the kitchen; it can be used as a natural beauty product, or for oral hygiene when oil pulling (see page 204).

COCONUT SUGAR

Coconut sugar is sustainably harvested from the nectar of the coconut palm tree and is an ideal substitute for brown sugar. It looks, feels and tastes very similar, but is a lot less refined and more nutritional – it is full of minerals. We use it in sweet baked goods and for balancing out savoury dishes.

DULSE

Rich in iodine, iron, magnesium and calcium, dulse is a seaweed (or sea vegetable) and has a salty, smoky taste compared to other seaweeds. It's great to add depth to dishes. You're unlikely to find dulse fresh; after harvesting it's quickly dried to retain its nutrients. We like the one from Atlantic Kitchen.

FILTERED WATER

Most tap water nowadays is chlorinated, which is meant to kill the disease-causing bacteria that either the water or the water pipes contain. Even though water varies greatly depending on where you live, we suggest using filtered water for consumption, especially when drinking water straight up, or using it in recipes. This is more important when a recipe requires fermentation as the chlorine contained in our water system will kill the friendly bacteria needed for the recipe to work! For a normal household a BRITA Filter will do, though some may go to the extent of fitting a reverse osmosis system. If you have neither, for recipes you could always use spring water.

FLAXSEED

Also known as linseed, flaxseed is great for digestion as it's full of fibre as well as omega-3 fatty acids and antioxidants. The whole seed is great sprinkled over salads, smoothies or baked goods but it's also great ground down and used in cooking and baking.

GHEE

Ghee is a clarified butter, which means that the whey has been removed from it. It is full of nutrients like vitamins A, D, E and K and has a very high smoking point, which means it's safer to cook with at higher temperatures than some oils. It's minimally processed so makes a better choice than margarine or refined oils; it also has the most incredible aroma and a little goes a long way! We found the best tasting ghee from Fushi.

HARISSA

Traditionally made mostly from roasted red peppers, this is a hot chilli paste used widely in North African and Middle Eastern recipes. We use it as a condiment or we add it to flavour tomato-based sauces; a little goes a long way with this feisty sauce! We love the one from Harry Brand because it has the fewest ingredients.

HEMP OIL

Hemp oil is high in omega-3 and omega-6 fatty acids, as well as being very high in protein, vitamins and minerals. It has a nutty taste and should not be heated. Drizzle it over salads or add it to dressings. We like the one by Biona.

KOMBU

Kombu is a seaweed and comes in freeze-dried strip form. It's great to add to soups, stews and broths. It's traditionally used in dashi, a delicious Japanese soup stock used as the base for miso soup. We buy ours from Clearspring.

NORI

Most commonly sold in sheet form or as sprinkles, nori is an edible seaweed high in vitamins A and C. We use the sheets to make wraps or crush them and sprinkle the nori over salads. We like the one from Clearspring.

NUTRITIONAL YEAST

The words probably don't conjure up very appealing images but nutritional yeast is simply a single-celled organism which is grown on molasses and then harvested, washed and dried with heat to kill or 'deactivate' it. Because it's not active, it doesn't froth or grow like baking yeast does so it has no leavening ability. It is mostly sold in the form of flakes and has a 'cheesy' flavour. Rich in vitamin B and high in protein, the taste makes it a great alternative to cheese for vegetarians and vegans; we add it to our 'nut cheeses' (see pages 179 and 180) for a stronger cheese flavour or to a Caesar dressing (see page 86). We like the one from Marigold.

POLENTA

A great gluten-free alternative to flour, polenta is derived from corn and often called cornmeal. Polenta is the coarse version – it's a little gritty and gives a great texture to cornbread and muffins. It can also be used to make a polenta 'mash' instead of starchy potatoes.

PROBIOTIC CAPSULES

Probiotics help stimulate the growth of healthy gut bacteria so are mainly used to aid gut health and healthy digestion. The capsules can be opened and the powder can be added to milk, coconut milk or nut spreads to start the fermentation process, making it probiotic-rich. We like to use OptiBac.

PSYLLIUM HUSK

Psyllium husk is most commonly used to help bowel movements and is a flavourless powder that can be added to almost anything. A high source of dietary fibre, it also lends itself to baking because it swells and binds, very much like eggs do, so can hold ingredients together. You can find it in most health food stores.

QUINOA

Quinoa is a very versatile and tasty nutritional seed – deriving from a plant related to beetroot and spinach. High in protein, magnesium, iron and fibre, it's also gluten-free. With a nutty taste, it can be used in place of glutinous carbs in a recipe. Widely available in supermarkets and health food stores, you can buy white, red, black or mixed quinoa.

SCHISANDRA BERRY

Schisandra berry has a long history in Traditional Chinese Medicine, but has only recently become popular in the West. Known for helping with fatigue, enhancing stamina, liver support, countering stress and heightening concentration, the powder is best used in smoothies and breakfast recipes.

SPIRULINA

Spirulina contains a crazy amount of chlorophyll, protein, vitamins, minerals, antioxidants and fatty acids. It is a bluey-green algae that grows all over the planet naturally in waterways, but now it is also grown commercially due to its increased popularity. Used in smoothies mostly, to disguise the mildly 'fishy' taste, do not dismiss this all-round superfood.

TAHINI

Either a light or dark paste made from sesame seeds, we use tahini for making salad dressings and it is essential in hummus (see page 183).

The dark version is a lot more nutritious, has a coarser texture and a much stronger flavour than the light version because the seeds have not been hulled. Some find the dark paste too bitter.

TAMARI
A type of soya sauce, brewed without wheat which makes it a great alternative for people with a gluten intolerance, tamari is perfect for seasoning and dressings. We like the one from Clearspring.

TURMERIC
Part of the ginger family (it looks like it too), turmeric is bright orange inside and can stain everything yellow, so be careful! It has been used for centuries to treat infections and inflammation. It also aids digestion and purifies the blood. It's a good 'all-rounder' spice – mild and subtle. We use turmeric root or as a ground powder and add it to our hot drinks, curries, broths and juices.

WAKAME
A variety of seaweed, high in magnesium and calcium, wakame is great used mostly in Asian recipes, soups and salads. It comes in freeze-dried form and can be found in health food stores and in your local Asian supermarket. We like the ones from Clearspring and Atlantic Kitchen.

CHAPTER ONE

For us, the morning sets the tone for our day so we find it really pays to break your fast well and set yourself up for the day the best way you can.

Most of the recipes in this section are based on one to two servings, but can easily be adapted to make more when you have extra mouths to feed or plan on spending a leisurely morning making breakfast. You may want to make the dal or either of the granola recipes beforehand, whereas the omelette or fruit and hemp seed bowl can be whipped up when you want them for a quick, simple start.

Make use of leftover potatoes or black rice from the night before – it's great to think outside the box when contemplating what to eat first thing. For us, anything goes! Whatever you choose, make sure you sit down to enjoy your morning. Appreciate this time you are giving yourself (and others if you're not solo-eating), even if it is only 10 minutes. You deserve that.

fruit and hemp
seed bowl

SERVES TWO

4 tbsp hemp oil

1 ripe banana

1 apple, cored

juice of 1 lemon

additional fruits of your
   choice, chopped

2 tbsp pumpkin seeds

2 tbsp sunflower seeds

2 tbsp linseeds

2 tbsp sesame seeds

This breakfast staple was introduced to us by our good friend Inger's mum, Françoise. It might look a bit puny, but it has lots of healthy fatty acids and proteins from the hemp oil and seeds, and carbohydrate from the fruits, which will keep you surprisingly full. We think it's the new porridge, especially if you find that grains in the morning don't sit well with you.

The seed mix can be made in advance, or if you make it on the day, be sure to make more than you need and store it so you have one less thing to do on future mornings. Use seasonal produce for the fruit base where possible. In spring, we like to use stewed rhubarb or blood oranges; the summer is for cherries, peaches, nectarines or strawberries; autumn sees us moving on to figs, blueberries, pears or plums; and finally in the winter, we go for passion fruit, clementines and pomegranate.

Place 2 tablespoons of the hemp oil in each bowl (we find shallow bowls easiest and most pleasing). Halve the banana, and mash each half into the oil. Chop your apple and divide it between the bowls, then squeeze the juice of the lemon over it to stop it browning.

Pile your other fruit into the bowls too.

In a blender, blitz the seeds together until you have a consistency you like – some like it more textured and some smoother, although beware of blitzing it too much as the oils start to bind the seeds and you will end up with seed butter!

Top your fruit bowls with the seed mixture (around 2 tablespoons per bowl), then mix everything together – this won't look very appetising but trust us, it's delicious, good for you and you will be excited to wake up in the mornings to it!

The leftover seed mix can be stored in the fridge and used for up to 1 week. You can also make this for one – just halve the ingredients (except the seeds if making more than enough), and keep the remaining fruit in the fridge.

savoury mushroom porridge

SERVES ONE

½–1 garlic clove, crushed
  (depending on your taste)
2 tbsp coconut oil or ghee
40g oats (jumbo or rolled –
  either is fine)
250ml almond milk (see page 158
  for how to make your own)
2 handfuls of mushrooms, chopped
  or sliced (we like shiitake, oyster
  and enoki)
1 tsp nutritional yeast
  (we use Marigold Engevita)
a pinch of dried chilli flakes
  (optional)
1 tbsp pumpkin seeds, plus extra
  to serve
1 spring onion, sliced
a handful of pea shoots
sea salt and black pepper

We admit this recipe might sound a little controversial as most of us are more familiar with sweetened porridge, but we don't always fancy a sweet start to our day. Because oats are so good at filling us up quickly, we thought we would experiment with making a porridge with a savoury note – it was a winner! Why not change your mindset and shake up porridge as you know it? This can be eaten at whatever time you fancy, not just in the mornings.

Gently heat the garlic in a pan with half the coconut oil or ghee, until soft. Add the oats, give it a stir and then pour in the almond milk. In another pan, sauté the mushrooms in the other half of the coconut oil or ghee.

Stir the nutritional yeast into the oats, season with salt and pepper and the chilli flakes, if using. Season your mushrooms too. A few minutes before the mushrooms are done, throw in the pumpkin seeds, toss them in the pan and wait for them to start popping.

Take the porridge off the heat and transfer it to a bowl, then top with the mushrooms, some extra pumpkin seeds, the spring onion and pea shoots. Enjoy!

—

green
omelette

SERVES TWO

4 eggs
a few sprigs of basil, flat-leaf parsley
*   and mint, roughly torn*
knob of unsalted butter or 1 tsp
coconut oil
a handful of spring greens, or any
*   other greens, such as kale, spinach*
*   or chard*
sea salt and black pepper

Some mornings call for a little more – something warm perhaps or simply just that bit more substantial. A simple omelette is great for mornings like these, especially when you don't have a lot of time. Remember to listen to your body – if it is hungry nourish it fully. We sometimes have a double breakfast – maybe the Fruit and hemp seed bowl (see page 22) before tucking into this omelette with its abundance of greens and the best-quality eggs we can find. When given the opportunity we like to sit quietly enjoying the textures that every mouthful brings, undistracted and present in the moment.

Crack the eggs into a bowl, add a little salt and pepper and beat together with a fork. There's no need to over-beat the eggs; we like there to be some changes in texture and runny pools of yellow in the eggy mixture. Stir in the herbs.

Take a heavy-based frying pan – 25cm or thereabouts – and place it over a medium heat. Once hot, throw the butter or coconut oil and swirl it around the pan as it melts, coating the entire surface. Add the egg mixture and shake it around the pan. Use a wooden spoon or spatula to pull the sides of the mixture into the middle, allowing the 'wet' egg to make contact with the base of the pan. Carry on like this until the omelette is almost set. Toss the greens on top and carefully fold the omelette in half before serving.

—

anytime
dal

SERVES FOUR

FOR THE DAL

1 tbsp coconut oil

1 white onion, sliced

*a thumb-sized piece of ginger,
    grated*

2 garlic cloves, finely chopped

2 tsp ground cumin

1 tsp ground turmeric

1 tsp ground coriander

1 tsp ground cardamom

1 tsp of dried chilli flakes

400g red lentils, rinsed

*1 litre boiling water (depending on
    how chunky you like your dahl)*

2–4 tsp vegetable stock powder

*a bunch of coriander stalks, chopped
    (use the leaves for the topping)*

4 generous handfuls of spinach

sea salt and black pepper

FOR THE TOPPING

*about 4 heaped tbsp of your choice of
    yoghurt (we use sheep's milk yoghurt
    for that extra tanginess)*

4 lime wedges

2 spring onions, finely sliced

a handful of coriander leaves

4 soft-boiled eggs (optional)

Dal makes a perfectly delicious crowd-pleaser or a warm and nourishing bowl for one (with enough to freeze for the days when you know you haven't the time to cook). We could eat dal any time of day. We keep it soupy for a light lunch, warm some chapatis or naan bread to have with it for dinner and enjoy the leftovers as a hearty breakfast with a soft-boiled egg.

We like throwing in some spinach at the end to make sure we get our greens in, although you can substitute spinach with anything that will wilt in the residual heat after cooking – kale leaves, chard leaves, spring greens, etc.

Boil the kettle and put a heavy-based pan over a medium heat. Add the coconut oil and fry the onion, ginger and garlic until soft, then add the spices to coat, stirring to make sure they don't catch on the bottom and burn.

Once fragrant, throw in the red lentils and stir again. Pour in 500–750ml of the water from the kettle, adding 1 teaspoon of vegetable stock for every 250ml of water. Throw in the coriander stalks, bring back to the boil and simmer for 20–30 minutes. If you like it soupier, add more water. Check and stir occasionally.

Check that the red lentils have thickened to your preferred consistency, season with salt and pepper to taste and turn off the heat. Stir in the spinach and allow to wilt.

Ladle the dal into your chosen vessels and top each one with a spoonful of yoghurt, a wedge of lime, a sprinkling of spring onion and coriander leaves – and maybe a soft-boiled egg!

—

brown rice congee
with ginger

SERVES FOUR

350g skinless, boneless chicken thighs

1 onion, quartered

2 thumb-sized pieces
   of ginger, chopped

185g brown rice

2 litres home-made chicken stock
   (see page 192)

tamari, to season

toasted sesame oil, to finish

4 spring onions, finely sliced

1 tbsp mixed black and white
   sesame seeds

chilli oil or flakes, to taste (optional)

Congee is a sort of soupy 'porridge' popular in Asian countries. Traditionally, it is made with white rice but it can also be made with different grains. We have used brown rice here to give it that characteristic nutty flavour that comes from the unrefined rice grain. It is the most comforting bowl to eat when you are feeling a little under the weather, especially when you have a sore throat. It takes a while to cook so we suggest making a batch at the weekend, or the night before you need it, but it's so easy to make because you can't really 'overcook' it. Just reheat it in the morning – it tastes just as good, if not better! When made with home-made chicken stock, our congee will be even more nourishing for your body. You can also add chilli oil or dried chilli flakes at the end to spice things up a bit.

Put the chicken, onion, ginger, brown rice and chicken stock into a large pot with a lid. Bring to the boil, then lower the heat to a gentle simmer. Partially cover with the lid and continue to simmer.

After 30 minutes or so, fish out the onion and ginger. Remove the chicken thighs and shred the meat with a fork. Return the shredded meat to the pot and place the pot back on the lowest heat possible on the smallest hob for about 1–1½ hours.

When it's ready the congee will resemble a thick porridge made with disintegrated rice. Season with tamari to your taste, then spoon into bowls and drizzle with the sesame oil. Top with the spring onions, sesame seeds and chilli (if using).

—

coconut and lemon potatoes

SERVES TWO

a large dollop of coconut oil

2 garlic cloves, thinly sliced (optional)

1 tsp dried chilli flakes

grated zest and juice of 1 lemon

5 medium leftover boiled
*   or roasted potatoes, cut into chunks*

2 eggs

sea salt and black pepper

a handful of chopped coriander,
*   to finish*

We discovered this simple recipe one dreary Monday morning when we had a handful of leftover potatoes from lunch the previous day and not much else in the fridge. Frying the potatoes gave them little golden crunchy corners and we felt we had discovered a real treat. The recipe is best made with pre-cooked potatoes, so it is worth boiling some the night before if you haven't any leftovers – or just ensure you cook extra at dinner time. Starting the day with a warm bowl of these fragrant, crispy potatoes feels so nourishing. Add an egg for a bit of protein to keep you going.

Place the coconut oil in a large heavy-bottomed frying pan over a medium heat. Once melted, add the garlic, if using, and move it around the pan with a wooden spoon so it doesn't brown too quickly. Now add the chilli flakes and lemon zest, quickly followed by the potatoes. Add more coconut oil if the mixture seems dry – you want the potatoes to get crispy and brown in places. Once they start to take on some colour, add a splash of the lemon juice along with a grind of black pepper and a sprinkle of salt.

Keep the potatoes warm while you poach or fry your eggs according to preference. Divide up the potatoes and serve with an egg on top of each portion, scattered with lots of coriander.

black rice, coconut and mango

SERVES FOUR

*200g black rice, rinsed then
    soaked in cold water overnight*
*1 x 400ml tin coconut milk
    (keep a little aside to pour over
    the finished dish)*
a pinch of sea salt
1 mango, peeled and stoned
almond or coconut flakes, for sprinkling
*1 tbsp maple syrup (or sweetener
    of your choice)*

This breakfast is for mornings that require something wonderful. It's the perfect morning meal if you have friends staying or if it's grey and rainy outside. Let the tropical flavours satisfy all your senses.

Drain the rice and rinse it well. Place in a heavy-based pan with the coconut milk, 125ml of water and the salt. Bring to the boil, then reduce to a simmer and cover the pan with a lid. Stir frequently until the rice is tender and most of the liquid has been absorbed (you still want a little liquid); this will take around 25–30 minutes.

While the rice is cooking, prepare the mango by cutting it into nice thick slices. Gently toast your almond or coconut flakes in a dry frying pan over a low heat. When the rice is ready, add the maple syrup and fold in to combine. Remove the pan from the heat and set aside.

To assemble, scoop your desired amount of black rice into bowls, top with the mango, almond or coconut flakes and a drizzle of reserved coconut milk.

sweet omelette

SERVES ONE

2 eggs

1 banana, mashed
   (we have also used blueberries,
   peaches, raspberries and
   strawberries)

a sprinkle of ground cinnamon
   (optional)

1 tsp coconut oil

1 tbsp coconut yoghurt

a small handful of blueberries

a sprinkling of seed mix
   (see page 22)

This is a sort of flourless pancake concoction, and the best way we could think to describe it was as a sweet omelette. Bananas and blueberries were the fruit we had to hand on the morning we were experimenting but other soft fruits work well too. This is lighter than a pancake, due to the obvious exclusion of flour, but it is really satisfying. We top ours with coconut yoghurt and some of the seed mix from our Fruit and hemp seed bowl recipe (see page 22).

Using a fork, whisk the eggs, then stir through the mashed banana. Add the cinnamon or any other flavours you like.

Melt the coconut oil in a heavy based frying pan and once hot, add the egg mixture. Let it cook for a few minutes and then flip it over to cook for a few minutes on the other side. Slide off on to a plate, and top with the coconut yoghurt and blueberries and before sprinkling some seed mix over the top.

black pepper granola

MAKES 1KG

250g rolled oats
250g buckwheat groats
65g cashews, roughly chopped
75g whole raw almonds,
 roughly chopped
65g pumpkin seeds
60g sunflower seeds
35g sesame seeds
30g chia seeds
black pepper, to taste
150g coconut oil
80ml maple syrup
1 tsp vanilla extract
2 tbsp ground cardamom
½ tsp fine sea salt

What you eat in the morning sets you up for the rest of the day and if you go for something too sweet you are more likely to have a sugar slump, which will temporarily disable your concentration soon afterwards. Shop-bought granola tends to be over-sweetened so we like to make our own; not only do we find it more cost-effective but it means we have control over what kind of sweetener is used and how much. This black pepper granola is subtly sweet and wonderfully spiced, the main flavour being the cardamom; the black pepper is only slightly noticeable. The flavour combination works really well with peaches, either fresh or poached. It is also a good recipe to make with children as it involves a lot of stirring and weighing – good jobs for little hands.

Heat your oven to 180°C/gas 4 and line a baking tray with non-stick baking paper.

In a large bowl combine the oats, buckwheat, nuts and seeds. Grind over a generous amount of black pepper.

In a small saucepan over a low–medium heat, melt the coconut oil. Once liquid, add the maple syrup, vanilla extract, cardamom and salt. Whisk together until smooth. Pour the wet mixture over the dry and fold in until evenly distributed.

Spread the mixture out in an even layer on the lined baking tray and press it down firmly with the back of a spatula to ensure that the mixture is compact.

Bake for 15–20 minutes. Remove from the oven, flip the granola, trying not to break it up too much to keep the pieces large, and place the tray back in the oven to bake for another 10 minutes, stirring every 3–4 minutes, until toasted and fragrant. The dark colour of the granola makes it hard to tell whether it is cooked or not, so go by smell. Another good way to test it is by tasting an almond, which takes the longest to cook – it should taste nutty and pleasantly roasted.

chocolate granola

MAKES AROUND 400G

50g oats (gluten-free oats work well too)
75g almonds
75g hazelnuts
70g sunflower seeds
4 tbsp cacao powder
3 tbsp maple syrup
1 tbsp coconut oil, melted
1 tbsp coconut sugar
a generous pinch of sea salt
35g coconut chips
1 tbsp cacao nibs

We like this granola recipe because it's not too sweet – it's made from cacao rather than sugary chocolate – but still feels like a breakfast 'treat'. We pour almond milk over it or use it to top a smoothie to give it some crunch. We even eat it by the handful as a snack. Play around with the ingredients as you wish: desiccated coconut can be stirred through at the end or adding around 50g of unroasted buckwheat groats gives it another level of texture.

Heat your oven to 160°C/gas 3 and line a baking tray with non-stick baking paper. Place all the ingredients except for the coconut chips and cacao nibs on the tray and mix thoroughly.

Bake for around 20 minutes, before taking the tray out of the oven and stirring through the coconut chips. Pop the tray back in the oven for another 10 minutes. Check on it occasionally to make sure that the granola doesn't burn. The dark colour makes it hard to tell whether the granola is cooked or not, so go by smell. Another good way to test it is by tasting an almond, as they take the longest to cook – it should taste nutty and pleasantly roasted.

Once done, remove from the oven and allow to cool on the tray, adding the cacao nibs once it's cooled and giving it one final mix before storing in a jar.

three breakfast
salads

We love a savoury start and salad for breakfast leads to a focused
and productive day. It contains no sugar so you will not get any
sort of blood sugar slump and the healthy fats in these, our three
favourites, will keep you feeling satisfied for longer. These can,
of course, be eaten at any time of day, separately or together.
We suggest adding a thick slice of our Everyday loaf (see page
175) covered in ghee, or a boiled egg to help make them a more
substantial start to your morning.

shaved
mushrooms

SERVES TWO

200g chestnut mushrooms,
*   very finely sliced*
truffle oil, for drizzling
black pepper
a few shavings of Parmesan

Lay out a layer of mushrooms on a serving plate, lightly drizzle with
truffle oil, then scatter over a generous amount of black pepper and
the Parmesan. Repeat until you've layered all the mushrooms.

—

cucumber, avocado and tomato

SERVES TWO

Chop the cucumber into quarters, cut the avocado into similar-sized chunks and do the same with the tomatoes. Toss them together in a bowl with the parsley, pour in the olive oil, add a squirt of lemon and season well.

½ cucumber
1 avocado, peeled and stoned
3 ripe tomatoes
a handful of flat-leaf parsley
a glug of olive oil
½ lemon
sea salt and black pepper

carrots and black sesame

SERVES TWO

Mix together the carrot, garlic, coriander and lemon juice. Drizzle with olive oil and season well. Gently toast the white sesame seeds in a dry frying pan over a low heat then scatter a sprinkling over the dish along with the black sesame seeds.

3 carrots, grated
1 garlic clove, finely chopped (optional)
a handful of coriander
juice of 1 lemon
olive oil, for drizzling
2 tsp white sesame seeds
4 tsp black sesame seeds
sea salt and black pepper

sweetcorn fritters

SERVES FOUR

150g buckwheat flour

¼ tsp baking powder

1 tsp ground coriander

1 tsp ground cumin

1 tsp sweet paprika

½ tsp sea salt

1 medium egg, lightly beaten

1 tsp lemon juice

350g fresh corn kernels, cut from
    about 3 large cobs

4 spring onions, thinly sliced

3 tbsp coriander, chopped

2 tbsp coconut oil

green salad, to serve

4 lime wedges, to serve

Are we allowed to have favourites? I mean, we do love all of our breakfast recipes but for this one we swoon, we salivate and we jump up and down in anticipation of every crispy morsel. Play with the spices – ramp them up or tone things down – and keep any accompaniments simple, the fritters are the star of the show. This is a special occasion kind of a breakfast!

Place the flour, baking powder, spices and salt in a bowl. Add the egg, lemon juice and 125ml of water and beat with a wooden spoon until you have a smooth batter. Now add the corn, spring onions and coriander and stir to combine.

Melt the coconut oil in a frying pan over a medium heat. When hot, add 2–3 spoonfuls of the fritter mixture. Flatten the mixture and fry for around 2 minutes per side. You want the fritters to be golden and cooked through. Serve with a green salad and the lime wedges.

baked eggs
with crispy sage

SERVES TWO

a large knob of unsalted butter
a handful of sage leaves
4 eggs
sliced sourdough bread, to serve

This recipe calls for so few ingredients that the quality of each is very important. Sage is quite an easy herb to grow so we tend to have a lot to hand and we like to use the best pasture-fed chicken's eggs we can, which have beautiful deep orange yolks. We buy our sourdough bread from one of our favourite bakeries, a process which in itself can be really enjoyable. This is a wonderful winter breakfast, to be taken leisurely at the weekend, wrapped in your dressing gown, with the papers or a good book.

Heat your oven to 200°C/gas 6. Melt the butter in a heavy-based frying pan and add the sage leaves. Fry the butter and sage together until the sage becomes crispy and the butter browns.

Crack the eggs into an ovenproof dish large enough for all four (the eggs should fill the base of the dish without being too thinly spread). Pour over the browned butter, keeping the sage to one side. Bake the eggs for 10 minutes – the whites will be set. Serve with a slice of sourdough bread and garnish with the crispy sage.

green juice

SERVES ONE TO TWO

4 celery sticks
½ large cucumber
½ fennel bulb
2 big handfuls of spinach
  (we use true spinach here; it's a
  lot stalkier and juicer than baby leaf)
a bunch of flat-leaf parsley
a thumb-sized piece of ginger
1 apple (optional)

Once you get into the habit of making green juice, you'll never look back. A juice is full of green goodness yet it's easier to consume than trying to fit in all these ingredients at mealtimes. We've added an apple to this recipe for those who enjoy a sweeter tasting juice or who are just transitioning to drinks made purely from vegetables – the apple will make this less daunting! Sometimes we make too much as the quantity of juice the veg yields depends on how 'juicy' your ingredients are and how good your juicer is (we like to use the Hurom cold press juicer), but it can be stored in a glass jar in the fridge for up to 3 days. The longer you leave it, the more it will have had time to oxidise and won't be as fresh and nutritious for you, but it's still better than shop-bought juice. This green juice is great to have with your breakfast, or as a mid-morning snack to keep you powering through to lunchtime!

Start by washing all the produce and chop the larger bits into pieces. Pass the ingredients through your juicer alternating between chunks and leaves. You can use the celery sticks and cucumber to help push the parsley and spinach through (we tend to bunch the leaves up as this helps make them more 'solid' and easier to juice). Once you have juiced all your bits, give it a stir and drink up the goodness as soon as possible.

berry cacao smoothie

SERVES TWO

500ml almond milk
    (see page 158 for how
    to make your own)
1 ripe banana
250g frozen berries (we use
    raspberries, blueberries
    and strawberries)
1 tbsp tahini
2 tsp cacao powder
1 tsp schisandra berry powder
    (see page 18 to find out a bit
    more about what this is)
1 tsp cacao nibs

When we fancy a sweeter treat in the mornings, this smoothie does the trick. It's also packed with goodness: mood-boosting cacao increases metabolism, fights fatigue and contains anti-oxidants and schisandra berry powder will give your libido a kick and soothe your nervous system. It's a super smoothie to power you through your day.

Load your blender with all the ingredients except for the cacao nibs. If your blender isn't very powerful, we tend to let the frozen berries sit in the almond milk first to defrost a little while we shower and get ourselves prepared in the mornings.

Blend until smooth. Sprinkle with the cacao nibs.

You can take this in a jar with you and have as a mid-morning or afternoon boost, just make sure you put it in the fridge until you're ready to drink it.

green
smoothie

SERVES TWO

1 ripe avocado, peeled and stoned

1 ripe pear, cored

a thumb-sized piece of ginger, peeled

2 handfuls of spinach

juice of 1 lemon

a handful of mint leaves

1 tsp spirulina powder

When we've had a period of heavy food, we tend to reset our body by drinking warm water with lemon upon waking (see page 200), followed by a green smoothie. Enough to keep you sated, but light enough to give your body a break from digesting, this smoothie will help you feel energised. It's great for breakfast, before or after a workout and as a snack. You can also make double and keep it in the fridge for the next day.

Put everything into a blender, with 300ml of water to begin with, and whizz until smooth. If you like your smoothies less thick, add more water as you see fit and blend again. Pour into a glass and enjoy!

turmeric latte

SERVES ONE

230ml almond milk
  (see page 158 for how to make
  your own)
1 heaped tsp ground turmeric
1 heaped tsp coconut oil or ghee
a grind of black pepper

So soothing and warming, this drink is a staple for us during the colder months, preferably enjoyed while reading a good book and watching the rain outside. Turmeric has anti-inflammatory properties so if you do any high-impact exercise or have joint pains, you can really feel them ease away after sipping a mug of this beautiful golden milk.

Pour the almond milk into a heavy-based pan. Place over a medium heat and whisk in the turmeric. Slowly warm the milk, adding the coconut oil or ghee and black pepper. Do not heat to a high temperature; it only needs to be warm. Pour into your favourite mug.

chaga latte

SERVES ONE

230ml almond milk
*   (see page 158 for how*
*   to make your own)*
1 tsp chaga powder
1–2 tsp raw honey
1 cinnamon stick

Although a type of mushroom, chaga grows on trees and is much harder than mushrooms you might be more familiar with – its texture and density is almost like wood. Chaga grows in harsh climates – mainly in Eastern Europe and in some parts of North America – where it survives by feeding and strengthening itself with the potent phytochemicals and nutrients from the tree. The Chinese call chaga the 'King of plants' and it has long been known for its potent anti-inflammatory and nourishing qualities; it aids the body in recovery and promotes longevity.

Chaga chunks can be steeped in water to make a subtle-tasting tea, but we like to absorb all its powerful benefits by sipping a warming latte made with powdered chaga and almond milk. Mixing it with the milk means that the flavour is milder than a tea and therefore not too overpowering for those trying chaga for the first time. We drink it as a daytime alternative to coffee, or just before bedtime.

Put the almond milk into a small pan set over a gentle heat. Place the chaga powder into your chosen cup or mug, add 2 teaspoons of water and stir or whisk the powder into a paste. Once the almond milk is hot (but not boiling), pour it into the cup, then stir in the honey and finish by adding the cinnamon stick.

CHAPTER TWO

This section is for those times when you're not ready for a meal but you'd like something to satisfy your taste buds, or perhaps you have people coming over and need some snacks. That said, most of the recipes can also work as side dishes or starters – there are no rules and we encourage you to enjoy them whenever you like.

Some people are natural
grazers while others' days are
dictated by three square meals
– neither is right or wrong; it's
simply important to listen to
your own body and what
it needs. If you are feeling
hungry (and you know it's
not just thirst), do not deprive
yourself, reach for something
in between.

baked green tomatoes

SERVES TWO

4 tbsp buckwheat flour
4 tbsp fine polenta
1 egg, beaten with a bit
   of almond milk (see page
   158 for how to make your own)
6–8 green tomatoes,
   cut into 5mm slices
ghee or olive oil, for frying
sea salt and black pepper

Green tomatoes are slightly more tart in flavour than their red friends and are available around October time. You can eat these baked tomatoes on their own, or try them with the Almond aioli on page 191; we think it lifts them to a whole new level.

Spread the buckwheat flour over a tray and do the same with the polenta on a separate tray. Place the egg mixture in a shallow dish and season with salt and pepper.

Coat each slice of tomato in the buckwheat flour, then shake off any excess before dipping in the egg mixture. Again, allow any excess egg to drain then coat the slice in the polenta and shake off any excess. Repeat this process for the rest of the tomato slices, and keep them on a plate or tray, ready for cooking.

Coat the bottom of a large frying pan with the ghee or olive oil and place it over a medium heat. When hot, add the tomatoes and fry for a few minutes until golden, then flip and fry the other side.

When cooked, remove each slice and set on some kitchen paper to drain. Sprinkle with more salt and pepper.

seaweed flaxseed
crackers

SERVES SIX

250g flaxseeds (not ground)
1 tsp tamari
2 tbsp green nori sprinkle
½ tsp sea salt
½ tsp dried chilli flakes

These are a welcome addition to your kitchen cupboard especially when you need something savoury or have people coming round – you'll be glad you have a stash. They are also a doddle to make and can be stored in an airtight container for up to a month. You can munch on them plain, or make them fancy with avocado, tomatoes or our Spicy turmeric hummus (see page 183).

In a bowl, mix all the ingredients together with 500ml of water, then cover with a tea towel and leave to sit for 1½ hours.

Heat your oven to 160°C/gas 3. Line a baking tray with non-stick baking paper.

Pour the mixture on to the lined tray, spreading it out evenly using a spatula, until it is about 5mm thick. Using a knife, score lines in the mixture to mark out the size of cracker you'd like. Bake in the oven for 12 hours (or overnight).

Once they are dry and brittle, remove the tray from the oven and allow the crackers to cool. Break them up using the marks you made and enjoy them however you want.

celeriac
chips

SERVES TWO

1 celeriac

2 tbsp olive oil, coconut oil or
   unsalted butter

2 garlic cloves, crushed

1 tsp dried oregano

1 tsp dried chilli flakes (optional)

4 rosemary stalks

sea salt and black pepper

We're not trying to replace potato chips by any means, but the slightly nutty and less starchy humble celeriac makes a delicious and healthier oven-baked alternative. The key is to flash-boil the celeriac first as this helps the outside crisp up in the oven. Try different dried herbs, according to your preference; we like to add chilli flakes to ours (we do to most things!) but you can leave this out if you don't fancy the heat. Enjoy with harissa sauce or your favourite condiments.

Heat your oven to 200°C/gas 6. Line a large baking tray with non-stick baking paper.

Peel your celeriac and cut it into wedges or big chip shapes (we like ours chunky).

Fill a pan with cold water and add your celeriac. Bring the water to the boil, and let the celeriac boil for 2–3 minutes. Drain and allow the celeriac to dry a little in its own steam.

Back in the pan, mix the celeriac with the oil or butter, garlic, oregano and chilli flakes, if using. Season generously and place on the lined baking tray, spreading the chips out evenly – you don't want them too close together, otherwise they will steam rather than roast. Add the rosemary stalks, and place the tray in the oven for 35–40 minutes.

They won't be as crispy as real potato chips, so be careful removing them from the tray – use a thin spatula where you can to separate the chip from the tray if you fear it might have stuck.

popcorn two ways: sweet and savoury

MAKES ONE LARGE BOWL

coconut oil, for frying
50g popcorn kernels

FOR SWEET
2 tbsp coconut oil
2 tbsp coconut sugar
2 tbsp ground cinnamon
a pinch of sea salt

FOR SAVOURY
2 tbsp coconut oil
2 tbsp nutritional yeast
2 tsp garlic powder/granules
½ tsp dried chilli flakes
sea salt and black pepper

Popcorn is a great and healthy alternative snack to have on hand when you're peckish, or when you have surprise visitors. It is so easy to make and sneak into the cinema as well, just adjust the flavours to your liking – anything goes so experiment.

In a large pot with a lid, heat enough coconut oil to cover the bottom of the pot over a medium–high heat.

To test if the oil is hot enough, drop one corn kernel in. When it pops, remove it and then add the rest of the kernels, shaking the pot to coat them evenly in the oil. Once the kernels begin to pop, put the lid on and listen to the popping sound, giving the pot a shake every now and then.

When the popping slows down and there's only a pop every so often, take the lid off the pan and make sure none of the kernels are burning at the bottom. This also lets the steam out so your popcorn doesn't become soggy.

In a smaller pan, heat the coconut oil for your flavours. Once melted, pour over the popcorn and add the remainder of either your sweet or savoury flavour ingredients and stir to coat. Tuck in!

vegetable corn muffins

MAKES EIGHT

1 carrot, grated

1 courgette, grated

100g sweetcorn

2 spring onions, chopped

2 handfuls of chives, chopped

2 handfuls of coriander, chopped

160g polenta

120g buckwheat flour

250ml almond milk (see page 158 for
    how to make your own)

1 tbsp sunflower seeds

1 tbsp pumpkin seeds

2 tbsp psyllium husk

1 tsp baking powder

½–1 tsp dried chilli flakes (to taste)

2 tbsp coconut oil, plus extra to grease

grated zest and juice of ½ lemon

black sesame seeds, to top

sea salt and black pepper

These are great to make ahead for the week for a snack when you're on the go or as something to take with you to the park or beach to enjoy. They can also step in as a quick savoury breakfast and are great with some smashed avocado as a light lunch. Experiment with different kinds of vegetables to get a variety of textures and tastes. This will keep the flavours interesting and act as an incentive to keep making them. You can also freeze them and warm them up in the oven again – if you're being extremely organised, you can bake the mixture in a loaf tin and then cut into slices before freezing.

Heat your oven to 200°C/gas 6. Grease eight holes of a muffin tin or a 450g loaf tin with coconut oil.

In a bowl, mix the carrot and courgette with the sweetcorn, spring onions and herbs. Add the polenta, buckwheat flour and almond milk and gently combine.

Now add the seeds, psyllium husk, baking powder, chilli flakes, coconut oil, lemon zest and juice and mix. Season with salt and pepper then continue to stir until it forms a sticky dough; if it's too dry just add a bit of water.

Spoon the mixture into your prepared tin, then bake in the oven for 20–25 minutes, until firm and golden on top. Remove from the oven and lift out of the tin, then place directly on to the oven rack. Bake for another 10–15 minutes – check the muffins or loaf are done by sticking a sharp knife in the centre; if the knife comes out clean, they are ready. Remove, scatter with the sesame seeds and allow to cool before tucking in.

CHAPTER THREE

Sometimes you might find
that you are dining alone, or
you need something small and
simple to make just for two
or three of you; these are the
dishes we turn to. They are
meals we come back to again
and again and make up most
lunches or dinners in our
households because they are
quick, easy and delicious –
some have even been known to
crop up in the mornings.

The majority of these can be scaled up to serve more, or we prepare a selection of them and serve them 'tapas-style' to make up a heartier dinner. They can also be part of a prep day – made in a batch so that you have something for the rest of the week, or a tasty surprise in the freezer when you come back home from a long day or weekend away and can't face lifting a finger in the kitchen.

chicken noodle soup

SERVES TWO (GENEROUSLY)

2 tbsp coconut or olive oil

1 large onion, chopped

3 garlic cloves, chopped

a thumb-sized piece of ginger,
    grated

½ red chilli, chopped
    (deseeded if you want less heat)

a handful of fresh oregano

2 large carrots, chopped

2 large celery sticks, chopped

a large handful of mushrooms,
    chopped

2 bay leaves

1 litre home-made chicken stock
    (see page 192)

200g cooked chicken, shredded
    (leftovers from a roast ideally)

1 x 200g tin sweetcorn

100g rice noodles (brown or white)

250g baby spinach

juice of 1 lemon, plus extra wedges,
    to serve

sea salt and black pepper

This is what we crave when it's cold outside and we want to be nourished with something tasty and warm. It's also amazing for when you are feeling a little under the weather – even more so if someone can make it for you! We always have fresh stock on hand and, occasionally, leftover chicken from a roast, so it's even easier to put this soup together. You can also make up a bigger batch and freeze it (without the noodles) so you'll always have home-made chicken soup for when you don't feel like making anything. This might not sound very groundbreaking as recipes go, but it really is the most soothing and comforting bowl of tasty goodness you can consume, packed full of vegetables and familiar flavours but with the sweetness of the corn and zing from the lemon.

In a large pot with a lid, heat your choice of oil (we use coconut), then fry the onion with the garlic, ginger, chilli and oregano over a medium–high heat.

Once softened, add your carrot, celery and mushrooms, along with the bay leaves. Season with salt and pepper, give it a good stir and cook for about 5 minutes.

Add the chicken stock and bring to the boil, then turn the heat down and leave to simmer for 15–20 minutes.

Now, add the chicken, sweetcorn and rice noodles, and cook for a further 10 minutes. The soup will have thickened with the rice noodles. Check the seasoning and that it is piping hot. Turn the heat off and throw in the spinach to wilt in the residual heat.

Give it a good stir to mix in the spinach, then serve in the most comforting bowls you can find and finish with a generous squeeze of lemon juice – this really makes the soup; we always have extra wedges on hand to add more.

mint and garlic chickpea soup

SERVES FOUR

2 x 400g tins chickpeas
2 garlic cloves, chopped
6 tbsp olive oil, plus extra to drizzle
2 tbsp lemon juice
¼ tsp cayenne pepper
2 tbsp mint leaves, chopped
2 tbsp flat-leaf parsley, chopped
2 tbsp pumpkin seeds
sea salt and black pepper

Tinned chickpeas are very much one of our store cupboard standbys (for more on these, see page 14). Ready to be turned into a tasty hummus, whipped into a hearty breakfast dish as an alternative to a bread-based breakfast, or simply added to salads and curries. This hearty soup is cheap and satisfying, as well as being absolutely delicious. Add more vegetables as you please or serve with a soft-boiled egg if you're feeling extra ravenous.

Drain the chickpeas, reserving the liquid and pouring it into a measuring jug before topping it up with water to make 900ml.

Place the chickpeas, chickpea liquid, garlic, olive oil and lemon juice in a food processor and blend until smooth.

Pass the purée through a sieve into a saucepan and add the cayenne pepper. Heat the purée, adding more water if you like a thinner consistency. Throw in most of the herbs and stir through. Once piping hot, season the soup with salt and pepper and adjust the level of lemon to your taste.

In another small frying pan, toast the pumpkin seeds until they start to pop, making sure not to burn them.

Serve the soup in bowls, scattering over the remaining fresh herbs and toasted pumpkin seeds. Drizzle some olive oil on top before settling down to enjoy.

chilled
almond soup

SERVES SIX

250g white sourdough bread
    (stale is best), crusts removed,
    torn into large pieces
900ml chilled water
150g blanched almonds
3 garlic cloves
2 tsp sea salt
6 tbsp olive oil
3 tbsp white wine vinegar
250g seedless white grapes, halved
olive oil, to serve
black pepper, to serve

Also known as *ajo blanco con uvas* (white garlic soup with grapes), this lively dish originates from Spain and is served chilled, very much like gazpacho. It packs a flavour punch – the sweetness from the grapes balancing the feisty garlic. This is a great starter to serve in the warmer months, or makes a light lunch served with a crisp salad and a slice of our Everyday loaf (see page 175).

Place the torn pieces of bread in the chilled water, and leave to soak while you get on with everything else.

Place the almonds, garlic and salt in a food processor and process until the almonds are finely ground.

Squeeze the excess water from the bread and add it to the processor, reserving the water. Turn the processor on again and trickle the olive oil in slowly, adding the vinegar, and then finally the water from the soaked bread.

Blend until smooth before transferring to a serving bowl. Stir through the grapes and keep the soup chilled, covered with cling film, until you are ready to serve. Add a drizzle of olive oil and a grind of black pepper to each serving to finish.

roasted cauliflower soup

SERVES SIX

FOR THE SOUP

1 garlic bulb

1 medium head of cauliflower,
    cut into florets

olive oil, for drizzling and frying

1 onion, chopped

1 carrot, chopped

1 celery stick, chopped

3 thyme sprigs, leaves picked

750ml good-quality stock (we use
    home-made chicken stock, but
    vegetable stock is also good, see
    pages 192 and 195)

250ml almond milk
    (see page 158 for how to
    make your own)

sea salt and black pepper

FOR THE ANCHOVY TOAST

4 anchovy fillets

5 tbsp unsalted butter, softened

baguette or toasted bread of
    your choice (enough for 6)

This is a super simple soup to make, especially in autumn and winter – it's cosiness in a bowl. The toast takes the soup to next-level deliciousness, especially if you're a fan of anchovies. Start off with a smaller quantity if anchovies sound a bit scary to you, but even if you're not a fan we'd say give them a go; they give the butter a lovely salty finish. You can keep the rest of the soup in the fridge or freezer if you don't need to make enough for six. It's always a bonus to have something you can just heat up when you've had a long day, especially something as comforting as this!

Heat your oven to 200°C/gas 6.

Cut the garlic bulb in half horizontally, place on a large piece of foil and drizzle with olive oil. Wrap the foil around it fairly loosely and place in the oven for 45 minutes.

Toss the cauliflower in enough olive oil to coat, season with salt and pepper and then transfer it to a baking tray. Roast for about 30 minutes until golden and slightly tender.

In a large pot, heat 3 tablespoons of olive oil over a medium heat. Add the onion and sweat until softened, then add the carrot, celery, thyme and stock. Bring to the boil, then reduce the heat and leave to simmer.

Once the cauliflower is ready, remove it from the oven and toss it into the pot. Leave to simmer for another 20 minutes. Meanwhile, remove the garlic from the oven and, when it is cool enough to handle, squeeze the cloves out of their skins and add them to the soup.

Combine the anchovies and butter by mashing together with a fork. Scoop out into a small bowl.

Turn the heat off the soup, add the almond milk and use a hand blender to purée the soup until smooth. Reheat gently if necessary. Serve in big bowls, with anchovy butter spread on top of the bread or toast, and plenty of black pepper.

—

mushroom
plate

SERVES TWO

6 king oyster mushrooms,
   thinly sliced lengthways
   (we find them at our local
   Turkish or Asian grocers)
2 tbsp olive oil
sea salt and black pepper

FOR THE HERB DRESSING

125ml olive oil
1 garlic clove, thinly sliced
a handful of flat-leaf parsley, finely
   chopped
1 tsp dried oregano
grated zest of 1 lemon
a handful of basil, chopped
a handful of mint, chopped

TO SERVE

1 quantity of Pickled mushrooms
   (see opposite)
1 red chilli, thinly sliced
a handful of flat-leaf parsley,
   chopped
juice of 1 lemon

This might seem like a lot of work for a very simple dish, but believe us, it is super delicious and makes a great and impressive starter. Once you've made this a couple of times, it will become a go-to recipe for dinner guests. The Pickled mushrooms (see opposite) and dressing can be made in advance and the latter can be drizzled on pretty much anything to be honest – it really lifts a dish. It's even nice to treat yourself to a plate of this for an uplifting solo supper.

Heat your oven grill on high. Lay the king oyster mushrooms in a roasting pan, making sure there's space between them so the mushrooms don't end up 'steaming' one another. Dress with the olive oil, and season generously with salt and pepper. Place under the hot grill for 2–3 minutes, or until the mushrooms begin to soften without colouring. Once done, take them out of the grill, and set aside.

For the herb dressing, heat half the oil in a pan and gently cook the garlic until it softens, then add the parsley for a couple of minutes. Take off the heat, transfer to a bowl or jug, add the oregano and lemon zest and allow to cool. Add the rest of the fresh herbs and olive oil, some salt and pepper to taste and give it a stir once the dressing has come to room temperature.

To serve, place the king oyster mushrooms on a plate, drizzle over the herb dressing, scatter the pickled mushrooms on top, along with the red chilli and parsley. Season to taste (if necessary) and finish with a squeeze of lemon juice.

pickled
mushrooms

SERVES FOUR OR SIX AS A SIDE

500g mixed mushrooms
(shimeji, shiitake, chestnut),
very finely sliced (use a mandolin
if you have one)
1 tbsp toasted sesame oil
4 tbsp tamari
4 tbsp apple cider vinegar
1 tbsp maple syrup
sea salt and black pepper

These very lightly pickled mushrooms are great for when your fridge raid lunch or dinner needs a facelift with something tasty and punchy. All too often they're an afterthought for us – a way of using up the mushrooms in the fridge, but when we do make them, we're pleased we did. They work well as a topping for a quinoa or rice bowl, in a wrap or on top of anything else you can think of.

In a bowl, combine all the ingredients and let them sit for 30 minutes, stirring occasionally to make sure the mushrooms are covered in the pickling liquid.

Use as you wish. They're that easy and honestly that delicious! You can store any you don't eat straightaway in a jar and pop them in the fridge for a few days.

—

harissa chickpeas, kale and fried egg

SERVES TWO

ghee or olive oil, for frying
1 x 400g tin chickpeas,
  drained and rinsed
1 tsp harissa sauce
grated zest and juice of 1 lemon
2 big handfuls of kale leaves,
  stalks removed
2 eggs
2 spring onions, sliced
sea salt and black pepper

Originally whipped up for brunch, this tasty dish has also been known to pop up at our lunch and dinner. It's easy to make for one as well (unless you're particularly famished), just halve the ingredients and pop the leftover chickpeas in a bowl in the fridge.

Harissa is a spicy chilli paste or sauce found in northern African countries. There are lots of brands and variations available but we like to keep it simple, that's why Harry Brand is great – it's just water, red chillies, fresh garlic and salt.

Heat some ghee or olive oil in a frying pan over a medium heat. Once hot, throw in the chickpeas, harissa and a splash of water. Once the chickpeas have been cooking for 5 minutes and are heated through, transfer to a bowl and stir through the lemon zest.

In the same pan, still on a medium heat, add a little more ghee or oil, and add the kale. Cook until wilted and soft, then season with salt and pepper.

While the kale is cooking, heat another pan with some ghee or oil and fry your eggs until they're done to your liking.

To serve, divide the kale between the plates, then add the chickpeas, a squeeze of lemon and top with the fried eggs and spring onions.

—

sardines with quick pickled shallots

SERVES TWO

1 shallot, finely sliced

1 tbsp apple cider vinegar

1 tsp coconut sugar

2 slices of bread of your choice
  (we use our local sourdough)

1 x 140g tin sardines in olive oil
  (we like Ortiz), drained

a glug of olive oil

a handful of flat-leaf parsley,
  chopped

juice of 1 lemon

sea salt

butter or ghee, to serve

We know we're not really breaking new ground with this recipe, but sometimes it's easy to forget how delicious the simplest things can be so we thought we'd remind you of what a timeless lifesaver a tin of sardines is. Sardines are naturally high in omega-3 fatty acids and amino acids and, to up the goodness, we've added a delicious home-made twist on a pickled onion. For us sardines on toast is a great, quick all-rounder meal – a breakfast, lunch or light dinner.

By all means cook fresh sardines on the grill and serve them the same way, but we find good-quality tinned sardines, such as the Ortiz brand, do the job and make this a lot quicker to whip up! Serve it with some cucumber for a bite of crunchy freshness.

First, put the shallot into a small bowl. Douse with the vinegar, sugar and a pinch of salt, give it a stir and set aside.

Next, toast your bread and while that's on, use the back of a fork to mash the sardines a little with the olive oil, two thirds of the parsley and some salt.

Once the toast is ready, spread it with a little butter or ghee, then top with the sardines and squeeze over some lemon juice too. Sprinkle the quick pickled shallot on top, along with the remaining parsley. Tuck in while the toast is still hot and buttery.

indian spiced cabbage

SERVES FOUR

2 tbsp ghee

1 tsp mustard seeds

½ tsp cumin seeds

1 garlic clove, crushed

a thumb-sized piece of ginger,
  finely chopped

1 small green chilli, finely chopped

¼ tsp ground turmeric

1 medium white cabbage, sliced

sea salt and black pepper

lime wedges, to serve

This aromatic and spicy dish makes a humble cabbage come alive. You can serve it simply with rice (see page 84 for our nutty Garlic brown rice) and some minty cucumber yoghurt, or it makes a great side dish to an Indian-spice rubbed roast chicken for an alternative Sunday roast (try using ground spices such as coriander, garam masala, chilli, cumin and turmeric as a marinade with lemon juice).

In a frying pan, heat the ghee over a medium–high heat. Add the mustard and cumin seeds and let them sizzle for a bit without burning. When they start making that popping sound, add the garlic, ginger, chilli and turmeric and stir so it doesn't stick to the bottom. Pop all the cabbage into the pan and coat it with the mixture, stirring continuously. Season with some salt and pepper to taste, and continue to stir until the cabbage begins to wilt a bit.

Once cooked to your liking (we think the cabbage should still have a bite to it!), turn the heat off. Serve with lime wedges.

sesame
seaweed salad

SERVES FOUR

30g dried dulse seaweed

30g dried wakame seaweed

juice of 1 lime

2 small carrots, thinly sliced

1 small cucumber, thinly sliced

a handful of shiitake mushrooms,
    stalks removed, thinly sliced

4 radishes, thinly sliced

2 tbsp toasted sesame seeds
    (white and black)

1 red chilli, thinly sliced

4 spring onions, thinly sliced

a handful of coriander leaves,
    chopped

sea salt

FOR THE DRESSING

2 tbsp apple cider vinegar

2 tsp maple syrup

a thumb-sized piece of ginger,
    grated

2 tsp tamari

1 tsp light tahini

1 tbsp toasted sesame oil

We love the saltiness and taste of the sea that comes from eating seaweed, but it's also packed full of flavour and goodness – dulse and wakame both contain ten times more calcium than milk and four times more iron than steak! We like to use both kinds for the different textures and tastes they bring to this dish, but there are lots of other types to try so experiment and mix and match according to your own preference. You can make a more substantial meal out of the salad by tossing chopped avocado through it; this is also a good way of adding some sustaining healthy fats.

Firstly, soak the seaweeds in a bowl of hot water for 10 minutes, until they soften.

While that is on the go, make the dressing by whisking together the vinegar, maple syrup, ginger, tamari, tahini and sesame oil.

Drain and dry the seaweed, then roughly chop it into 5cm pieces. Toss the seaweed in half the dressing along with the lime juice. Spoon the salad into your dishes and top with the sliced vegetables. Drizzle over the remaining sauce, gently toss again and sprinkle over your toasted sesame seeds, chilli, spring onions and coriander. Season with salt if necessary, although you might find that the seaweed and tamari are salty enough already.

garlic
brown rice

SERVES FOUR TO SIX

500g short grain brown rice,
soaked in cold water
for at least a few hours
4 tbsp ghee or coconut oil
2 garlic cloves, crushed
sea salt

We love nutty brown rice – it's full of fibre and is hearty and filling. We make up this simple rice dish and toss it through greens, such as Tenderstem broccoli with some tamari and chilli for a quick and simple midweek supper or serve it as a side dish to a main.

Drain and rinse the rice, place in a saucepan with a lid and cover with 1 litre of fresh water. Bring to the boil, then turn the heat down and allow to simmer, covered loosely with the lid, until the rice is cooked through but still has a bite – this usually takes 20–30 minutes. Turn the heat off and keep the lid on. The rice should have absorbed all the liquid.

In a frying pan, gently heat the ghee or coconut oil and fry the garlic lightly until golden. Now throw in the rice and stir to mix thoroughly. Season generously with salt and serve hot.

—

quinoa tabbouleh

SERVES FOUR

400g quinoa
  (we like mixed to add colour)
1 cucumber, diced
8 plum tomatoes, diced, or 400g
  cherry tomatoes, quartered
4 spring onions, chopped
2 tbsp olive oil
2 garlic cloves, crushed
juice of 1 lemon
a handful of mint leaves, chopped
a handful of flat-leaf parsley,
  chopped
sea salt and black pepper

Quinoa is lighter on the stomach than couscous and it's wheat-free for those avoiding wheat. We think it gives this traditional recipe a nuttier flavour and a bit more texture than couscous would but by all means use couscous if that is your heart's desire. The tabbouleh can be kept in the fridge until you need it, but add the herbs just before you serve it so they're still perky.

Place the quinoa in a medium saucepan over a medium heat and allow it to toast until it starts to smell fragrant. Add 500ml of water and bring to the boil. Pop the lid on and allow to simmer, stirring occasionally, until all the water has been absorbed and the quinoa has expanded and has little 'tails'. This should take about 10–15 minutes, possibly a little longer if you are using red or black quinoa too. Once cooked allow to cool to room temperature at least.

Place the quinoa in a big bowl and add the cucumber, tomatoes and spring onions.

Whisk the olive oil, garlic and lemon juice together to make a dressing, seasoning with salt and pepper. Mix the dressing into the bowl of salad, stirring in the fresh herbs just before serving. Season to taste.

kale caesar
salad

SERVES TWO (GENEROUSLY)

500g kale, stalks removed

75g cashew nuts, soaked in cold water for a few hours then drained

65g macadamia nuts, soaked in cold water for a few hours then drained

4 tbsp nutritional yeast

2 garlic cloves

1 tbsp tahini

juice of 1 lemon

1 tbsp Dijon mustard

1 tsp dried chilli flakes

35g pumpkin seeds, toasted

sea salt and black pepper

Although entirely vegan, this is a creamy, cheesy-tasting generous side salad – a really tasty but nutritionally super-charged version of the classic. The nutritional yeast brings the 'cheese' flavour and it is a plant-based source of complete protein – full of vitamins and minerals. You can add more toppings as you desire to make it more substantial or keep this as a side. Another way we like to eat this is to roll it up inside a sheet of nori with thin slivers of carrot, cucumber, sprouts and our Sauerkraut (see page 168), for a quick and simple lunch.

Massaging the kale will help break down the cellulose, making the leaves more sweet than bitter, a more vibrant green and above all softer which means it is more easily digestible so you can eat it raw! Soaking the nuts beforehand will make the blending process a lot easier for your machine.

Wash your kale and dry the leaves well, then place in a bowl.

Place everything aside from the kale, chilli flakes and pumpkin seeds in a blender with 250ml of water and blend until smooth. Season with salt and pepper to taste.

Depending on how 'saucy' you like your salads, start by pouring half of the dressing into your bowl of kale, then, with clean hands, 'massage' the kale so the sauce starts to break down and soften the leaves – this should take between 5 and 10 minutes. Keep at it – the salad will taste so much better.

Once softened, pour in any more dressing you feel it may need or keep the rest refrigerated in a jar for another day, another salad or to use as a dip! Top the salad with the chilli flakes and pumpkin seeds, and mix.

solo
salmon

SERVES ONE WITH

LEFTOVERS, OR TWO

80g white rice

2 tbsp tamari

1 tbsp toasted sesame oil

2 organic salmon fillets, with skin

2 spring onions, chopped

½ red chilli, finely chopped

250g green vegetables

  (such as 125g of Tenderstem

  broccoli and 125g of sugar

  snap peas), trimmed

1 tbsp black sesame seeds

1 tbsp green nori sprinkle

juice of ½ lemon

a handful of coriander, chopped

sea salt

We've called this 'solo salmon' because it is a nourishing meal we've each come to depend on at times when we've needed something just for one. It's something you can cook midweek or at the weekend when you need a quick, simple and tasty meal that is also really good for you – full of healthy fats and greens! Often salmon fillets are sold in packs of two, so we usually make extra for the next day or invite a friendly face over to share our plate of goodness.

Heat your oven grill on high.

Get your rice on the go by adding it to a pan of boiling water. Allow it to simmer according to the packet instructions.

Prepare a steamer to cook your greens and line a baking tray with foil.

In a small bowl, mix the tamari and toasted sesame oil. Brush this mixture over the flesh side of the salmon, then place on the baking tray and season with salt. Flip the fillets and do the same to the skin side. Flip back over and top with the spring onions and chilli.

Once the steamer is ready, place your vegetables inside and steam for 6–8 minutes depending on how big they are – you don't want to overcook them. At the same time, place your salmon under the grill for 6–8 minutes until the skin is crispy, the spring onions are browning slightly and the marinade is bubbling – cooked this way the salmon will still be moist and full of its healthy oils.

Check your rice is cooked and fluffy, then serve it on your plate or bowl of choice and sprinkle with the sesame seeds and nori. Add the vegetables and sprinkle over some lemon juice. Lastly, serve up the salmon, along with the juice that has collected at the bottom of the tray, then scatter the coriander on top. Sit down and enjoy.

coconut greens

**SERVES FOUR AS A SIDE,
OR TWO EATEN WITH RICE**

2 tbsp coconut oil
4 garlic cloves, sliced
2 small shallots, chopped
*1 red chilli, thinly sliced
    (deseeded if you'd
    like it less fiery)*
*a thumb-sized piece of ginger,
    finely chopped*
*a bunch of spring onions,
    finely sliced*
*a bunch of cavolo nero, ribs
    and stems removed, leaves sliced*
*a bunch of spring greens, ribs
    and stems removed, leaves sliced
    (Savoy cabbage can be a great
    substitute)*
125ml coconut milk (from a tin)
sesame seeds, to sprinkle
sea salt
lime wedges, to serve

This makes a healthy and fragrant side dish to any main meal, or it can become the star of the show by simply adding it to a bowl of fluffy white rice spiked with tamari.

Heat the coconut oil in a large frying or sauté pan over a medium heat. Add the garlic first, and cook until golden, then add the shallot, chilli, ginger and half the spring onions, stirring until soft.

Add handfuls of the cavolo nero and spring greens, letting each wilt before adding some more. Season with salt. Stir until the greens are cooked through, but still have a bite to them, about 6–8 minutes. Add the coconut milk and warm through.

Transfer the greens to a serving bowl and top with the remaining spring onions. Sprinkle with sesame seeds and serve with lime wedges.

CHAPTER FOUR

We believe in the importance of making time in your week to sit down with family or loved ones and share some good food. In this chapter you will find a combination of larger dishes that can entertain a few friends and also some really simple family meals. When time is on our side, cooking a feast can be very meditative and a highlight

in a busy week. We like to
plan ahead and get organised,
choosing our ingredients
according to the season and
taking into account our mood.
The cooking never takes over
the evening though. You don't
need a full feast every day but
scattering something a little
more special throughout your
week is well worth the effort.

spring onion
pancakes

SERVES EIGHT

200g buckwheat flour, plus extra
*   for dusting and rolling*
1½ tsp sea salt
4 spring onions, sliced
about 1 tbsp sesame oil, plus extra
*   for frying*

A variation of spring onion pancakes made with wheat flour can be found all over South East Asia. Our version uses buckwheat flour so that they're lighter on the stomach and easier to digest. Sometimes we top our pancakes with a simple lemony spinach and cucumber-ribbon salad, and when we're hungry, some smoked salmon too. If you want to stay authentic though, seek out some hoisin sauce without any nasty additives and use it as a dipping sauce.

Bring 125ml of water to a boil. Sift the buckwheat flour into a large bowl and combine with the sea salt. Slowly pour the water into the flour mixture. Knead the dough until it is no longer sticky and the surface becomes smooth – you might need to add a little more flour or water. The kneading should take about 10 minutes. Add the green parts of the spring onions, knead again and roll into a big ball. Cover the dough with a damp cloth and set aside for 30 minutes.

On a lightly floured surface, divide the dough into eight small balls. Take one dough ball at a time, and with a floured rolling pin, roll the ball out into a flat disc shape (around 15cm wide), dusting as you go (turn the page for a photograph). Once rolled out, brush it with sesame oil on both sides to prevent from sticking.

Once all your discs are ready, it's time to get a frying pan on to a medium–high heat. Sometimes we find that the pan needs a bit of oil and other times the oil on each pancake is enough. Fry a pancake for 1 minute on each side, until bubbles start forming. Repeat with the rest of the pancakes, adding more oil if necessary (kitchen paper might come in handy here too, to soak up the excess oil!). Serve hot.

—

paprika potato
cakes

SERVES SIX

1kg waxy potatoes, such as
  Cyprus or Charlotte
2 large eggs
a handful of flat-leaf parsley, chopped
1 white onion, finely chopped
2 tsp paprika
coconut oil, for frying
sea salt and black pepper

When we fancy something filling on a weeknight and don't want to eat meat, these are great served with a simple green salad tossed in an olive oil and lemon dressing. And on weekends, they work well as a side dish to a meaty main if you've got friends over. We recommend eating them hot out the frying pan but they're delicious cold as well so we often make more than we need to have them for the next day. If you're feeling extra decadent, serve them with soured cream.

Peel and finely grate your potatoes then put them straight into some cold water. Drain and dry them as much as you can using a tea towel and colander – this helps remove the starch.

In a bowl, crack open and beat the eggs lightly. Add the potato, parsley, onion and paprika. Season with salt and pepper, then mix well.

In a frying pan set over a medium–high heat, melt enough coconut oil to cover the base of the pan. Drop a serving spoonful's worth of potato mixture into the pan. Flatten the cake slightly, then lower the heat to make sure you cook it evenly. Once brown on one side, flip the cake over and do the same on the other side.

Once done, remove and set on some kitchen paper to soak up any excess oil and keep warm in an oven set at the lowest temperature while you cook the other potato cakes.

roast tomato potatoes

SERVES FOUR

*1kg waxy potatoes, such as
Cyprus or Charlotte, peeled
and chopped into equal chunks*
*400–500g juicy plum tomatoes,
quartered*
5 garlic cloves, crushed
1 tsp paprika
1 tsp dried chilli flakes
80ml olive oil
1 lemon, cut into quarters
sea salt and black pepper

Waxy potatoes, like Cyprus potatoes, work best for this recipe as they don't soak up too much of the juice from the tomatoes and lemon, which would make them soggy. We also find them sweeter in taste. Great with simply grilled white fish or roast chicken and wilted spinach or watercress and friends round a table, or just on their own with a simple lemony green salad. Make more than you need so you can have them the next day, reheated, crushed and pan-fried.

Heat your oven to 220°C/gas 7.

Spread your potatoes out in a roasting tray, then add the tomatoes, garlic, paprika, chilli flakes and olive oil. Squeeze over the juice from the lemon, and drop the shells into the tray. Season generously with salt and pepper, then use your hands to give it all a good tumble so everything is coated nicely and spread out evenly.

Roast in the oven for around 40 minutes. Check and give them another mix before turning the oven down to 180°C/gas 4 and roasting them for another 15–20 minutes until they are crisp on the outside, squidgy on the inside and some of the juices have caramelised.

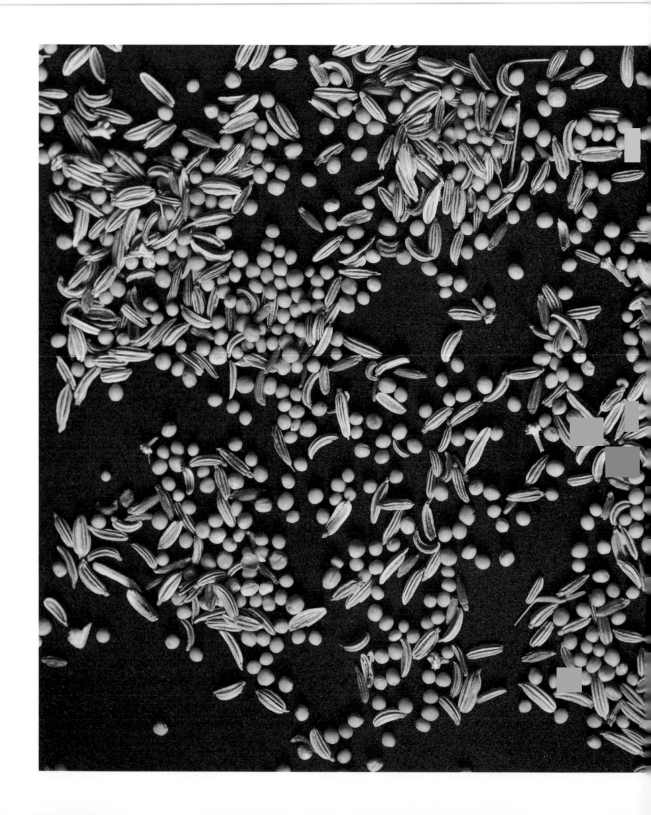

kitchidi

SERVES SIX

1 tbsp ghee or coconut oil

*a thumb-sized piece of ginger,
     grated*

1 tsp ground cumin

1 tsp ground turmeric

1 tsp ground coriander

a pinch of ground cinnamon

*200g mung dal (split yellow mung
     beans), soaked in plenty of cold
     water overnight*

190g basmati rice

*1.5–1.75 litres boiling water (or your
     choice of stock)*

1 tbsp mustard seeds

1 tbsp fennel seeds

2 handfuls of baby spinach

a handful of frozen peas

*a handful of coriander leaves,
     plus extra to garnish*

sea salt and black pepper

lemon wedges, to serve

Also known as kitchari, this dish is said to be the inspiration for the Anglo-Indian dish kedgeree (which is also very tasty!). It's an ancient Ayurvedic dish, made up of two grains (mung dal and rice) and is cooked and eaten for its cleansing and nourishing properties. It's so easy to make a big pot of it, which means you can just reheat it and run some more ghee through it and a squeeze of lemon at a later date (it keeps well in the fridge for a few days, or freezer for a couple of weeks). If you want more colour, just gently steam some leafy greens and have them on the side. This is great to have after a particularly overindulgent weekend or occasion, as it grounds you and helps reset your digestive system but it's important to soak the grains overnight, or for at least 4–6 hours before cooking, to aid digestion.

Heat the ghee or coconut oil in a large pot with a lid over a low–medium heat and gently fry the ginger. After a few minutes, add the cumin, turmeric, ground coriander and cinnamon. Stir gently then add the drained mung dal and rice, and stir again to mix with the spices.

Pour in the water or stock, cover with the lid and allow to simmer for around 20 minutes, or until the grains soften. In a frying pan, dry-fry the mustard seeds and fennel seeds until they start to pop, then remove from the heat. Pop them into your pot of grains.

Throw in your green bits (that's your spinach, peas and coriander), stir through and cook for another 5 minutes until the spinach is wilted. Turn the heat off, and season to taste.

Ladle the kitchidi into bowls, sprinkle over the extra coriander leaves and serve with the lemon wedges.

celeriac and chanterelles

1 large celeriac

3 garlic cloves, crushed

a few thyme sprigs

sea salt and black pepper

FOR THE GREEN SAUCE

2 handfuls of flat-leaf parsley, and
   other herbs if you have them to
   hand, such as chervil, dill,
   tarragon and the celeriac leaves

2 tsp capers, rinsed

2 tsp Dijon mustard

2 tbsp of sherry vinegar

2 tbsp olive oil

2 tbs cold water

TO FINISH

2 large handfuls of chanterelle
   mushrooms

a thumb-sized knob of
   unsalted butter

4 garlic cloves

a few sprigs of thyme

2 tbsp sherry vinegar

We recently hosted a series of dinners with our friend Nick Balfe, head chef of his lovely restaurant Salon in Brixton, and this was one of the stand-out dishes. We love these frilly mushrooms and they partner well with sturdy celeriac. It's an earthy-flavoured dish that can happily sit alone or be served with white fish. The green sauce pulls it all together by adding a lovely zingy element.

Heat your oven to 200°C/gas 6. Wash and trim off any long roots and shoots from the celeriac (if it comes with its stalks and leaves save the stalks for a soup or stew and use the leaves in the sauce). Wrap the whole thing in foil (there's no need to peel it) with the garlic, thyme and some salt, then bake for 1 hour, or until you can stick a skewer into the centre without too much resistance. When the celeriac is cooked, set it aside and leave to cool. Once cool, trim off the skin with a sharp knife and dice the flesh into 1cm cubes.

Now make the green sauce. Finely chop the parsley (and other herbs if you have them) along with the capers. In a bowl, mix these with the mustard and vinegar, then gradually add the olive oil and 2 tablespoons of cold water, stirring as you go, until the mixture has a loose but viscous consistency. Add a pinch of salt and pepper and a little more vinegar if you think it needs it.

Clean the chanterelles by brushing any dirt and leaves off them with a pastry brush. Cut off any damp, mushy ends – these will taste like the forest floor, but not in a good way.

When you are ready to serve, heat a large frying pan over a medium-high heat. Add the butter and allow it to foam a little before adding the celeriac. Don't move the pan too much to begin with as you want to get a bit of colour on the celeriac. After a minute or so, toss the pan to flip the cubes so they can colour on another side. Add the garlic and thyme, then the chanterelles. Let everything sizzle together before tossing again, then add the vinegar and a pinch of salt. Give everything a final swirl in the pan and check the seasoning. Serve in warm bowls with plenty of the green sauce drizzled over the top.

crunchy vegetables
and peanut sauce

SERVES FOUR TO SIX

360g brown rice
4–6 soft-boiled eggs, to serve

FOR THE VEGETABLES

1 small red cabbage, shredded
2 carrots, grated
2 beetroots, grated
2 handfuls of green beans,
   blanched
a handful of boiled potatoes, diced
a handful of chestnut mushrooms,
   thinly sliced
½ cucumber, diced
4 spring onions, thinly sliced
a bunch of coriander
a handful of peanuts, crushed
   or roughly chopped
lime wedges, to serve

FOR THE SAUCE

1 tbsp sesame oil
2 garlic cloves, minced
1 small red chilli, finely chopped
a thumb-sized piece of ginger,
   grated
1 generous tbsp smooth
   peanut butter
1 tbsp tamari
juice of 1 lime
2–4 tbsp hot water

This is our version of a gado gado – an Indonesian salad dish made up of lightly boiled and raw vegetables, topped with tofu or egg and then this incredibly delicious, moreish peanut sauce, which pulls the dish together. Great for gatherings, it's interactive, incredibly tasty and good for you. And the bonus is sometimes there'll be leftovers, so you will have the makings of lunch the next day, or another dinner. You can swap any of our suggested vegetables for ones you have in the fridge or what you fancy, that's the beauty of it. We make like the Indonesians and top ours with a soft-boiled egg for an added protein hit.

Start by cooking the brown rice in boiling water according to the packet instructions. Drain and rinse and transfer to a serving bowl.

While that is happening, prep your vegetables (and eggs, if using) as necessary and place in different serving bowls.

Then make the sauce. Pour the sesame oil into a small pan and fry the garlic, chilli and ginger over a medium heat. Once soft, scoop in the peanut butter then add the tamari and lime juice. Now start to trickle in the hot water and whisk until you have a sauce of a consistency you like (we like it like a salad dressing). Adjust the lime juice and tamari to your taste. Once you're good, transfer the peanut sauce into a jug or a bowl with a spoon for serving.

Allow everyone to gather round and help themselves to vegetables, rice and to put their own toppings on, before pouring over the peanut sauce, mixing it all up and finishing with the spring onions, coriander, crushed peanuts and a squeeze of a lime wedge.

—

celeriac
gratin

SERVES FOUR

150g cashews, soaked in cold water
   overnight, or for at least 7 hours
2 garlic cloves
4 tbsp nutritional yeast,
   plus a little extra to sprinkle
100ml almond milk (see page
   158 for how to make your own)
1 slice of stale sourdough bread
1 small celeriac
grated zest of 1 lemon
a few thyme sprigs, leaves stripped
sea salt and black pepper

This recipe is a surprisingly satisfying alternative to a potato gratin. The light celery flavour works really well with the nutty cashews and the nutritional yeast provides a tangy cheesy taste. It's also very cheap, and any leftovers can be reheated the next day.

Soaking the cashews breaks down their enzyme inhibitors, which block and reduce the cashews' nutritional quality. This process also makes them easier to digest and easier on your blender.

Heat your oven to 180°C/gas 4.

Drain and rinse the cashews thoroughly. Put them into a blender along with the garlic and nutritional yeast. Blend, adding the almond milk as you go, until the mixture is smooth.

Pop the slice of sourdough into a food processor and process it to crumbs.

Slice the celeriac into the thinnest slices you can manage by hand. In a small square baking dish, spread out one layer of celeriac slices overlapping them slightly, then sprinkle over some lemon zest, thyme leaves, salt, pepper and a few spoons of the cashew sauce. Repeat until all the celeriac is used up. Top with an extra sprinkle of nutritional yeast and the sourdough crumbs.

Bake in the oven for 45 minutes to 1 hour, or until the celeriac is tender. If the top looks like it might burn then cover it with foil. Serve with a simple green salad.

spiced cauliflower and potatoes

SERVES FOUR

1 tbsp coconut oil

1 onion, roughly chopped

4 garlic cloves, finely chopped

3 tsp chilli powder

1 tsp garam masala

1 tsp ground coriander

1 tsp sea salt

2 medium tomatoes, chopped

500g waxy potatoes, such as
   Cyprus or Charlotte, peeled and
   cut into chunks

1 medium head of cauliflower,
   broken into florets

black pepper

a handful of coriander, to serve

We like the spices to be hot – the cauliflower sucks up the flavours with its branches and the potatoes end up coated in spice. Have this as part of an Indian feast or alone with rice and yoghurt.

Heat the coconut oil in a casserole or heavy-based saucepan, add the onion and fry for around 6 minutes, until it is starting to turn golden and sticky. Add the garlic, chilli powder, garam masala, coriander, and the salt and some black pepper and fry for a further 2 minutes.

Add the tomatoes and cook until broken down and slightly mushy, then add the potatoes and 400ml of water. Bring the mixture to a simmer, cover and cook over a medium heat for 10 minutes. Add the cauliflower and continue to cook, covered, for a further 7–8 minutes until the cauliflower and potatoes are tender enough for your liking.

Serve sprinkled with the coriander.

prawn burgers

SERVES FOUR

600g raw prawns, peeled
*   and deveined*
4 spring onions, chopped
1 red chilli, finely chopped
a thumb-sized piece of ginger,
*   finely chopped*
a handful of coriander,
*   finely chopped*
juice of 1 lemon
1 garlic clove, crushed
2 tsp coconut or olive oil
8 butter lettuce leaves
*   (Little Gem works well too)*
lime wedges, to serve

FOR THE SALAD

1 x 200g tin sweetcorn, drained
1 mango, firm but ripe, diced
1 red onion, diced
4 tomatoes, diced
1 x 400g tin black beans
a handful of coriander,
*   finely chopped*
½ cucumber, diced
juice of 1 lime
1 tbsp olive oil
½ red chilli, deseeded and chopped
sea salt and black pepper

Super zingy and fresh with the coriander, ginger and spring onion flavours coming through, this is a light supper dish that can easily be made during the week when you're busy. If want to make a bigger meal of it serve the burgers in buns, but we find that the beans in the salad are satisfying enough. In the summer these are great cooked on the barbecue, and when the weather is cooler, the chilli and ginger are warming on the palate and a perky little reminder of those lighter days.

Divide the prawns in half. Roughly chop half, then blend the other half in a food processor to a coarse paste.

Place both prawn mixtures in a bowl, then add the spring onion, chilli, ginger, half the coriander, the lemon juice and garlic, and mix together with your hands. Divide the mixture in four and shape into patties (you could also do smaller ones and make eight).

In another bowl, prepare the salad by mixing all the ingredients together. Season with salt and pepper to your liking.

In a frying pan, heat the oil and fry the patties for around 6 minutes on each side or until browned and cooked through.

To serve, place a couple of lettuce leaves on each plate, top with a burger and scoop the mango bean salad on to the side of the plate. Serve with lime wedges.

prawn, tomato and chilli tagliatelle

SERVES TWO

*a glug of olive oil, plus extra for
    griddling*
600g baby plum tomatoes, halved
2 garlic cloves, sliced
160g dried tagliatelle
1 tsp dried chilli flakes
*a bunch of basil leaves,
    roughly chopped or torn*
*12 raw king prawns, peeled
    and deveined*
sea salt and black pepper
wedge of Parmesan, to serve

This is a dish that of course we're not trying to claim as our own – it has countless incarnations across Italy, let alone the rest of the world, but it is a meal that has been refined to such pleasurable simplicity that we could eat this at least once a week and often we do, so we had to include our version. Incredibly quick and easy to make, a shop-bought sauce has nothing on the real thing. Shellfish pasta and risotto dishes don't call for Parmesan – in fact, it's an Italian no-no because traditionalists feel that cheese would be too overpowering for delicate seafood flavours, but we find the Parmesan here just really finishes off this beautifully simple dish.

Pour the olive oil in a medium saucepan to cover the bottom of it. Turn the heat on to medium–high and, when the oil is hot, throw the tomatoes in (be careful as they will sizzle from the hot oil). Add the garlic and be generous with a seasoning of salt and pepper.

When the tomatoes start to become saucy, and you can squish them with the back of your stirring spoon, put the pasta on and cook it according to the packet instructions. Once the sauce has thickened, and the skins of the tomatoes have peeled off and it actually looks like tomato sauce instead of just tomatoes snuggled in a pan, add the chilli flakes, turn the heat down low and throw in the basil to wilt.

While the pasta is cooking, drizzle olive oil over the prawns and season them generously on both sides.

Once the pasta has only 5 minutes left, place a griddle (or frying) pan over a high heat. Drop in the prawns, turning them over as soon as they've started to brown on the first side – you don't want to overcook them as they will become rubbery. Once cooked, take off the heat.

Drain the pasta, throw it into the pan of tomato sauce and mix thoroughly before adding the prawns at the end. Transfer to pasta bowls and help yourself to a generous grating of Parmesan.

—

fish tacos

SERVES FOUR

4 corn cobs

a knob of unsalted butter

1 x 400g tin black beans,
    drained and rinsed

3 avocados, peeled, stoned
    and chopped into chunks

1 mild red chilli, finely sliced

600g firm white fish (such
    as haddock, line-caught cod
    or pollack), skinless and boneless

a little flour, for dusting the fish
    (optional)

1 tbsp coconut oil

8 soft corn tortillas
    (we like ones from the Cool
    Chile Co)

sea salt and black pepper

FOR THE SALSA

a bunch of small radishes,
    cut into small cubes

½ cucumber, cut into small cubes

splash of olive oil

squeeze of lime

TO SERVE (OPTIONAL)

4 lime wedges, on a small plate

¼ white cabbage, shredded,
    in a bowl

a bunch of coriander,
    roughly chopped

200ml soured cream or
    coconut yoghurt

Having spent a little time in Los Angeles we became aficionados of fish tacos. While LA is packed with places to find them, we had trouble finding any in London that match our expectations so we created this version to satisfy cravings. We don't bother with batter as is traditional; we want to taste the freshness of the fish (batter can also be a nuisance to cook). And we love the extras as much as we love the fish. You don't have to include everything we suggest; we just think it's fun to have lots of ingredients on the table, in bowls. Interactive food at its best!

Heat your oven grill on high or a griddle pan over a medium–high heat.

Bring a pan of salted water to the boil and cook the corn cobs for 8 minutes. Pop them on to a tray under the grill (or into the griddle) to blacken the yellow kernels slightly. Pay close attention when doing this to make sure they don't burn, then slice off the kernels into a bowl. Toss with the butter and some salt.

For the salsa, put the radishes and cucumber into a serving bowl and mix with the olive oil, lime juice and salt and pepper to taste.

Mix the black beans and avocado together in a bowl. Try to just fold them together so that the avocado doesn't get too mushy. Scatter the chilli on top.

Dust the fish with the flour, if using, and season well. Put the coconut oil into a frying pan and leave to melt, then add the fish and fry over a medium heat for around 4 minutes on each side, until golden and just cooked through. Remove from the pan and allow the fish to cool slightly, then flake it into big chunks and place in a bowl.

For the tortillas, heat a dry frying pan until medium hot. Warm each side of the tortilla until toasty warm but still soft. Wrap in a tea towel to keep warm.

Lay the fish on the table along with bowls of all your chosen accompaniments and allow everyone to build their tacos.

—

baked haddock with almond

SERVES FOUR

½ white cabbage, shredded
1 fennel bulb, thinly sliced
1 bunch of asparagus, cut
    lengthways into quarters
4 tbsp olive oil
800g skinless, boneless
    haddock fillets
juice of 1 lemon

FOR THE LEMON YOGHURT

4 tsp lemon juice
300g plain yoghurt
1 garlic clove, crushed
a handful of flat-leaf parsley,
    chopped
sea salt and black pepper

FOR THE ALMOND GREMOLATA

2 tbsp olive oil
50g almonds, roughly chopped
2 shallots, finely chopped
grated zest of 1 lemon
1 garlic clove, finely chopped

This recipe was a step-by-step discovery. It began with some uncooked leftover cabbage and the realisation that cabbage can be baked – and works really well with fish as it happens – then later we added the crunchy 'gremolata' topping for texture. A traditional Italian gremolata – the garnish used for sprinkling over meat and fish dishes – is actually made from parsley, but we wanted a little bite so have swapped the parsley for almonds. Make a double quantity of the gremolata and store it in the fridge for sprinkling on salads.

Heat your oven to 200°C/gas 6.

Start by preparing the lemon yoghurt. Mix the lemon juice with the yoghurt, garlic, chopped parsley, and some salt and pepper to taste. Place in the fridge.

To make the gremolata, heat the olive oil in a heavy-based frying pan, add the almonds, shallot, lemon zest and garlic until the almonds have taken on some colour and the shallot and garlic have softened. Remove from the heat.

For the haddock, lay the cabbage, fennel and asparagus out in a large baking dish. Add the olive oil and some salt and pepperand use your hands to mix and coat the vegetables thoroughly. Bake in the oven for 10 minutes. Remove from the oven and place the fish on top, seasoning it well. Squeeze the lemon juice over the entire dish and sprinkle over the gremolata. Bake for a further 10 minutes or until the fish is just cooked through.

Serve with the lemon yoghurt on a summer evening.

pancetta, eggs
and spaghetti

**ENOUGH FOR TWO
HUNGRY PEOPLE**

a glug of olive oil

2 garlic cloves, thinly sliced

200g diced pancetta

160g spaghetti

70g Parmesan, grated

70g pecorino, grated

2 eggs, plus 1 yolk, beaten
    together lightly

a handful of flat-leaf parsley,
    chopped

dried chilli flakes, to taste

sea salt and black pepper

This is our comforting version of carbonara, with added garlic and green bits! Super satisfying, and tasty, it's quick to whip up, with minimal ingredients. We only use eggs (which is how carbonara is traditionally made – without cream), but we like to throw garlic and chilli flakes in to spice things up and then parsley at the end for some herby goodness. A classic to us now, and a recipe we know off the top of our heads – this is on rotation in the colder months! In springtime, we like to throw in some wild garlic to wilt at the end too – delicious!

Start boiling a large saucepan of water for your pasta.

Splash the olive oil into a frying pan and gently cook the garlic over a low–medium heat until golden. Remove it with a slotted spoon and set aside.

Throw the pancetta into the same pan and cook until its fat is crisp and golden, then lower the heat to keep it warm.

Once the water has reached a rolling boil, cook the spaghetti according to the packet instructions. Put half of the Parmesan and half of the pecorino into the egg mixture and stir it together. Add a generous grind of black pepper.

Once the pasta is cooked to al dente, drain it well and toss it into the pan of pancetta. Add the garlic and egg mixture and stir to coat. Turn the heat off at this point to make sure you don't scramble the eggs! Stir through the parsley towards the end, and season to taste. Serve in big pasta bowls, sprinkle over the remaining cheese and add some fire to your pasta with the chilli flakes if you like.

greens, butter bean and chorizo stew

SERVES FOUR

1 tbsp olive oil

400g cooking chorizo, sliced

2 white onions, chopped

6 garlic cloves, sliced

2 tsp smoked paprika (optional;
    see introduction)

50ml dry sherry

2 x 400g tins chopped tomatoes

100ml home-made chicken or
    vegetable stock (see pages 192
    and 195)

1 x 400g tin butter beans
    (or use 100g dried beans,
    soaked in cold water
    overnight and pre-cooked)

125g spinach or any other greens

crusty bread or sourdough, to serve

We've added sherry to this hearty stew, which gives it a more complex flavour, and we always throw in lots of greens. If you would prefer not to use tinned beans then remember to soak the dried beans overnight to make them easier to digest. You will also have to pre-cook them for 20 minutes to use them in this recipe. Leftovers are very welcome when we make this stew as it tastes even better the next day.

Although both cooking and cured chorizo will work for this recipe, our preference would be for the cooking chorizo as the texture of the chorizo ends up being a little more tender. If using cured, you may not need to add paprika as the flavour from the smoked sausage might be enough.

In a large casserole heat the olive oil over a medium heat, add the chorizo and allow it to cook for 5 minutes, or until sealed. Using a slotted spoon scoop out the cooked chorizo into a bowl on the side.

Add the onion to the olive oil and chorizo fat and let it soften for a few minutes before adding the garlic and paprika. Now pour in the sherry, this should make a satisfying sizzle, then allow the alcohol to cook off for about 5 minutes. Add the cooked chorizo, tomatoes and stock and bring the mixture to a simmer. Leave to simmer for at least 10 minutes, until it all starts to thicken and reduce slightly – the longer you leave it the deeper the flavours become.

Throw in the butter beans and spinach towards the end and cook for a further 5 minutes to allow the spinach to wilt and the beans to warm through. Serve with lots of crusty bread.

baked nori
chicken wings

SERVES FOUR

4 heaped tbsp buckwheat flour
2 heaped tbsp nori sprinkles
1 tsp dried chilli flakes
2 garlic cloves, finely chopped
1 tbsp sesame seeds
50ml sesame oil
8 chicken wings
sea salt and black pepper
a big bowl of brown rice, to serve
Quick red pickled cabbage (see
*   page 172), to serve*

A healthier version of fried chicken wings, these are particularly moreish so we have allowed for 2–3 chicken wings per person and then an extra one to nibble on after you think it's all over. Adjust according to your appetite and the size of chicken wings you buy. The wings are great served with nutty brown rice and our refreshing Quick pickled red cabbage (see page 172). This recipe can easily be doubled or trebled if you have more people coming over, and makes a great hands-on meal for friends over a drink or two.

Heat your oven on to 200°C/gas 6.

In a bowl, mix the buckwheat flour, nori, chilli flakes, garlic, half the sesame seeds, a generous pinch of salt and a grind of black pepper.

Grease a baking tray with a little of the sesame oil and place the rest in a shallow bowl. Now rub each chicken wing with the sesame oil, then transfer it to the bowl and coat it with the buckwheat and nori mixture. Once evenly coated, place the wing on the tray and repeat for the remaining wings. You may need to use more sesame oil, depending on how generous you are with it and the size of your wings.

Once all the wings have been coated and are on the tray, sprinkle with the remaining sesame seeds and place in the oven for 30–45 minutes. They are ready when they are brown and beginning to crisp a bit. Again, this will depend on the size of your wings.

—

spiced chicken
legs and thighs

SERVES SIX

6 shallots, finely chopped
2 garlic cloves, crushed
1 tbsp olive oil
6 tbsp tamari
1 tbsp ground black pepper
½ tsp chilli powder
2 tbsp ground coriander seeds
2 cinnamon sticks
1 tbsp ground nutmeg
8 chicken thighs
8 chicken drumsticks
4 tbsp clear honey
   (we like to use raw honey
   but any would work)
sea salt

TO SERVE
boiled white rice
sliced cucumber
a bunch of coriander, chopped
20 lime wedges

The spice combination in this marinade is very well balanced, there's some heat, a little sweetness and just the right amount of saltiness. Try to use good-quality chicken so that the meat remains really juicy. You can marinate the chicken overnight for extra flavour and hold back on the spices if sharing with children. This has to be served with fluffy white rice, sliced cucumber, fresh coriander and lime.

Mix the shallot, garlic, olive oil, tamari and dried spices with some salt in a large bowl. Add the chicken and coat each piece in the mixture before placing in a large roasting tray. Cover and leave to marinate for as long as you can, ideally overnight.

Heat your oven to 190°C/gas 5.

Place the tray of chicken in the oven for 30 minutes, then turn the chicken pieces over and add some water to the pan if the sauce is starting to dry up. Cook for a further 15 minutes and then drizzle the honey all over the chicken. Return to the oven for a final 15 minutes.

Serve with fluffy white rice, sliced cucumber, a scattering of fresh coriander and lime wedges.

lamb shoulder with tomatoes

SERVES SIX

a bunch of flat-leaf parsley,
   chopped
200g cooking chorizo, sliced
1 shoulder of lamb (about 2kg),
   preferably on the bone for flavour
2 x 400g tins chopped tomatoes
1 bulb of garlic, cloves peeled
   but left whole
200g kalamata olives, pitted
400g cherry tomatoes
40ml olive oil
sea salt and black pepper

This dish has seen a few variations over the years but below is the recipe at its best – it is a real celebration of tomatoes. We serve this with some simple boiled new potatoes and a herby crunchy salad. Sometimes not all of the tomato sauce will get eaten, so on those rare occasions save it for another evening and stir it through some pasta.

Heat your oven to 150°C/gas 2.

Spread the parsley over a large roasting tray. Lay out the chorizo in a single layer in the middle of the tray on top of the parsley, then place the lamb shoulder on top. Pour the chopped tomatoes around the edge of the lamb, then bury the garlic cloves and olives in the tomatoes. Add the cherry tomatoes and drizzle the olive oil over them. Season well.

Roast the lamb in the oven for 3 hours, or until the meat is cooked through and beautifully tender. If the tomato sauce looks like it's drying out or the lamb is browning very quickly, add some water or cover with foil.

To serve, carve the lamb and spoon the tomato sauce over the top.

roast chicken
orzo

SERVES FOUR (WITH LEFTOVERS)

1 chicken (about 1.5kg)

a bunch of thyme sprigs

25g unsalted butter

juice of 2 lemons (keep the shells)

125ml olive oil

1 tbsp dried oregano

400g orzo

a bunch of flat-leaf parsley,
    chopped

25g Parmesan

sea salt and black pepper

Because of its grain-like shape, orzo is the type of pasta that pretends to be rice – the name is also the Italian word for barley, although the pasta is generally made from semolina flour, which is a hard form of wheat. Orzo is a firm favourite with kids but this one-pan meal is a big hit with adults too. The flavours aren't challenging, they are comforting and familiar but we feel they really satisfy and that this makes a great, slightly indulgent weekend meal. You don't need a large portion and only need a simple salad on the side. Be prepared to fight over the crispy bits that stick to the edges of the baking dish. They are a delight!

Heat your oven to 180°C/gas 4.

Clean your chicken under cold running water, ensuring the insides are clean and any excess fatty skin removed. Pat dry and place in a large roasting tray.

Stuff most of the thyme, all of the butter and the lemon shells into the chicken's cavity. Drizzle the olive oil over the skin of the chicken, then scatter with the oregano, remaining thyme (take the leaves off the stalks and just use them) and half the lemon juice. Season very well and pour 300ml of water into the base of the tray.

Cook for 50 minutes, then remove from the oven and stir the orzo into the chicken juices, spreading it out evenly. Add the remaining lemon juice and a further 300ml of water and mix well.

Cook for a further 40 minutes, or until the orzo is cooked but slightly al dente. The top layer will be nice and crispy. Remove from the oven and allow the chicken to rest for 10 minutes.

To serve, remove the chicken from the tray, carve and place the pieces back into the tray. Sprinkle the parsley and Parmesan over the whole dish. We just place the dish in the middle of the table for guests to help themselves.

—

CHAPTER FIVE

Excessive consumption of sugar has been in the spotlight for a while now as a potential cause of many modern diseases and mounting evidence indicates that this is indeed the case. But the important thing to focus on in that sentence is the word 'excess'. There are times when a small sweet treat is exactly what we all need – there's absolutely nothing wrong with indulging that pleasure and we shouldn't feel guilty about it. The problem, for many of us, is that our palate has become used to overly sweetened and processed sweets and puddings. But once we train our palates to appreciate natural sweetness – using unrefined sugars, such as coconut, date and maple sugars as well as all fruit sugars – there is no reason we shouldn't enjoy a pudding or sweet snack when we feel like something sweet. The recipes in this chapter will enable you to pull out a pudding when friends come round or rustle up a sweet snack in the blink of an eye.

roast rhubarb

SERVES FOUR

600g rhubarb stalks
80g coconut sugar

Rhubarb season is one we look forward to because rhubarb is such a versatile ingredient and lends itself to many things – sweet and savoury. This recipe is a good starting place. We head straight down to our favourite local shop – Leila's – to purchase her bushy, pink stalks. Roast rhubarb in bulk as we do here and keep it in a glass jar in your fridge for up to a week. Dollop it on top of your morning granola or layer a ramekin with rhubarb and custard for a simple dessert. We have chosen coconut sugar here as it is a slower-releasing sugar than refined sugar and we really like the flavour.

Heat your oven to 200°C/gas 6.

Rinse your rhubarb and shake off any excess water. Trim the ends and cut the rhubarb into finger-sized pieces. Place the rhubarb in a shallow dish or roasting tin, sprinkle the sugar over it, give it a mix and then spread the rhubarb fingers out into a single layer.

Cover the dish with foil and roast for 15 minutes until the sugar has dissolved. Remove the foil and bake for a further 5 minutes or until the rhubarb is tender and juicy. We like the rhubarb to keep its shape rather than turn to mush, but that's personal preference.

blood orange
and pistachio

SERVES FOUR AS

A LIGHT DESSERT

4 blood oranges

50g unsalted, shelled pistachios,
*   roughly chopped*

50g sesame seeds

2 tbsp maple syrup

Blood orange season is another exciting time of the year. It's hard to tell from the outside what colour the flesh of a blood orange will be so slicing one open is fun. We let this aesthetically perfect fruit shine in this simple and refreshing recipe. We usually serve it for dessert but it's great at any time of day.

Heat your oven grill on medium.

Peel your oranges and slice them carefully into thin rounds, trying to keep them even. Mix the pistachios with the sesame seeds on a baking tray and pop the tray under the grill. Be careful not to let the nuts and seeds burn – you just want them to brown ever so slightly, bringing a warmth to the flavour.

Mix the maple syrup with 2 tablespoons of water. Layer the orange slices on plates, sprinkle the pistachio and sesame mix over the top and drizzle with the maple liquid.

—

coconut, cacao and strawberries

MAKES AROUND 10–12 SMALL BARS

FOR THE FILLING

12 strawberries, hulled
25g desiccated coconut
1 tbsp coconut oil, melted
¼ tsp vanilla extract
3 tbsp maple syrup

FOR THE COATING

100g cacao butter
1 tbsp coconut oil
6 tbsp cacao powder
2–3 tbsp maple syrup

We love the winning combination of the bitter cacao and the sweetness of the strawberries. A great all-round mood enhancer, and a lovely treat to store in the freezer for when you need a chocolate break, this is your healthier alternative to a chocolate fix full of refined sugar and empty of nutrients.

Line a 20 x 20cm container or baking tray with non-stick baking paper, leaving plenty of overhang.

For the filling put all the ingredients into a food processor and pulse until you have a mixture with a coarse texture.

Pour the strawberry mixture into the lined tray and spread it out evenly. Pack it down tightly, making sure the top is smooth. Lightly score the mix into bar shapes – how big or small these are is up to you. Pop the container or tray into the freezer for an hour or two.

Meanwhile, prepare the coating. Heat a saucepan of water over the lowest heat and place a heatproof bowl on top. Place the cacao butter and coconut oil in the bowl and, once melted, stir in the cacao powder with a whisk, until smooth. Add the maple syrup, then taste and adjust the sweetness to your liking. Take the bowl off the heat and set aside.

Line a fresh large tray with non-stick baking paper. Once the strawberry mixture has frozen, take the tray out of the freezer and pull the mixture out using the baking paper. Cut into your scored bars and dip these in the cacao mixture, coating them evenly. You may have to do this a few times with each bar to get the coating nice and thick.

Transfer to the lined tray. Once you're done with the dipping, place the tray in your freezer so the bars can set. You may have to wait another hour to eat them if you can.

We like to store these in the freezer because they are less crumbly and once you take them out the coating melts quite fast depending on how warm the room is. They can be kept in the freezer for up to a month, but trust us, they won't last a few days!

dates with sesame
and sea salt

SERVES ONE (OR TWO IF
YOU'RE BEING FRIENDLY
AND GENEROUS)

1 tbsp light tahini

a splash of almond milk or water (see
    page 158 for how to make your own
    almond milk)

a pinch of sea salt

a handful of Medjool dates, pitted

Satisfyingly both sweet and savoury this is something we love as a snack – it's super simple, delicious and quick. Tahini is packed full of protein so it will keep you full and the dates are great for fibre. However, although dates are a natural way of keeping your sweet tooth satisfied, we don't advise gorging on them constantly, they should still be considered a treat, because even though the natural fruit sugar in dates is better for you than refined sugars, it is still a form of sugar. Snack mindfully!

Whisk the tahini with the almond milk or water, adding the salt and stirring until it has a dipping consistency. Tweak the ingredients to your own preference, you may want more tahini, salt or liquid.

Grab your dates and dip away!

banana
crumble

SERVES FOUR

125g oats (jumbo or rolled
    according to preference)
120g pecans, very finely chopped
a pinch of sea salt
2 tbsp coconut oil
2 tbsp maple syrup
5 very ripe bananas, mashed
vanilla ice cream, to serve

Natali's daughter Frankie has apple crumble on Fridays at school. She talks about it all week. When a few of the bananas in Natali's fruit bowl were looking particularly black and blue, she decided to make Frankie's Friday come early – but with banana crumble. The banana caramelises around the edges of the ramekins to create this gooey, sticky delight.

Preheat your oven to 180°C/gas 4.

In a mixing bowl combine the oats and pecans with the salt. Melt the coconut oil and maple syrup in a small pan over a low heat, then pour over the oat mixture and stir to combine.

Divide the mashed banana equally between four ramekins then pour over the oaty topping. Place the ramekins on a baking tray and bake for 20 minutes or until the crumble is a lovely golden brown. Serve with vanilla ice cream.

almond
lychee jelly

SERVES FOUR TO SIX

1 tbsp agar flakes

280ml almond milk (see page
  158 for how to make your own)

2 tbsp coconut sugar

1 tsp almond extract

4 oranges

20 lychees

Natali's mum has been making this recipe since she was tiny and we both love the mixture of textures and the mild, gentle flavours; they are comforting and familiar. It's a perfect summer dessert.

Have ready a 23 x 23cm container or baking tray.

Place 280ml of water in a small pan and heat it gently, then sprinkle over the agar flakes and allow them to dissolve. Add the almond milk, sugar and almond extract and mix well.

Pour into the container and leave the mixture in the fridge until completely set – at least 3 hours.

Not long before serving, peel and segment the oranges. Peel and cut the lychees in half, removing the stone. Place the fruit into serving bowls and mix gently then cut the jelly into neat 2cm squares and arrange them in and around the fruit.

—

almond
rice pudding

SERVES SIX

200g sushi rice

40g coconut sugar

a pinch of sea salt

1 tsp ground nutmeg

1 tsp ground cardamom

1 tsp ground cinnamon

1.2 litres almond milk
  (see page 158 for how
  to make your own)

chopped pistachios, to serve

seasonal fruit, to serve

A good rice pudding requires a little patience. Grab whichever book you have on the go, pour yourself a drink and enjoy the process. Another lifelong favourite but we now make ours with almond milk. It really is just as indulgent and creamy. We would suggest using home-made almond milk (see page 158) or The Pressery almond milk, naturally.

Place the rice, sugar, salt, spices and about 500ml of the almond milk in a saucepan. Heat the mixture over a medium heat stirring regularly. As the liquid starts to steam, turn the heat down slightly. Keep a close eye on the mixture, stirring regularly and adding more almond milk in stages – as the mixture gets thick and sticky. This will take around 30–35 minutes depending on whether you like a nutty or a mushy texture to your pudding.

Serve sprinkled with chopped pistachios and seasonal fruit.

peaches
on sourdough

SERVES TWO

2 slices of sourdough bread
butter, for spreading
2 ripe peaches, thinly sliced
black pepper, to taste

This was pulled together after a long car journey for a weekend away with a group of friends. We were in charge of getting all the food together and we arrived ahead of the crowd. We were hungry and knew that the rest of the gang would take a while to arrive. Natali's daughter loves peaches and we had just bought a really nice sourdough loaf so we simply put the two together. We sat up on the kitchen counter with mugs of tea and plates of this wonderful fresh sweet toast.

Toast the bread and butter it generously. Lay the peach slices on top and grind over a little black pepper. Serve immediately!

—

CHAPTER SIX

These might not all seem 'basic'
or like staples to you, but we
promise they are easy to make
and having a few of them in
your fridge or cupboards will
ensure midweek meals and
snacks are easy to pull together.
Use the tahini dressing to
perk up a salad, slather the
seed loaf with a generous smear
of anchovy spread, nut cheese
or hazelnut cacao butter for
a tasty snack and add flavour

to just about anything with the stocks. Almond milk is great in smoothies or splashed over your breakfast and we also use it to make soups, salad dressings, muffins and desserts. We make these basics often, usually on a Sunday when we normally take stock of our kitchen and top up on any that we want for the week ahead. Preparation makes everything easier.

almond milk

MAKES AROUND 1 LITRE

*150g almonds, soaked in
plenty of cold water overnight
or for at least 12 hours*
750ml to 1 litre filtered water

This is the most basic recipe for almond milk. You can add your choice of sweetener into the mix (like dates, maple syrup or honey) and sea salt, which helps bring out the sweetness, but we like to keep ours simple which means the almond milk can be used in both savoury and sweet recipes. It's worth trying to source 'raw' almonds, as these are sweeter, with more natural oils than pasteurised nuts which are dried out during the pasteurisation process, and they also retain more of their living enzymes and nutritional value. Most supermarket bags of almonds have been pasteurised which means they have been heat-treated. If they are genuinely raw, the packet should state that they are raw almonds, and you will find that they are less crunchy. Don't let not being able to track down the raw stuff stop you from making your own almond milk though! Nothing can compare to home-made almond milk.

Drain your almonds from the soaking water and rinse them thoroughly.

Tip your plump almonds into a high-speed blender with 750ml of the filtered water, and blend until the almonds are mixed with the water (if you're choosing to sweeten it, this is a good point to add your choice of sweetener). If you like a slightly less creamy, looser milk, add more of the water.

Line a jug or bowl with a muslin cloth or nut mylk bag. Pour the mixture into the vessel, then gather the edges of the cloth or bag up around the nuts and begin to squeeze and drain the 'milk' into the jug or bowl. Make sure to give it a good squeeze to get all the almondy goodness out. There should be no bits in your milk.

Pour the milk into a bottle and pop it in the fridge. It should keep for up to 4–5 days if refrigerated. If it sours, it is still drinkable (it's just a question of whether you like the flavour). Turn to pages 162–5 to see photos of the whole process.

The leftover almond pulp can be spread evenly over a baking tray lined with non-stick baking paper and then left to dehydrate in an oven set at the lowest temperature (usually around 65°C) until completely dry (about 6–8 hours, depending on your oven; we usually leave ours overnight). Then you can blend it into a fine flour to use as gluten-free flour (store it in an airtight container for up to 3 months).

Or you can use the pulp fresh to make energy balls. Place it in a food processor or high-powered blender with a handful each of pitted dates and nuts (almonds and cashews work well), and a tablespoon of a 'superfood' powder (such as maca) for example. Bring the mixture together then roll it into balls. Leave the balls to set in the fridge – they will keep for up to a week.

anchovy spread

MAKES ABOUT 60G

1 x 50g tin anchovies packed in oil
2 garlic cloves
60ml olive oil
grated zest of ½ lemon
½ tsp dried chilli flakes
sea salt and black pepper

If you like anchovies and savoury dishes, you will want to keep this in your fridge. We can eat this on anything and with anything – it livens up most dishes. Stir it into salad dressings or simple pasta dishes, mix it with yoghurt to make a dip for raw vegetables, spread it on hot buttery toast for eggs and soldiers, or it also makes a great sauce for fish if you add a bit of parsley and lemon juice to it.

Firstly, drain and rinse the oil from the anchovies and blot them dry with some paper towel.

In a food processor, pulse the garlic, a pinch of salt and the anchovies until nicely mixed. Then, with the food processor running, pour in the olive oil in a slow stream, adding a generous grind of black pepper, then the lemon zest and chilli flakes to taste at the end. If you don't have a food processor, a pestle and mortar works well too with some elbow grease. You're aiming for a spreadable texture. Store in the fridge for up to a week.

—

cucumber kimchi

FILLS A 1 LITRE JAR

1.5kg cucumber, finely sliced
150g sea salt (for the brining),
*   plus an extra tbsp*
75g Korean chilli powder
*   (Gochugaru for authenticity)*
1 tbsp tamari or amino acids
100g coconut sugar or honey
3 large spring onions, chopped
a thumb-sized piece of ginger,
*   chopped*
1 bulb of garlic, cloves peeled
*   and chopped*

Kimchi is a traditional Korean dish made from fermented chilli and vegetables – usually cabbage. Because of the fermentation process, kimchi has great bacterial cultures (like yoghurt), and is good for your gut. This is something that takes a bit of patience to make (just like the Sauerkraut overleaf), but once you have it, it's great to plonk on rice dishes or in wraps to add some punchiness. Allow two days to prepare the mixture for fermentation, then up to a week to ferment before you can put it in the fridge and use it. If cucumber isn't your bag, replace it with radish or carrot.

In a large mixing bowl, cover the cucumbers in the salt and using your hands, mix them together. Cover the cucumber with enough filtered water so that all of it is submerged, then place something heavy on top of it (like a plate) to weigh it all down and allow it to sit overnight.

The next day, sterilise your jar (see page 168). Drain the cucumbers and submerge them in fresh filtered water. Drain again, and taste; they should taste slightly salty. If too strong, wash and drain again until to your taste.

Place all the remaining ingredients in a blender and blend until smooth. Use your hands to mix the cucumber with the chilli mixture then stuff the lot into your sterile jar, making sure you pack it down really tightly. Place a smaller sterilised jar, filled with water, inside, to weigh the mixture down so that everything is submerged in its own liquid. Either loosely screw the lid back on, or place a piece of muslin over the jar to allow air flow for fermentation to take place – do not restrict it. You may need to place a plate underneath the large jar, to catch any overflow during fermentation! Leave the jar in your kitchen, or somewhere at room temperature for 5–7 days. Taste the mixture after 5 days. When it is ready there should still be a crunch and it should be tasty and a little acidic but it should not smell or taste 'off'. If it has started growing black mould, sadly you will have to throw your efforts away. If on the surface you see white mould, then you can safely remove this and what you will be left with will taste amazing!

sauerkraut

FILLS A 1 LITRE JAR

1 medium white cabbage
1½ tbsp sea salt
1 tbsp of caraway seeds

Fermented foods like sauerkraut contain a lot of gut-friendly bacteria. Shop-bought stuff just doesn't compare as it usually has to be pasteurised or controlled, so it won't be as tasty as home-made, or contain as much of the natural goodness. Once you see how easy, cheap and delicious making your own is, you won't go back! We spoon this over almost everything, every day – it works wrapped up in a nori sheet with our Kale caesar salad (see page 86), spooned over the Solo salmon (see page 89) or just to top any healthy bowl of goodness you may be making. One important thing before you start is to make sure all your utensils and storage jars are sterilised properly so that the good bacteria has a chance to survive and thrive. If you have a dishwasher, make sure your jar has been through a cycle. Failing that, rinse it with boiling water to sterilise. This goes for the knife you will use to shred the cabbage and any other utensils used. Wash your hands thoroughly too – they will be used!

Remove the outer leaves of the cabbage and the core, and slice it into very thin ribbons. Place in a big mixing bowl along with the salt. Begin massaging the salt into the cabbage with your hands. This should take about 10 minutes, and you will feel the cabbage becoming limp and less crunchy. You will also notice water coming out of the cabbage. Add the caraway seeds and massage it all in a bit more.

Now, transfer the cabbage to your sterilised jar, making sure to keep it as compact as possible (even using your fist to pack it all in), pour any liquid from you massaging the cabbage into the jar as well and, if it helps, place a smaller jar filled with water or something heavy into your jar of cabbage to weigh it down and keep the cabbage submerged in liquid. It may take some time for the cabbage to become even more limp and the liquid to submerge the rest.

Cover the jar with a muslin cloth and an elastic band, this will prevent dust and anything else entering your sauerkraut, and allow the air to flow freely. Leave on the side for 24 hours, checking it every few hours and press down on the heavy jar to help submerge the cabbage.

—

If after 24 hours, the liquid hasn't risen above the cabbage, dissolve 1 teaspoon of sea salt in 250ml of water and add it to the mixture until submerged.

Leave the cabbage to ferment for 3–10 days, out of direct sunlight. Check on it every day to make sure it's completely submerged, if not, have a go at packing it down again. If a white residue forms on top, just scoop it off and discard and continue with the ferment. This will not affect the sauerkraut that is in liquid. Start checking the taste after 3 days; you can leave it to ferment for up to 10 days and even more, it is entirely up to you how funky you like your sauerkraut and how warm your kitchen is. Once you are happy with the flavour, pop the lid on and stick the jar in the fridge. It will keep fermenting, but at a much slower pace. You can keep this for several months or longer – as long as it tastes and smells good to eat, it will be. You will definitely know if it has gone wrong!

quick pickled
red cabbage

FILLS A 1-LITRE JAR

1 small red cabbage

50ml apple cider vinegar

50ml olive oil

1 tbsp maple syrup

a handful of coriander, leaves
  picked and chopped

1 tbsp black sesame seeds

sea salt and black pepper

This was thrown together one evening to give a refreshing crunch to the richness of another dish. Now a firm favourite, it's easy to make, and it keeps in the fridge for a couple of days. This tastes delicious as a side dish and is also great added to salad bowls and wraps made from nori.

Finely shred the red cabbage, taking out any hard bits (like the core), and place in a big bowl. Add the vinegar, olive oil, maple syrup and season. Next, use your hands to massage the mixture together for about 10 minutes to soften the cabbage and set aside.

After about 30 minutes, throw in the chopped coriander and black sesame seeds, give it a stir to bring it all together and serve as you please or keep in the fridge until you are ready to use it.

everyday loaf

SERVES SIX

130g pumpkin seeds

90g flaxseeds

150g gluten-free oats

3 tbsp psyllium husk powder

1 tbsp nori sprinkles

1 tbsp nutritional yeast

1 tsp sea salt

2 tbsp chia seeds

65g hazelnuts

4 tbsp ghee or coconut oil, plus
   extra to grease

We like to have this on our kitchen side or sliced in our freezer at all times. It is not really 'bread', it is more of a seed and oat loaf, but we feel that it is a suitable alternative for those wanting to limit the amount of gluten and processed foods in their diet and it is tasty as well as being a great source of energy. You really only need one slice at a time as it really fills you up. We have tried out many recipes for gluten-free, seedy loaves and this is an amalgamation of what we believe to be the best elements. The nori sprinkle and nutritional yeast add complexity to the flavour in addition to their nutritional benefits – iron from the nori and B vitamins from the nutritional yeast. We have it in the morning with a boiled egg or toasted on the side of a salad. You should also try it as a snack smothered in ghee and our Hazelnut cacao butter (see page 186).

Mix all of the dry ingredients in a large bowl.

Melt the ghee or coconut oil and whisk it into 350ml of water. Add this mixture to the dry ingredients and stir until combined. The dough will be very thick but you should still be able to stir it. Add a couple of additional teaspoons of water if needed.

Transfer the dough to a 900g loaf tin; a silicon one is the most practical but a standard metal loaf tin will work too. If using a metal tin then make sure to grease it well with ghee. Smooth the surface of the dough with a spatula, it will have a heavy, thick and slightly gelatinous texture. Once evenly spread set aside for 2 hours. If leaving it for longer, cover with a tea towel.

Heat your oven to 180°C/gas 4.

Place the tin in the oven and bake for 20 minutes. Remove from the oven and turn the bread out (it should come out easily; if it doesn't place it back in the oven for 5 minutes and try again). Place the bread directly on the wire rack in the oven and bake for a further 30–40 minutes. If the loaf sounds hollow when you tap it then you know it is ready. Leave to cool on a wire rack and do not try to slice it until it is completely cool.

Once cool, cut the loaf in half, then slice one half and insert squares of greaseproof paper between each slice. Transfer to a freezer bag and place in your freezer to use for toast. Put the other half in an airtight container – it should keep for up to a week.

date sauce

MAKES A SMALL JAR

10 dates (Medjool are the sweetest),
*   pitted and soaked in cold water*
*   overnight*
40g coconut sugar
50ml water (you can use the
*   soaking water)*

This is a ridiculously simple way of making a caramel sauce to fix a sweet tooth calling without the refined sugar. However, we must point out that even though dates are a natural sweetener, you should still limit the amount you consume and count anything sweet as a treat. This sauce is perfect for drizzling on baked fruits as a dessert or dipping some chopped apples in for a snack. Sometimes we even stick some peanut butter and a pinch of sea salt in the mix too!

Put the dates and sugar into a high-speed blender with 50ml of water (you can use the soaking liquid) and blend until smooth.

The sauce should keep in the fridge for up to a week; if it hardens, just loosen it with a few teaspoons of water and give it a good shake, or stick it through the blender again.

simple nut cheese

MAKES ABOUT 300G

*300g cashews, soaked in cold water
    overnight*
3 tbsp filtered water
*1–2 probiotic capsules
    (powder only)*

'Nut cheese' is great for those trying to cut down their consumption of dairy. Although it's hard to replicate the taste of dairy cheese, the texture is similar and we love it because it's tasty, tangy and full of good fats from the nuts. The keys to making your own nut cheese are in the strength of your probiotics (we like Optibac) and the temperature at which you ferment it. Fermentation will be slower in a cooler environment, and therefore will take a little longer. For a tangier, more pungent cheese, leave at room temperature for longer than we suggest, then once it's to your liking, transfer it to the fridge. It will become a stronger and harder cheese as it sits in the fridge.

Once you've got the hang of the basic recipe you can play around with flavouring the cheese. Try adding salt and pepper, nutritional yeast, a garlic clove and a tablespoon of chives or shallots; or even sweeten it with a teaspoon of honey and spread it on toast.

Drain and rinse the cashews, then blend them in a high-speed blender with the water until they are the consistency of a smooth, thick purée. Depending on the strength of your probiotic (some are sold as 'extra strong'), tip either 1 or 2 capsules of the powder into the purée and mix well.

Place the mixture in a sterilised container or bowl (see page 168) and cover with a muslin cloth to allow it to ferment at room temperature overnight. Check the flavour by tasting it the next day, and if you wish to ferment it longer, do so. If there has not been a lot of change or the mixture is not tangy enough for your taste, try adding more probiotic.

Once happy, you can pack it into your chosen vessel (we use Tupperware or a few glass ramekins) and place it in the fridge. You can either use it as a spread, or leave it to harden for a 'rind' and you will be able to slice it, although it will still have the texture of a soft cheese rather than a hard one. You can keep it for up to a month in the fridge – it will continue to get tangier in flavour. If for any reason it starts to smell a bit funky, it has gone off.

macadamia
nut cheese

MAKES ABOUT 250G

250g macadamia nuts, soaked in
  cold water overnight
2 tbsp filtered water
2 tbsp coconut oil
juice of 1 lemon
1 tsp sea salt
2 tsp nutritional yeast flakes
1–2 probiotic capsules
  (powder only; optional)

If you don't want the tanginess of a fermented raw nut cheese, as in the previous recipe, you can omit the probiotics and go for this one which you can serve straight away. This one also has a much creamier consistency – very much like ricotta – because the combination of the softer macadamia nuts with the other ingredients doesn't allow it to harden. It's spreadable and can easily be mixed into sauces for pasta or risottos, just as you would use ricotta. Try it with everything – the flavour will be creamy and slightly tangy from the lemon juice.

Drain and rinse the macadamia nuts, then blend them in a high-speed blender with the water, coconut oil and lemon juice until you have a smooth consistency. Remove from the blender, add the salt and nutritional yeast flakes and mix well. Store in an airtight container in the fridge for up to a week.

To make this into a tangier fermented nut cheese, you will need to add the probiotic powder towards the end of blending then follow the recipe for Simple nut cheese on the previous page.

spicy turmeric hummus

MAKES A SMALL BOWL

1 x 400g tin of chickpeas,
    drained but reserve 2 tbsp
    of the liquid
juice of 1 lemon, or more to taste
3 garlic cloves
½ tsp dried chilli flakes
2 tsp ground turmeric
1 tsp ground cumin
2 tbsp tahini
4 tbsp olive oil, plus extra to serve
sea salt
pinch of paprika, to serve

A slightly more exotic take on the humble hummus, we find that we tweak this every so often according to our tastes on the day we make it. The main components to consider are the lemon, tahini, salt, olive oil and garlic, so play with these ingredients to get your desired flavour. Some days we like a strong, garlicky hummus, and sometimes a zestier one with more lemon; olive oil and tahini offer a smoother and nuttier finish, and finally salt will even out the creaminess.

Place everything (including the chickpea liquid but not the olive oil or paprika) in a food processor. With the machine running trickle the olive oil in slowly to get the consistency you like. You may need to scrape down the sides and process again. Once happy with the consistency and seasoning, transfer to a bowl and top with a sprinkling of paprika and a drizzle of olive oil. Happy dipping!

hazelnut
cacao butter

FILLS A 500ML JAR

400g hazelnuts
1 tbsp coconut oil
3 tbsp cacao powder
1 tsp vanilla extract
2–3 tbsp maple syrup
a generous pinch of sea salt

Who doesn't have childhood memories of Nutella? They disguised it as a healthy hazelnut spread, but really it was just a sugary chocolate one. This is a cleaner version, without all the added nasties like palm oil (bad for the environment) and refined sugar (bad for you), and with healthy fats from the nuts. This can be kept in a clean jar, in the fridge for up to a month – but we don't know anyone who hasn't eaten it all before then! We love to have it as a staple in our cupboards, ready to be snacked on, spooned into our morning porridge or smoothie, spread on buttery toast for an indulgent breakfast or used as a dip for strawberries.

Heat your oven to 180°C/gas 4. Spread the hazelnuts out on a roasting tray, and once the oven is hot, pop them in for 10–15 minutes, until the skins are brown and roasted. Watch them carefully.

Once the hazelnuts have cooled a little, remove their skins by wrapping the nuts in a clean tea towel and rubbing them on the kitchen top. Removing the skins makes for a creamier finish!

Place the nuts in a food processor with the coconut oil and process. Eventually, after about 8–10 minutes, the nuts will turn into a butter. Scrape down the sides as needed during the processing and give your food processor a break every now and then.

Now add the cacao powder, vanilla extract, maple syrup and salt and blend again until they're all incorporated. Taste and add more of anything to your heart's desire. Store in a clean jar in the fridge for up to a month.

lemon tahini
dressing

FILLS A 150G JAR

6 tbsp tahini
4 tbsp lemon juice
2 garlic cloves, crushed
sea salt and pepper

This is a really simple and creamy dressing that will liven up anything. We drizzle it on roasted vegetables, on top of a bowl of quinoa, inside a filled nori wrap, over a fried egg or even use it as a dip. It's very versatile and keeps well in the fridge for a few days.

Blend or whisk your ingredients together with 6 tablespoons of water, seasoning generously and adjusting the lemon juice to your liking. Add more water if you like a runnier consistency.

—

almond aïoli

SERVES FOUR

50g blanched almonds
2 garlic cloves
juice of 1 lemon
2 medium egg yolks
250ml olive oil
250ml sunflower oil
sea salt

We obviously like anything that involves almonds and this nutty and garlicky mayonnaise is great for dipping and serving with a roast chicken (see page 132), but also goes well with fish. Whizz it up and keep it in the fridge for up to a week.

Turn your oven on to 150°C/gas 2.

Spread the almonds out on a roasting tray and stick them in the oven to toast for around 20 minutes, until golden. Take out of the oven, let them cool and then chop them roughly.

Grab your mortar and pestle, and with a generous pinch of salt, crush the garlic until smooth. Add the lemon juice and mix some more before transferring the garlic paste to a mixing bowl.

Whisk in the egg yolks, then very, very slowly add the oils. Watch carefully that the mixture emulsifies and turns into a mayonnaise consistency, before adding the oil in a quicker stream.

Taste to see if you'd like more salt or lemon. When you are happy, add the chopped almonds and give it another stir until they're all incorporated.

chicken stock

MAKES ABOUT 2 LITRES

1 chicken carcass

1 onion, chopped

2 carrots, chopped

2 celery sticks, with leaves, chopped

2 leeks, chopped

4 garlic cloves, peeled

a handful of flat-leaf parsley, with stalks

2 thyme sprigs, leaves only

2 bay leaves

8 black peppercorns

a big pinch of sea salt

2 tbsp apple cider vinegar

There's been a recent fashion and a resurgence for making what our parents and grandparents did instinctively – 'bone broth', which is is essentially some kind of stock. Bone broth has been around for centuries, although it has only recently been recognised as a superfood. This liquid gold has many restorative qualities due to its ability to heal the digestive system and we need a healthy, smooth-running digestive tract in order for our bodies to take in the nutrients we feed it. The apple cider vinegar we've used in our recipe helps draw out the wonderful nutrients from the bones as they cook.

Drinking 1–2 cups of bone broth a day can really help the body repair itself and you will notice the difference. Have a cup in the morning, as a snack in the day or you can sneak it in with your cooking where water or stock is needed. Using a chicken carcass from a roast is a great base for a stock so that you don't end up wasting anything but if you don't fancy the clean up from a roast, you can also buy bones from your local butcher – just ask, sometimes they might even be given to you for free! And if you don't have time to make stock after your roast, just throw the chicken carcass in the freezer and take it out when you do.

Throw everything into a big pot, and cover with around 2.5 litres of water – top it up if you need to, to make sure everything is submerged. Bring to a boil, then turn down the heat and allow the liquid to simmer gently, uncovered, for 2–4 hours, skimming any foam or scum that rises to the surface.

Once ready (taste it to check you're happy with the flavour), strain the stock and let the liquid cool before transferring it to your preferred vessel and storing it in the fridge. A layer of fat will form on the top when the broth is cooled, there is nothing wrong with this and once you heat it up it will melt.

Gently reheat to enjoy on its own, or use it as a cooking liquid in recipes that call for chicken stock.

fish stock

MAKES ABOUT 1.5–2 LITRES

800g fish bones (heads, tails and
   trimmings of non-oily fish and shellfish)
1 large leek, finely chopped
1 large carrot, finely chopped
1 small fennel bulb with
   fronds, finely chopped
a handful of flat-leaf parsley, with stalks
2 thyme sprigs, leaves only
6 peppercorns

Use this broth in all fish recipes where stock is required, or, very much like the chicken stock, you can sip on it during the day for a nourishing drink. All white fish make great fish stock, but avoid oily fish such as mackerel, sardines and herring as they just give the broth a very strong fishy flavour, rather than a light, delicate one. Shellfish will add a surprising amount of depth to the stock as well.

Clean the fish bones thoroughly with cold water, being sure to get rid of any scales, gills and blood.

Place all the ingredients in a large pot with 2 litres of water. Make sure the water covers everything and bring to the boil. Turn the heat down and allow to simmer for 20 minutes with the lid off, skimming any foam or scum that rises to the surface.

When ready, strain the stock. Allow the liquid to cool before transferring to your preferred vessel and refrigerate.

Gently reheat to enjoy on its own, or use it as a cooking liquid in recipes that call for fish stock.

vegetable stock

MAKES ABOUT 1 LITRE

*25g unsalted butter (can be
replaced by coconut or olive oil
if vegan)*

1 large onion, chopped

1 large carrot, chopped

*1 large celery stick, with leaves,
chopped*

*3 large handfuls of chopped
mixed vegetables, such as
leeks, mushrooms, broccoli,
fennel, tomatoes, courgettes, etc.*

*a handful of flat-leaf parsley,
with stalks*

2 thyme sprigs, leaves only

2 tbsp tamari

2 strips of kombu

With so much chat about bone broth, what about the vegetarians? This vegetarian stock is super quick and tasty to make and is a great replacement for when recipes call for bone broth. Use any vegetables you have lying around. We've added kombu to the liquid, which is a type of kelp known as the 'King of seaweed', and it is incredibly nutrient-dense, packed with lots of calcium and iron. Kombu adds a rich depth of flavour to the recipe. Sautéing the vegetables first will also bring out the flavour in the broth and should not be skipped!

In a large pan, melt the butter (or oil) on a medium–high heat, and throw in all the vegetables. Cover the pan and allow the vegetables to sweat a little, for around 10 minutes or until soft.

Now add the parsley, thyme and tamari. Pour in around 1 litre of water, making sure everything is covered and drop in the kombu. Bring to the boil, then turn the heat down and allow to simmer for 20 minutes.

Strain the stock, taste and add more tamari if necessary. Let the liquid cool before transferring it to your preferred vessel and storing it in the fridge.

Gently reheat to enjoy on its own, or use it as a cooking liquid.

CHAPTER SEVEN

The challenges surrounding
the day-to-day running of our
company encouraged us to
come up with coping methods.
These quickly became our tools
for life and they have become
the foundations of our book
– the food that we eat and
share, the lotions and potions
we concoct and the rituals we
try to follow. In this chapter
we have curated some of our
favourite rituals, beauty recipes
and advice. Please use it as
inspiration – we don't want you
to feel overwhelmed and we are
certainly not suggesting taking

them on board or starting them
all at once. You have a greater
chance of creating lifelong
habits if you move slowly.
We find that rituals can provide
little anchors throughout the
week and can help with the
inevitable ups and downs.
However, they should be
personal so find out what
works for you and tweak them
to suit your schedule. Be kind
and gentle with yourself. Do
not scold yourself. If you break
a good habit just begin again.
Talk to yourself as you would
a most treasured friend.

warm water
and lemon

Drinking warm water with lemon in the morning is a lovely routine to form and for us it is an anchor. We feel the day develop mindfully when we bring small repetitive rituals of self-care into our daily lives. However if we forget, we do not judge ourselves.

There are many benefits to drinking warm lemon water in the morning: lemon juice helps flush out toxins and aids the digestive tract. Naturally high in vitamin C, it is also immune-boosting and even though they taste acidic, lemons are alkalising, which means they help balance your body's pH. It is believed that disease can only thrive in an acidic body so keeping your pH balanced is really important.

You don't want boiling water mixed with your lemon as that will affect its vitamin C content, nor do you want cold water, which isn't gentle enough for your body first thing in the morning. We prepare our warm water and lemon by pouring boiling water into our favourite glass or mug, then leaving it on the counter while we step into the shower or settle down to our morning meditation. By the time you have finished this the water will have cooled down slightly. Squeeze the juice of half an organic lemon into the water, then take a seat and sip slowly while pondering your day ahead or chatting with a loved one.

oil pulling

You may or may not have heard of oil pulling, but this method for whitening teeth and improving oral health is an age-old remedy with Ayurvedic roots. Some research into oil pulling shows that it can help with infections (like a cold), due to the fact that many believe bacteria and infections can enter the blood through the mouth, and swishing cold-pressed organic oil around it can help draw out toxins.

In India, sesame oil is traditionally used, but coconut oil (melted) and olive oil work well too. Some people prefer to use coconut oil as they like the taste better and because of its natural antibacterial qualities. One thing to keep in mind though, is to make sure you use 100 per cent cold-pressed organic oil because you don't want to be drawing out toxins and replacing them with oil that has been processed with chemicals.

To oil pull is very simple. Put 1 tablespoon of your chosen oil into your mouth and swish it around for 20 minutes. We suggest doing this when you're in the shower – we find that you can take your tablespoon of oil, pop the kettle on, do some dry brushing (see page 206) then hop in the shower, and before you know it it'll be time to discard it! Timing is key, this length of time has been measured for its effectiveness in breaking down plaque and bacteria but it is not so long that the toxins are reabsorbed into the bloodstream.

As it is mixed with your saliva, the oil will get thicker, whiter and double in volume. Spit the oil out when your 20 minutes is up, then rinse your mouth and brush your teeth as normal.

And now bin your shop-bought mouthwash which will have harsh chemicals in it. We try to oil pull every other day, but when we're short of time, once a week is enough. When you're feeling under the weather is a particularly good time to draw out the toxins.

mouthwash

*We would rather forgo mouthwash than use the commercially available
options as they can be incredibly toxic, sugary sweet and not refreshing
at all. Fortunately, it is really easy to make your own and doesn't cost much.*

MAKES ABOUT 200ML

6 drops peppermint oil
3 drops myrrh
150ml distilled water
25ml colloidal silver (optional)

Mix all the ingredients together and transfer to a sterilised dark glass
bottle. Store out of direct sunlight. Shake well before use. This mixture
will keep for up to 2 weeks.

dry brushing

Your skin plays an essential role in eliminating bodily impurities and you can give it a helping hand with this through dry skin brushing, which strips off the dead skin cells and stimulates the lymphatic system. Your complexion and energy levels will reward you!

Use the brushing time to relax and clear your mind at the same time. All you need is a good, rough bristle brush and some coconut oil for moisturising afterwards. We aim to do this twice a week and ramp it up if a sunny holiday is on the horizon as a greater proportion of skin is likely to be on show.

Make sure you choose a brush made from natural vegetable fibres, rather than synthetic ones, which may contain toxins. Something like jute fibres are perfect. They may seem rough and harsh at first, but the bristles quickly soften with usage and your skin will become accustomed to the feeling. The firmer the bristles, the greater the beneficial effect on your circulation.

You'll want to get a brush for your body, and a softer brush (or cloth) for our face, which is more sensitive.

It's best to brush dry skin, before showering as a shower cleanses the body of the impurities and dead skin cells that the brushing removes. Make sure your brush is totally dry before you start, so clean it in advance. The process is uplifting and invigorating, so it's preferable to do it in the morning, rather than in the evening, when you need to wind down.

Start with the extremities: begin by brushing the soles of your feet, making small, circular movements. As you move upwards, brush in longer strokes with an upward sweeping motion. You should always brush towards the heart, following the path of the lymphatic system, avoiding any areas that are irritated or sore. If you're new to brushing, begin gently, allowing your skin to habituate itself to the process. You want to remove the dead skin cells on the surface layer of your skin, without irritating the softer skin beneath.

Moving towards the abdomen, use gentle circular, counter-clockwise motions, making particularly light brushes over the breasts. Brush upwards from your elbow towards your shoulder, thinking again about directing your movements towards the heart. Using the same motion, brush from the wrist up towards the elbow.

You'll need a brush with a handle for your neck and back. Brush upwards from the base of the spine to the neck, and then down again from the neck. Finally, cleanse your body with a shower, alternating between hot and cold water – this stimulates blood flow and will leave you feeling invigorated. Afterwards rub gently with a towel to remove any remaining impurities.

Many people forget about the face and neck when dry skin brushing, but all the beneficial effects of dry skin brushing the body also apply to the face, strengthening the skin and delaying ageing. Just make sure to use gentler, softer movements and a face-appropriate bristle strength.

Use your brush to lift the facial muscles gently upwards, then swirl downwards to finish the stroke, making an upside-down 'U' shape. Use this motion on both sides of your face, working your way gradually upwards from chin to forehead. If this is your first time dry skin brushing, don't go too far. You can gradually increase the pressure over a few weeks or months. The motions should leave a pleasant tingling (never stinging) sensation on the skin, which is invigorating and energising.

face mist

Misting your face is a great skin prep before moisturising with a cream, serum or oil as the moisture from the mist will be locked in. It can also be used during the day to perk up your tired face and is great to carry around and use on long journeys, especially on flights, which are particularly drying for your skin. We have also used it as make-up remover after applying a thin layer of oil (coconut, or our Face and body oil works well, see page 212) and removing gently using cotton wool pads or a muslin cloth in the shower.

Rose water is a by-product of rose oil production; it helps balance out the skin's pH levels and control excess oil. You should always make sure you buy 100 per cent organic pure rose water, which is distilled without any chemicals. Its anti-inflammatory and antibacterial properties mean it can help reduce redness of the skin and aid in healing. The astringent-like qualities mean it works well at cleaning the pores and toning.

Colloidal silver is a natural mineral solution containing silver ions and very small charged silver particles suspended in a medium (distilled water). In the past, silver was used to make cutlery and serving utensils and used in 'upper class' households for its antibacterial properties, so some of the silver would have been ingested and entered the bloodstream to help fight off infections (the 'lower class' ate from pewter which often caused lead poisoning (!)). Nowadays, we don't actually need silver in our diets, but we can still use it for its antibacterial properties, as research has found it is antimicrobial and can help boost the immune system. Some people even keep a small spray of pure colloidal silver on them to use on their daily commute instead of the usual antibacterial gels full of harsh chemicals and drying alcohol.

MAKES 100ML

70ml rose water
30ml colloidal silver

Mix the two liquids in a sterilised dark glass bottle (see page 000) with a gentle spray nozzle. Store out of direct sunlight. It feels even better used straight from the fridge as a cooling mist. Spray on to your face morning and night before moisturising.

face mask

Every now and then, when you can find the time, it's great to have a little
pampering session. One way we like to do this is to mix our own face mask,
lie back and do some reading while it works its magic.

Bentonite clay is made from aged volcanic ash and is one of the most effective
and powerful healing clays. It helps to draw toxic pathogens and environmental
toxins out of the body. It is known to be perfect for all skin types and aids the
cleansing and healing process of the skin. Due to its detoxifying properties,
bentonite clay can be drying, hence we advise moisturising well afterwards.

FOR ONE MASK

2 tsp bentonite clay
1 tbsp coconut oil
2 tsp water

Mix the ingredients together to form a paste and apply to the face in a thick
layer. Make sure to avoid letting bentonite clay come in contact with metals as
this will make its detoxifying less effective, since it will draw the properties of
the metal it's touching rather than from you. You can use wood, glass, ceramic
or stone to mix the paste together.

Leave for 20 minutes – it will dry up and start to crack! Rinse off with warm
water, then follow with a hydrating spray and moisturiser.

face and body oil

Over the years, as we have begun to realise that what we eat really has an effect on our bodies, we have become increasingly aware that what we put on our skin does too. After all, the skin is our largest organ and it faces the elements every day, so it makes sense to protect our skin from all the pollution. There is something satisfying about concocting your own skin oils and then the ritual of putting them on. You can also tweak them to how you like them – their scent and texture, for example – and making your own usually also works out cheaper than buying ready-made versions if you buy the base ingredients in bulk.

Everyone's skin is different, so we don't propose this is a miracle oil for all. Try different amounts of the ingredients and work out what feels best for you and your skin. Make sure you find organic cold-pressed oils as these will have been processed the least and all the good qualities of the natural oils will have been retained.

Jojoba oil is non-allergenic and is the safest oil to use. Because it is structurally and chemically very similar to human sebum it does not clog pores and will not irritate sensitive areas like the eyes. Acting as an antibacterial substance and antioxidant, it will protect you from the free radicals we face every day. It contains lots of natural minerals and vitamin E, which is great for promoting healthy skin.

Sweet almond oil is anti-inflammatory, therefore great for soothing sensitive skin. It works amazingly at moisturising excessively dry skin and eliminating dark circles. It's also known for being a muscle relaxant because it contains magnesium, so when applied topically it can help aid stressed and aching muscles. Almond oil can also help scars heal faster, so has been known to be good for stretch marks if used daily.

Sesame oil is very much like sweet almond oil in its anti-inflammatory properties – constant use has been shown to lead to a decrease in skin infections and joint pain. It can improve skin texture and works as a mild sunscreen due to its natural SPF. Massaging sesame oil into the skin can help eliminate toxins in the body, therefore it is great for detoxification and will improve the blood circulation.

Essential oils are natural plant oils with potent properties. They are extracted from the plant by distillation and have the scent of the plant from which they have been taken. The oils have different therapeutic and health benefits and are often used in aromatherapy. The choice of essential oils you put on your face and body is completely up to you and your preference and needs. There's lots of information on the web about the benefits of different essential oils, so ultimately it depends on what scent you'd like to apply every day and what benefit you're seeking (for example, lavender is great for relaxation, grapefruit lifts the senses and frankincense comforts).

MAKES 250ML

100ml jojoba oil
100ml sweet almond oil
40ml sesame oil
10ml mixture of essential oils of your
    choice (we like bergamot for its scent
    and rose otto for its balancing properties)

Mix all the ingredients together in a sterilised dark glass bottle with a gentle pouring nozzle. Store the oil in a cool, dry place if possible. This means it will keep longer, because it will be protected from direct sunlight and heat, which could turn the oils rancid more quickly.

To apply to your face, after misting your face (see page 210), pour 2–3 drops of the oil into the palms of your hands. Rub and pat the oil on to your face. This will help keep the moisture from the spray in. For a more intense treatment at night, increase the drops and massage the oil into your face with slow circular movements, taking extra care to be gentle around the eyes (you do not want to drag the skin).

On your body the oil is best applied after a shower or bath when your skin is still damp. Massage the oil in circular movements or sweeping in the heart direction to help blood circulation. Try not to rush this and enjoy this treatment for yourself.

preparation

It's true what they say: 'fail to prepare, prepare to fail'. There are weekends where everything is spontaneous in life, you're out and about, everything is hunky-dory and fine, then Monday comes around and you wake up with an empty fridge, rushing around and buying a quick sandwich to eat en route to your next priority and it all goes downhill from there. We're not advocating staying in all weekend to prep your meals, or even doing it every weekend. But when you spend time preparing your food for the week ahead, your body (and sanity) will thank you for it. It's also a nice ritual to get into and its rhythm can be therapeutic.

TIPS FOR PREPARATION

1. Write a rough meal plan to determine what you will need to buy. It's always handy to consult a seasonal chart so you know you are eating the best local produce at the time you're supposed to.

2. After shopping, set aside what you think you will need for the next 3–4 days. Fill your sink or a large bowl with water and a splash of apple cider vinegar, and soak your fruit and vegetables for 10 minutes, making sure to scrub anything with dirt attached, then rinse well.

3. Dry your produce (leaves in a salad spinner, everything else with a tea towel), chop them up if needed (though chopping can mean some vitamins will be lost) and divide into BPA-free storage containers or bags. BPA is an industrial chemical that is used to make plastics and research has shown that it can seep into the food or drink from the containers used. You can now find lidded glass dishes for storage too – they are an initial investment, but by storing like this, your produce will be kept longer and you can save on washing up by using the same dish to store and cook.

4. Cook multiple things at once. You don't need to set aside more than an hour or so for your preparation, and spending that time now will save you lots of time during the week. Choose simple things that can then be turned into meals easily, or cook batches of things that can then be reheated.

SOME IDEAS OF THINGS WE LIKE TO DO ON OUR PREP DAYS ARE:

— making a big pot of dal or soup, then storing some in the fridge and some
  in the freezer
— cooking plenty of quinoa/rice/pulses to use as the base for quick meals
— roasting a variety of veggies and storing them in the fridge ready to make
  up a quinoa/rice bowl or wrap, or for using to top a soup
— chopping vegetable sticks and making a dip for snacking
— boiling eggs for on-the-go snacking or to use as a topping for all kinds
  of breakfast, lunch or dinner dishes
— making a big batch of granola or sauerkraut

EXTRA TIP:

Hang unripe bananas to let them naturally ripen. When they do, use some and
chop some up for the freezer to add to smoothies quickly in the morning. If you
need to ripen an avocado quickly, sit a ripe banana next to it and let them hang
for a bit. You can also cube and freeze avocado for quick smoothie-making.

meditation

On a quest to find an easy way to nourish, balance and strengthen our hormones, and endocrine and nervous systems, we finally stumbled upon what every other person has been talking about for a number of years. Meditation can help transform your relationship with stress, soothe your nervous system, aid restful sleep and give you a feeling of profound awareness you will have lacked before.

Willing to adopt any new tool that will help us in this frantic, modern world, we can safely say we have tried a few forms of meditation and it's not one-size-fits-all! Each and every person has their individual needs, coupled with the fact that our schedules, priorities and situations are all different too.

If you're new to meditation, then starting with a guided one is probably best. There are many apps for smartphones and online that you can access. Guided meditation is what it says on the tin: you are guided by words through the session, prompted with breathing and visualisation techniques that help you achieve a state of calm. Try a few out, or read reviews and ask your friends what they prefer. Some exercise studios even have meditation classes; some with meditation alone, some that involve yoga beforehand.

If you are confident in your practice or would like a challenge that will benefit you even more, try vedic meditation. Vedic meditation originated in India a very long time ago, but it is simple and effective for the modern day – just what we like! It has been scientifically proven that vedic meditation can provide positive, long-term benefits to a person's well-being. You aren't forced to clear your mind so it works very well in our information overload society.

To perform, all it requires is for you to sit comfortably with your eyes closed, back supported, and to repeat a sound or a mantra in your mind. If it helps, visualise something as well, for example, a scene or an object. Despite it being so simple, people have reaped the benefits of the meditation in the form of heightened concentration, better memory and an ability to learn new tasks and control levels of stress and anxiety. There are lots of studies on vedic meditation and people who can teach you, but ultimately it's about you, a comfortable seat, your breathing and settling the mind.

All it takes is two 20-minute sessions of your day – once in the morning and once in the evening. According to some experts, 20 minutes of vedic meditation is the equivalent of 2 hours' sleep. But if you don't have that much time to spare, 5 or 10 minutes is truly better than nothing. The best part is taking the time to reconnect with yourself, and from that, you will start to listen to your body more, helping you realise your full potential in all aspects of your life.

movement

Movement is an essential component in the quest for a healthy mind and regular exercise is vital for achieving a state of well-being. This doesn't mean that you have to smash four high-intensity workouts each week, unless you find that enjoyable; it's about finding the kind of exercise that works for you. Everyone is different. You have a much higher chance of making something a lifelong habit if you actually enjoy it.

RUNNING

Running is a real divider. We like running but haven't always. Some people find running repetitive and boring, we actually enjoy the monotony of it. It can be a battle with your mind. Sometimes you will win that battle and have a really good run and other times your mind will defeat you. That is fine and to be expected. It is most likely your body telling you that it is tired. Take a couple of days off or mix in some restorative yoga and then get back out there. If you are a social runner there are so many running clubs, which can really help keep the motivation up. We also find signing up for 10km races or even half marathons gives you a focus and a goal, further strengthening your drive to get your kit on come rain or shine.

YOGA

Yoga has incredible healing qualities. It is moving meditation, time for your mind to withdraw from the never-ending to-do list and to connect with your body and breath. We tend to take part in more classic and restorative yoga practice rather than the dynamic options, but that is just a personal preference. When you are in the class, try to keep your mind calm, not competitive. Switch off from others in the class, focus on your own practice and don't let anyone distract you. This is your time, keep compassion in your heart and be kind to yourself.

PILATES

This is really effective for your core and a strong core keeps everything
in check. Your posture will improve, you will avoid back pain and a strong
core will help your progress in other forms of exercise too. If you are a runner,
pilates is a really good support exercise, strengthening all of the necessary
muscles that help prevent injury. Post-pregnancy it is a great exercise to
restore strength to your middle and pelvic floor.

SWIMMING

Swimming feels inherently natural – we are 60 per cent water after all.
The ability to glide, weightless, through silky water clarifies both the mind
and body. The slow lane is a serene haven to take your time behind other
daydreamers. For the more energetic swimmers there are strokes to perfect
and length times to beat. We also love using the water to stretch – try writing
the alphabet with both of your toes for starters. One of the most glorious uses
of a swim is to cure a hangover: dive into the water and it almost slips away
behind you. Remember, you will always feel better for it.

moon rituals

Our bodies are mostly made up of water, so it makes sense that we are somewhat governed by the moon, which also controls the sea and its movements. You may find that your body and mind will behave differently at different times of the month (you may also notice a pattern from month to month). The more we became attuned about what we were putting into our bodies via food and drink, the more we also became aware of listening to our bodies and in turn attuned to the cycles of the month. This prompted us to look into moon cycles, and what can benefit us from learning about the different energy that comes from the moon and how we can harness that energy for our bodies and mind.

There are two important dates in the moon's cycle to which we pay attention: one being the new moon; the other the full moon. This changes every month, so you will need to consult a calendar of the moon phases in your part of the world – it's easily found on the internet.

A new moon marks the beginning of a cycle, so during the new moon phase, we plant our seeds of intention and ask the universe to help us manifest everything that we need in our lives. This is just the basic law of attraction whereby all it takes is to get clearer about what you want and lose the negative thoughts, replacing them with positive ones.

TO MANIFEST

1. Check when the next new moon will be sighted in your part of the world and note the time. It's important to manifest closest to the time the new moon is at its most powerful (though we don't encourage getting up at 3am if it's going to tire you out for the rest of the day).

2. Set yourself up with a pen and some paper (keeping a notebook specifically for manifesting is quite useful), some nice calming tea and burn a candle or palo santo stick to ground yourself.

3. In your notebook or on your piece of paper, write the date and the following: 'I accept these things into my life now, or something greatest for the highest good and the highest good for all concerned.'

4. Next, write down what you'd like to manifest in your life – nothing is too great or small. Anything you'd like, such as 'I wish health and happiness to all my friends, family and loved ones', or 'I will master the crow in yoga this week'. Always write in an affirmative and positive tone, such as 'I will' or 'I am' as opposed to 'I need'.

5. When you are done, read over what you've written (in silence or out loud) and really visualise your list manifesting into reality.

6. Each month, open your list again and rewrite it, taking off anything that you have managed to manifest in between and adding anything more you wish the universe to help you with.

You should never manifest more than what you think you deserve and more than what you see in line with your karma, for example, if you cheated in an exam, you shouldn't ask for a top score in the exam. Aside from those rules, manifest to your heart's desire. It's a very powerful ritual and really gets the positive energy in your life moving – who doesn't want more of that?

moon rituals
continued

A full moon is a time for getting rid of things that no longer serve you. During this phase the moon will reach its fullest and brightest, highlighting what is and what isn't working for you. It's a perfect opportunity to remove anything that is standing in your way from making progress with your new moon intentions. You may have noticed intensified energy around you during the days leading up to a full moon, so it is a great time to release physically, mentally, emotionally or even spiritually.

Weather permitting, you can perform your ritual outside under the light of the full moon. Failing that, inside with a window you can see the full moon from is good enough. Just acknowledge its presence. If you have crystals, you can also lay them out during your cleanse and bathe them in moonlight – some believe this recharges them with positive energy.

TO CLEANSE

1. Check when the next full moon will be sighted in your part of the world – it always falls two weeks after a new moon, and as before, note the times it will be at its most powerful and try to do the cleanse within 8–12 hours of this window.
2. Gather together pen, paper and things that will help you, such as trinkets you love, candles and incense sticks to scent the room to your liking, photos that will help you visualise and any crystals from which you may feel energy. Make sure to have a vessel on hand if you want to burn your list. Burn a sage stick – it is one of the oldest and purest methods of cleansing a person, people or space.
3. Take a few deep breaths to set your intentions of releasing. Write down all the things that no longer serve you, for example, 'I release my fear of...'.
4. Now, get rid of your list either by ripping it up or burning it in your vessel. Sit for a moment and visualise all that you're letting go of and see yourself freed from the heaviness of what used to weigh you down.
5. You can close the cleanse by doing something healing for yourself like having a cup of herbal tea, taking a bath or performing some light stretching.

sleeping
and waking

Nowadays, there's a general assumption that the less you sleep, the harder you're working. However, at what cost? Getting some precious shut-eye is vital to regulate the hormones you need to keep your body in check, as well as keeping your energy levels up. There are more and more studies to show the importance of sleep and how our health, productivity and happiness can be negatively affected by a lack of it. According to recent studies adults need between 7 and 9 hours of sleep a night and your body works best at repairing and healing itself between the hours of 10pm and 2am. We try and aim to go to bed by 10pm. Of course that doesn't always work – life gets in the way – but when we can, we really do feel the benefits when we wake up naturally refreshed at 6am after 8 hours of sleep. Of course, we also know that there are human alarm clocks that wake us before we've had enough sleep, and extra stresses that can affect our sleep patterns. But there are ways we can try and help ourselves to a better night's rest.

TIPS FOR SLEEPING

1. Stop screen time. The blue light that is emitted from our screens wreaks havoc with our sleep-inducing hormone, melatonin. Make it a priority to shut off any screens 30 minutes to 1 hour before your bedtime to allow your body to relax. That means no working from your laptop, watching programmes from your computer or scrolling through social media on your phone.

2. Instead of chilling in front of the latest box set, try a different bedtime ritual. Take a bath, read a book, write in your gratitude journal or do some stretching. Train your body and mind to this pre-bedtime routine, as you would with children (bath, bedtime story, etc.).

3. If you always aim to be in bed but find yourself pottering about two hours later, maybe try setting a bedtime alarm. This may sound strange and might not work for everyone, but if you set an alarm to get up in the morning, why not do the same for bed? You will be gently reminded by your alarm to anticipate sleep, therefore your body will begin to recognise that it is time to wind down anything your mind is engaged in, knowing that it is soon bedtime, just like babies with a bedtime routine. We appreciate using a gentle alarm for the morning and evening, rather than one that 'jolts' you into action – your alarm shouldn't be alarming.

4. Allow two hours between your last meal and sleep. It's important that your body has digested the bulk of the food you've consumed during the day by bedtime, otherwise it's still working and not resting. You'll often find that your sleep is disturbed if you eat too close to bedtime or you fall asleep on a full stomach – the next morning you will feel a 'food hangover'. If you find that you get home late and tired, eat something light such as steamed vegetables or soup – just enough to satisfy you without affecting your sleep.

5. As well as screen stimulation, you should also cut down on other stimulants. Avoid caffeine after 2pm, don't have any sugar just before bed and resist the temptation to 'relax' with alcohol if you've had a stressful day, because again, these can disrupt the body's natural sleep hormones. We love a glass of wine or two, but they should be enjoyed and not used to help aid sleep. Have some camomile tea or almond milk instead.

6. Things on your mind? Write them down. If it's a list of things you need to do or you're worrying about, get them down on paper and off your mind. It works.

sleeping and waking

continued

7. Making sure your bedroom is in complete darkness and at the right temperature are important in making sure you get to sleep. Studies show that the perfect room temperature for sleep is between 15 and 18°C. Basically, keep your room cool and make sure there's a constant air flow where possible.

Once they get their sleep pattern regulated, many people will find that their body wakes naturally without an alarm – the transition from sleeping to waking will be a lot gentler and easier on their nervous system.

TIPS FOR WAKING

1. Get up straight away. Don't you find that sometimes you'll be awake before your alarm, then you hit the snooze button and somehow it becomes harder to get out of bed? Respect the time that your body is telling you to get out of bed and start your day.
2. Meditate (see page 218). Even if it's only for five minutes, take the time to ground yourself and set the tone for the day.
3. Write in your gratitude journal. Again, this helps set a positive tone for the day and your general well-being.
4. Sip warm water with lemon (see page 200). This is great for flushing out your system first thing in the morning and alkalising the body. Generally, drinking a lot of water before your morning cup of coffee or tea helps the body wake up and work more efficiently throughout the day.
5. Exercise if you can. Early movement will help invigorate you for the rest of the day and means you don't have to dash off to fit in an exercise class at lunchtime or after work when you are too tired. Even if it is just a short 10-minute interval workout in your bedroom, get your heart pumping.
6. Write your day's to-do list. This will keep you from feeling overwhelmed first thing in the morning. Even if you don't get round to finishing your daily to-do list, you can move things on to tomorrow's list. The key is to write things down, in the order of priority and work through them. A physical checklist means you have less on your mind and more room to focus.

acknowledgements

CHI

With this book, I feel like my life has come full circle. It's always been about food and drink, and sharing it with the people you love. Those are...

My mum and dad, who taught me the importance of eating together and making food from scratch. Beyond that, they have surprised me time and again with their unwavering support of the next project I want to embark on. Thank you for trusting me.

My brother Joe who, being six years younger, always bore the wrath of me when we were kids, but would still look up to me. I hope I've made up for it since.

Alex, without whom I would never have made it to this point. Holding me up since we met in 2010, making our way through the life waves together and more recently, embarking on the most exciting adventure yet – welcoming our baby girl into the world. Words cannot describe how much you mean to me, so I won't even try. Thank you for being you.

All my girlfriends; you know who you are. Always there for me, through thick and thin, ups and downs, trials and tribulations. I owe a lot of who I am today to the strong, empowering and amazing group of women I call my chosen family. You inspire and expand me in many ways; I hope I do the same for you.

All my guy friends; you know who you are. The best guy friends a girl could ask for. Always there with the best advice or making me laugh when needed. I'm lucky to have a group of wonderfully talented and supportive friends I can call upon for anything. Thanks for being the best bunch.

To our lovely publisher Liz, who took a chance on us at the very beginning and has been our cheerleader ever since. Thanks for believing in us. To Imogen, our editor, who understood us from day one. Without her, we wouldn't have survived the whole process. Thanks for going above and beyond to make this book happen. To Charlotte, whose eye for detail captures our aesthetic brilliantly, while turning the book into something beautiful and functional for people's homes. To Emma, Lucy, Seiko and Emily for the wonderfully chilled shoot days together – you really were the dream team. I hope we can work together again soon one day.

NATALI

The team behind this book have been incredible throughout the whole process. We stuck an image of a blank book upon our manifesting wall at the beginning of The Pressery – Liz and Yellow Kite made this dream a reality. Thank you for guiding us gently and being such a great support during the writing period and on our shoot days.

My mum and dad, David, Bob and Shirl, the Stoneley Crew, Ginevra, Nick, Tarek, Cece, Gabi, Sonjay, Mattias and Anna, Orlando and Natalie, Torie and Indy, Henry, Alex Little, Alex Shepherd, Micke, Kris, Raul, Estewen and Ciaran – I love you.

For Frankie-Mae, my daughter. You have been with me throughout The Pressery's journey, witnessing the highs and the lows. You have provided me with constant joy and I remain determined to create something you will be proud of.